TRANSLATION

Applications and Research

Contributors

AUTHOR	AFFILIATION
R. Bruce W. Anderson	Department of Sociology, University of Texas at Arlington, Arlington, Texas
Richard W. Brislin	Culture Learning Institute, East-West Center, Honolulu, Hawaii
David Gerver	Department of Psychology, University of Stirling, Stirling, Scotland
Harry Hoemann	Department of Psychology, Bowling Green State University, Bowling Green, Ohio
Rudolf Kassühlke	United Bible Societies, International Headquarters, Stuttgart, West Germany
Eugene Nida	American Bible Society, New York, New York
Lila Ray	Professional translator, 233 Jodhpur Park, Calcutta, India
Danica Seleskovitch	Université de Paris Sorbonne Nouvelle, Paris, France
Peter Toma	LATSEC, Inc., La Jolla, California
Harry Triandis	Department of Psychology, University of Illinois, Champaign, Illinois
Ryan Tweney	Department of Psychology, Bowling Green State University, Bowling Green, Ohio
Wolfram Wilss	Institute for Translation, University of Saarlandes, Saarbrücken, West Germany

TRANSLATION

Applications and Research

EDITED BY
RICHARD W. BRISLIN
East-West Center

GARDNER PRESS, INC., New York
Distributed by Halsted Press
A Division of JOHN WILEY & SONS, INC.

NEW YORK · LONDON · SYDNEY · TORONTO

GARDNER PRESS, INC.
32 Washington Square West
New York, New York 10011

Distributed solely by the HALSTED PRESS Division of John Wiley & Sons, Inc., New York

Library of Congress Cataloging in Publication Data

Main entry under title:

Translation: applications and research.

  Includes indexes.
  1. Translating and interpreting—Addresses, essays, lectures. I. Brislin, Richard W., 1945–
P306.T7   418'.02   75–40295
ISBN 0–470–14994–9

PRINTED IN THE UNITED STATES OF AMERICA
1 2 3 4 5 6 7 8 9

Contents

Introduction

RICHARD W. BRISLIN

THE MAGNITUDE OF THE TASK of translating from one language to another has led to such statements as the following: translating is "probably the most complex type of event yet produced in the evolution of the cosmos (Richards, 1953, p. 250)." Eugene Nida, who is probably the world's leading scholar on translation, ends his chapter in this book with this quote, and it provides a good starting point to introduce all the chapters. It is easy to overemphasize the importance of one's own speciality, and yet the range of skills demanded of a good translator make the quote by Richards defensible. Just the necessity for communicating the following terminology begins to show the range of translators' skills. *Translation* is the general term referring to the transfer of thoughts and ideas from one language (source) to another (target), whether the languages are in written or oral form; whether the languages have established orthographies or do not have such standardization; or whether one or both languages is based on signs, as with sign languages of the deaf. *Interpretation* is one type of translation, and it refers to oral communication situations in which one person speaks in the source language, an interpreter processes this input and produces output in a second language, and a third person listens to the source language version. When both terms are used in the same discussion by a given writer, as in the chapter by D. Seleskovitch, *translation* becomes a more specific term and refers to the processing or written input, and *interpretation* to the processing of oral input.

In this book the following topics are covered, providing even more of a basis for Richards' assertion: the encyclopedic knowledge demanded of a translator; the necessity for attention to nuances of the social situation, above and beyond the words actually used in communication; the necessity for sensitivity to affect and emotion; the reasons behind the limited success shown by machine translation in contrast to human translation; the sensitive social role of the translator vis-à-vis others attempting to communicate across language barriers; the translator as an indispensible colleague in cross-cultural research; and the translator as mediator between people using an oral-written language and people using a sign language.

The chapters in this book have the common element of increasing our understanding of the range of skills a translator must have and the range of places in which the skills of a translator can be used. At the same time the authors of the chapters make more precise exactly what translators do and what they must do to be better in their work. The authors are specialists in various areas, including linguistics, psychology, sociology, literature, and education. This interdisciplinary group covers a wider range of translation issues than discussed previously in one collection or even in any potential collection of scattered journal articles. All the authors contribute to a total picture by working through and expanding upon their specialities. My own work has been largely concerned with the measurement of translation quality and the use of translation as a research tool in cross-cultural studies, and I suppose that in introducing the various chapters this background will form the basis for the way certain issues are discussed.

Types of Translation

Nida's chapter is itself an introduction to a wide variety of ideas directly relevant to translation, and it is best introduced by referring to it often throughout the discussions in this introductory chapter. Nida reviews a three-part division of approaches to translation, the philological, linguistic, and sociolinguistic (the last division is the most recent approach, at least in its terminology, and it is discussed more fully later in this chapter). Another set of categories to show the various purposes of translation that I have found useful is that of Casa-grande (1954) who wrote of the four "ends" of translation. The expansions on each of the four types draws from analyses done since 1954. Type one is pragmatic translation referring to the translation of a message with an interest in accuracy of the information that was meant to be conveyed in the source language form. Pragmatic translation is *not* concerned with other aspects of the original language version (e.g., aesthetic form) that would be considered as part of the other three ends of translation (see below). The clearest example of pragmatic translation is in the treatment of technical documents in which information about, say, repairing a machine is translated into another language. Mechanics should be able to repair the machine using the translated materials. Translators would have no concern other than getting the information across in the second language. This approach contrasts sharply with type two, aesthetic-poetic translation, in which the translator takes into account the affect, emotion, and feelings of an original language version; the aesthetic form (e.g., sonnet, heroic couplet, dramatic dialogue) used by the original author; as well as any information in the message. The clearest examples are in the translation of literature, and this book benefits greatly from Lila Ray's treatment of such translation. For instance, her analysis of the poem, "Edé Subito Sera" is a very good example of this approach to translation.

The third type is ethnographic translation, and its purpose it to explicate the cultural context of the source and second-language versions. With this as their goal, translators have to be sensitive to the way words are used (e.g., yes versus yea in American English), and must know how the words fit into the cultures that use the source and the target languages. This type is similar to that discussed by Nida under the heading, "Sociolinguistics and Translation," and his most compelling example for me was the description of the translation from the Bible used by students who were protesting social injustice in a Latin American country. Their translation was in common, everyday language, and it was mimeographed on the type of paper often used in the past for their activist communications. The translation and the form in which it appeared thus fit the cultural context. At a meeting I attended in Australia recently, an-

thropologists were discussing how people from specific cultural groups (e.g., Aboriginal Australians) used certain words
very roughly translated into English such as myth, folklore,
narrative, tale, story, and fable. The conference participants
were interested in how the people themselves use the terms
(*not* the anthropologists studying them), and they were concerned with the context in which the terms would be used.
They called for an *Oxford English Language Dictionary* type
of analysis in which the terms would be given (in long passages
with as much context as possible) as they are actually used. This
is another example of ethnographic translation, because the
concern is with use in a social situation. It also introduces the
importance of context in translation, which will be covered
below.

The fourth type of translation is called *linguistic,* and it is
concerned with "equivalent meanings of the constituent mor-
phemes of the second language (Casagrande, 1954, p. 337) and
with grammatical form. Nida uses the same term in his chapter
and discusses this type of translation fully. In his chapter on
machine translation Peter Toma points out the necessity for
linguistic analysis of both the source and target languages. The
corresponding structures specified in the analysis become a
central part of the computer program that constitutes the step
between the source language input and the machine's target
language output. Lack of such analysis has been a major reason
for past failures in attempts at machine translation (see also the
chapter by Wilss).

It is natural for people to ask whether the tremendously
influential (on linguistic theory generally) contributions of
Noam Chomsky and transformational grammarians have any
use for translators. Nida's answer seems to be that analysis in
terms of deep and surface structures may be helpful, and he
shows how this approach may work, indicating that some
translators have been doing such analyses for a long time. Lila
Ray presents examples of actual poems that she has translated,
and her analyses show concern with layers of meaning below
the surface structure, even though she does not use the
Chomsky terms. The question, Is this approach going to be an
aid for me in the analysis of this particular passage? is the right
one for a translator to ask. It is easy to feel out of date in the

fast-moving field of linguistics because every issue of *Language* brings up new arguments and new approaches to issues long thought settled. But if one of the "older" ideas from transformational generative linguistic theory, like kernel sentences, is useful in a specific translation effort, it should be used. This would be the same criterion that would be applied to any new contribution from linguistic theoreticians.

For those people involved in translation who (like myself) are overwhelmed by the fast-moving nature of linguistic theory, it is reassuring to remember that the average life (in the sense of active readership) of a well-done translation is much longer than the average life of a good journal article on linguistic theory.

Of course, any one translation can rarely be categorized into only one of Casagrande's four types. Certain information that would be a concern of pragmatic translation, for instance, is conveyed by the way certain words are used in a cultural context, with Lila Ray's discussion of the word gentleman. Likewise, certain aesthetic-poetic forms used in long narratives designed to tell a long story, such as heroic couplets, do not fit today's social context in such places as the United States, where readers are accustomed to long narratives in the form of novels. Awareness of Casagrande's four types should help the translator choose more exactly his goals in a given translation, because compromises must be made between elements subsumed under the four types, depending on what the translator decides to emphasize.

Research on Translation

There are two topics covered in the various chapters and in this introduction that, because of their similarity, might be difficult to distinguish. One is research on translation, and the other is translation as a research tool. The chapter by David Gerver on simultaneous interpretation and that by Ryan Tweney and Harry Hoemann on sign languages are reviews of research on translation. These scholars are behavioral scientists who have applied research methods (e.g., experiments, content analyses) to discover exactly what translators do and what the nature of their output (in a second language) is relative to the original-language input they receive. Later in the present chapter the nature of translation as a research tool will be covered. Here the focus is on how behavioral scientists use translation to discover other important aspects of human behavior, especially when they make comparisons across cultures, as in surveys carried out in two or more countries. Work in one of the topic areas enriches the other. Research on translation helps behavioral scientists who want to use translation as a tool, because the users will know what they can and cannot expect of a bilingual colleague on the research team. People who use translation as a tool often have experiences, both successes and failures, that can suggest further research on translation itself.

In introducing the two chapters concerned with research on translation, I wish to emphasize those research findings that have been replicated (or discovered through practical experience) by a number of investigators working independently. I also refer to related work in language-oriented research that has application to an understanding of translation.

The largest body of research information on language that has application to translation is composed of studies on learning, memory, and reproduction of material learned (Zimbardo and Ruch, 1975, have a readable introduction). The approach of current research in this area is to view the person who learns as an *active processor* of information, rather than as an automation that learns by rote. Viewing the learner as active is actually a revolution in psychology; the classic paradigm has been the S-R approach, in which there was a search for stimulus conditions (S), such as a body of material to be learned, and responses (R), or the output of the learner. Historically, emphasis was on developing stimuli that would lead to similar responses in large numbers of people, with little attention being given to what the learner actually did. More recent research, however (reviewed by Cofer, 1973) has looked at the classic paradigm differently, symbolized by the letters S-O-R. The S and R stand for the same concepts, but the O is the organism, and increasing attention has been given to the way O processes input and how O actively intercedes between stimuli received and responses emitted. This newer approach was just beginning to be commonly cited in the mid-1960s. Examples of emphasis on O include the learner's idiosyncratic methods of remembering large amounts of material, the clustering of information around several themes for more efficient "storage" in memory, and the nature of learning rules that help organize seemingly diverse material, thus leading to faster learning and more accurate reproduction. The person as an active, introspective thinker has replaced the reactive, "empty organism."

Gerver reviews the research on the interpreter as an active processor of information, as in his citation from an interpreter's (R. Glement) description of his work, in his discussion of such concepts as "units of meaning," and in his model of the simultaneous interpretation process. Similarly, Tweney and Hoemann deal with this approach in their discussion of the simultaneous generation of spoken and signal messages. They point out that research on this complex task should help in understanding those cognitive processes that occur during the encoding of language and which are applied by all people, not just interpreters.

The importance of context and redundancy. Researchers who have investigated translation quality have indicated that context and redundancy in the original language version has major effects on the quality of the translated version. Experienced practitioners have come to the same conclusion. Gerver, Seleskovitch, and Tweney and Hoemann indicate various positive effects of translating from documents with large amounts of redundancy and context. Redundancy helps in the construction of material likely to be translatable, because if there are two phrases in a passage that refer to the same concept, this allows the translator to be sure of the passage's meaning. It also allows any translation-checker to note errors when one of the phrases in the translation is different in meaning when compared with the other. As an example of applying knowledge about redundancy, Campbell (1968) has made suggestions about research in which questionnaires are to be used, with the goal of using the questionnaire to interview large numbers of people who speak different languages. He has suggested that every concept under investigation be represented by at least two questions, differently worded if at all possible. If the two or more questions show similar results, a researcher may have more faith in his measuring instruments, and can also add more credence to his claim that the obtained results are not due to translation errors.

Descriptions of the advantages of redundancy are also found in the writings of information theorists. A quotation from one of the most prominent proponents of information theory in psychology, George Miller, (1953, p. 8) points out the advantages of redundancy for all communication.

It is reasonable to ask why we are so redundant. The answer lies in the fact that redundancy is an insurance against mistakes. The only way to catch an error is to repeat. Redundant information is an automatic mistake catcher built into all natural languages.

The principle of providing ample context for difficult terms has been suggested by various analysts. Werner and Campbell (1969) point out that a word is translated least adequately when it is translated as a single item. Translation improves when a word is a part of a sentence, and is even better when the sentence if part of a paragraph. Longacre (1958) writes that in translating Bible passages, the long passages are easier to translate than short ones because long passages provide more context for any one concept. Phillips (1960) noted that the translation procedure of the well-known anthropologist Bronislaw Malinowski included a careful addition of clarifying terms to provide more context.

Chapanis (1965, p. 73), a psychologist interested in human factors engineering, described context cues for improving understanding of human speech. "A word is much harder to understand if it is heard in isolation than if it is heard in a sentence." And in discussing the NATO alphabet, Chapanis (p. 75) said that it "is a specially selected one, full of context and redundancy for getting the maximum amount of information across."

This emphasis on the writings of Chapanis provides a background for a set of rules he designed for a "language to be used under adverse conditions" (p. 75). To cite Richards (1953) again, the translation process can be considered as an example of an adverse, difficult state of affairs. Chapanis's rules should have value in writing the original language form a researcher wants bilinguals to translate. Three of his five rules apply (pp. 75–76):

"2. Use as small a vocabulary as possible and make sure that vocabulary is known to all the communicators.

3. Use familiar rather than unfamiliar words. [Chapanis suggests the Thorndike-Lorge (1944) word count as a source.]

4. Supply as much context for your words as possible. Put the difficult ones in a sentence if you can."

Chapanis's principles of maximum communication with human speech seem to echo researchers and practitioners' suggestions for maximum translatability.

Another research area that has yielded similar results from a number of investigators working independently is the analysis of the types of errors made by translators and interpreters. The question asked by researchers in this area is whether there is a limited number of categories into which the output of translators can be placed so that their work can be described in summary terms. Gerver reviews the categories developed by Henri Barik, and the research reviewed by Tweney and Hoemann has benefited from the use of such a system of categories. I was developing a system for the analysis of written translations at the same time that Barik was developing a system for the output of interpreters, and yet we did not know about each other's work until it was published (again, at about the same time: Brislin, 1970; Barik, 1971). I was struck by the similarity of our categories. The system I developed was also used in the study of the translation of technical materials (Sinaiko and Brislin, 1970, 1973, to be reviewed more fully later in this chapter), and we found, like Barik, that different readers could examine a translation and use the same categories to summarize the same translation. This is an indication of the reliability of the categories.

The examples to be reported are the original English and the English back-translation, which is the third step of this sequence: original to target language to original language. The back-translated English is provided by a bilingual working from the target version with no knowledge of what was in the original version. The advantage of the back-translation technique is that a person who does not know the target language can examine both English versions to gain some insight into the quality of the of the translation. Reporting results that compare the original and back-translation also communicates what happens in translation to the greatest number of people, because every person reading this book knows English, but everyone would not know another target language that might be chosen for illustration. Back-translation is explained in greater detail later in this chapter. The categories, and examples of each from the technical translation study (the source of the original English is a helicopter maintenance manual), are as follows.

First, of course, a translation can be accurate:

Original: "leaks occurring beyond relief valve could cause some indication of low oil pressure."
Back-translation: "If oil is leaking at the outside of the pressure relief valve, it can activate the warning of oil low pressure."

Second, an omission can occur:

Original: "This chapter provides all the instructions and information necessary for maintenance authorized to be performed by organizational maintenance activities on the Power Train System."
Back-translation: "This chapter lists all the instructions and information necessary for the maintenance of the Power Train System. The maintenance has to be assigned to an authorized unit." (Note that "organization" is omitted; this is important as it indicates the exact administrative unit that is supposed to do the maintenance.)

Third, the translator makes a substitution, usually of a term from another section of the original.

Original: ". . . two gear boxes through which the tail rotor is driven . . ."
Back-translation: "These gear boxes activate the tail fan blade."

Fourth, translators garble terms that result in definite changes of meaning; and they leave an ambiguous, sometimes nonsensical, phrase in the back translation.

Original: "Troubleshooting precautions."
Back-translation: "Preventions while repairing."

In the original study (Brislin, 1970) there was also a category called additions, referring to material added by the translator that was not part of any section of the original, but there were few such errors in the technical translation study. In the omission, substitution, and addition categories, the errors can also be broken down into subcategories of major and minor errors, based on the readers' feelings of how much a given error affects the total meaning of the translation as compared to the original. Again, there is good agreement across different readers.

My guess is that explicit attention to such categories as applied to the work of translators and interpreters would be a good teaching device. Translators could have their work analyzed to determine if they frequently make errors of a certain type, and then they could work on the specific problems that are diagnosed. One practical outcome of such error analysis has been the development of rules for helping people write English that is likely to be translatable, which is reviewed later in this chapter.

Machine Translation and the Translation of Technical Material

Nida comments in his chapter that the machine translation system designed and operated by Peter Toma is the world's only commercially successful operation of its type, at least of which he is aware. Machine translation has had a history closely associated with high-speed computers possessing large memory capacities. Computer specialists often point out that these machines allow people to ask questions that they simply would not ask otherwise. Just as in 1920 when no one asked, while in New York City at breakfast time, for luncheon reservations in San Francisco (a plausible event now with jet travel), no one asked about translation by machine until computers were developed. The request seemed reasonable enough: design a system that can take material in one language as input, can have a transfer system as throughput, and can produce material in a second language as output. Much of the early work was devoted to English-Russian systems. Later (1969–1970, especially) a great deal of effort in Washington, D.C. was spent in trying to organize a system that would allow for translation between English and Vietnamese. I worked in Washington, D.C. at the time and did some work published openly (Sinaiko and Brislin, 1970; 1973). Perhaps some comments on my experiences will help shed light on the reasons behind the successes and failures of machine translation.

In the late 1960s and early 1970s the United States was trying to disengage itself from an unpopular war in Vietnam, and the method of doing so was "Vietnamization." This coined word referred to a large number of activities that had the common goal of turning jobs over to the Vietnamese people that were previously held by American advisers stationed in Vietnam. Many of these jobs were technical in nature, demanding mastery of complex equipment. Training people to handle such equipment may seem straight-forward enough, but it is easy to forget that tremendous numbers of technical documents, both for instruction in and maintenance of this equipment, must accompany any transfer from one group of operators and maintenance specialists to another. Estimates of many thousand documents involving millions and millions of words were frequently heard, and it is no wonder that administrators thought of machine translation. Those of us who worked on the problem sometimes joked that a high-placed administrator read about machine translation in some Sunday-supplement article and then decided that this was the solution.

Thus, despite warnings that machine translation was frought with difficulties (e.g., the volume by Pierce et al., 1966, was easily available but I never met an administrator who had read it), large numbers of well-trained behavioral and social scientists were asked to work on different aspects of the problem. Memoranda read at meetings included the feeling on the part of the highest-level administrators that there was no problem of greater importance in the United States' efforts at Vietnamization than the translation of the technical documents accompanying machinery.

I do not mean to provide a description of administrators as "bad guys" and behavioral scientists like myself who later returned to academia as "good guys." The magnitude of the problem of providing material in the Vietnamese language was enormous, and in retrospect it is very understandable why the administrators turned to computers, which were so highly publicized at the time as the century's great breakthrough. It is likewise understandable why they did not particularly want to hear about negative information (see Janis, 1971, on such decision making) regarding the potential of machine translation (such as the issues discussed in Toma's chapter), based on previous work between the English and Russian languages. I suppose that it would have been lax of the administrators not to investigate machine translation systems for English to Vietnamese.

Because I had some experience with translation, while doing my doctoral dissertation work (Brislin, 1970), and because my co-worker had also worked extensively with various aspects of translation and interpretation (Sinaiko, 1963), we had the advantage at early meetings of a special translation task force of being able to specify what we wanted to study before others had an opportunity to "stake out their territory." We decided to focus on the more general problem of translating between a language that has many technical terms (e.g., English) and a language that has very few technical terms (e.g., Vietnamese). We felt that no matter what the decision regarding translation was to be made (by people *much* higher than ourselves) concerning machine versus large numbers of human translators, some knowledge about the special nature of translating technical materials would be useful. We then hired twelve highly skilled professional translators, all native speakers of Vietnamese, and began to work with them. We presented them with technical documents on engine maintenance to determine exactly what they did in translating between English and Vietnamese.

Among our findings were that the translators could work effectively at a rate of 400 words/hour, or about 2400–3000 words maximum for a full day's work. This figure is significantly lower than the 1000 words/hour that the translators claimed they could do with nontechnical prose (e.g., a *Reader's Digest* article). We concluded that much of the time involved in a translation session is not in translating itself, but rather in *understanding* (see the chapter by Seleskovitch) such complex phrases as "nose and hydraulic system reservoirs must be properly serviced." A further time-consuming effort is the thinking of or explaining technical terms like "hydraulic system reservoirs." My favorite example of the material we worked with was the following, from a helicopter maintenance manual, and I still feel guilty about having presented the translators with such an English sentence: "Reinstall bolt connecting actuator to governor control level, adjusting actuator shaft rod-end to obtain 0.010 inch clearance between governor stop arm and upper stop screw, measured with a feeler gage."

The translators, then, had to spend time understanding the technical terms and explaining them in simple Vietnamese. For instance, the translators looked at the word tachometer and then had to spend time understanding that this meant a rotation measuring device. They then translated the latter three words to Vietnamese. This transformation of technical English words to simpler English, and *then* to Vietnamese, was labeled the explain-around technique. Wickert (1957) noted that he experienced the same technique when he asked Vietnamese to translate abstract concepts. Another example of "explaining around" we encountered was the translation of the technical term by-pass valve. The simpler English actually translated was "a valve used to pass fluid in the way not normally used." Wilss covers similar issues in his chapter with examples of translations between German and English.

Our other line of research concerned the assessment of translation quality. Again, we reasoned that no matter what translation approach was to be eventually chosen, machine versus human, knowledge of how to assess whether a translation is good, mediocre, or bad would be useful. A number of authors in this book, Nida and Seleskovitch especially, discuss what is "good" translation, and their message is that any definition of "good" depends on the translator's (or the employer's) purpose. A translation of a Bible passage or piece of literature may be good for aesthetic reasons, but bad for communicating the information meant to be conveyed in the passage. The definition or explanation of good translation, then, becomes more complex but is more a mirror of translators' work, which involves different approaches to different tasks. For our work on translating maintenance documents, and probably for all such technical translation, any criterion of good translation centers around the amount of information and knowledge conveyed. In operational terms, the criterion meant that people using the translated materials should be able to maintain the equipment as well as people using the material in its original language form.

Three techniques for assessing translation quality were used:

1. the analysis of back-translated Vietnamese, based on the technique in which one bilingual translates from English to Vietnamese, and another bilingual (who does not know about the first bilingual's work) translates back from Vietnamese to English. Nida discusses this technique briefly in his chapter. The advantage of the technique is that a person who does not know the language from the middle of the sequence (Vietnamese, in this case) can gain some insight into the quality of the translation by comparing the two English versions. Brislin (1970) has discussed this and other advantages, as well as the major disadvantage, that the technique can lead to a false sense of security if the two English versions are equivalent. I have known skillful bilinguals doing the back-translation (second) step, for instance, who could read a poorly done, garbled translation (from the first step) and put it back into good English. Just as all readers of this book can understand broken, poorly formed English sentences and, in effect, put them into good English, some back-translators are able to understand garbled second-language versions and put them into a proper first-language form. For this and other reasons Brislin (1970; Brislin, Lonner and Thorndike, 1973) recommended that another assessment method always be used in conjunction with back-translation so as to provide an additional quality check. The weakness of back-translation alone as a research tool was also a motive behind the development of Triandis' research approach, covered in his chapter.

2. The second assessment method was the measurement of translation quality through knowledge testing of Vietnamese readers in their own language. Readers of a Vietnamese translation of some technical document received a questionnaire about the contents of the document. Our reasoning was that if readers of the translation could answer accurately as many questions as the readers of the original version, then this was an indication that the translated version was conveying the same information as the original.

3. The third method involved the assessment of technical

material, both translated Vietnamese and the original English text, through performance testing of technicians who must use the material to repair or adjust part of a piece of equipment, as described in the material.

Results showed that the back-translation technique could yield an ordering of different translations (of the same original material) from best to worst. It also gave insight into the types of phrasing in English, or more generally, types of word usage, that did not translate well. Our assumption was that if over half of our translators had trouble with a phrase, then the problem was with the English phrasing, not with the translators. Indeed, the list of potentially helpful rules for writing translatable English in the section (this chapter) on "Translation as a Research Tool" were developed using the back-translation technique with a large number of translators. In this specific research project, the back-translation technique yielded three translations that we called best, medium, and worst, and these were further subjected to knowledge and performance testing.

Knowledge testing, in which people read a translation and answer questions about it, proved highly sensitive to differences in translation quality. Average scores varied by more than a factor of two, for example, an average of 6.1 questions answered versus 2.1 questions answered on a ten-item test, for the best and worst translations, respectively. Scores on these knowledge tests correlated positively with independent ratings (when all translations of the same material were compared by the same person) by experts on quality of translations, and they correlated positively with an error analysis of back-translations. Disadvantages of the technique are that lengthy amounts of time are necessary for its preparation and administration. The technique is somewhat time-consuming to administer, and it requires that test questions be written and translated. Also, testtakers' answers must be scored for the translated version, meaning that a scorer must be able to read answers in the language of the translated materials.

Performance testing is a way of measuring the quality of technical translations by having readers perform a task using the translations. To the extent that such performance is good or bad, the translation is assumed to be good or bad as well.

Our experiments showed that different quality levels of a translated technical manual were directly reflected in the work of crews of helicopter technicians, soldiers in the Vietnamese Air Force. The best translation into Vietnamese resulted in performance on a very difficult, multistep task at a level that was approximately equal to that of United States Army technicians who used the English manual (at the time of these experiments, the Vietnamese were being trained to take over the jobs of the United States Army technicians). Error-free performance was observed for 73 percent of the tasks done by each group, United States Army and Vietnamese Air Force. Lesser-quality translation brought the corresponding figure as low as 11 percent. Vietnamese technicians using English, *the language in which they had been trained,* worked at a 41 percent error-free level, showing the superiority of the best-translated version. Performance testing is the most time-consuming of the quality assessment methods we used. It also requires the availability of equipment (UH-1H helicopters in this case) and the close cooperation of expert technical observers to evaluate people's performance.

Informal, subjective opinion, as a method of evaluating quality of technical translation, is both inaccurate and misleading. This comment refers to the common practice of showing an expert a translation, with nothing else for comparison, and asking for an opinion. We found two reasons for making this negative assertion. In the first case, some of the Vietnamese technicians, working with the best available translation, expressed dissatisfaction with having to read unfamiliar terms; in fact, however, the performance of these technicians was much better than that of other Vietnamese airmen who used the English manual on which they were trained. In the second case, technically competent bilingual reviewers called the poorest quality translation ". . . not bad . . ." when actual performance with that translation was the worst measured.

Another of our findings, hardly surprising, was that when translators had the aid of dictionaries giving Vietnamese equivalents of technical English words, their translations were of higher quality and were done in less time than when no such dictionaries were available. These dictionaries had been prepared by Vietnamese Air Force officers, on their own time, to help their men being trained with the use of English-language manuals. As well as being beneficial to the trainee technicians, the dictionaries provided a useful aid to the translators who worked with us.

Based on our research, we made a number of recommendations. These included a proposal for a dictionary that could be put into a computer. Using such a computer system, as soon as a translator coined a word, or thought of an "explain around" Vietnamese term, he or she could enter this new technical Vietnamese phrase into the computer from any number of terminals. Other translators could do the same, because various terminals would have access to the same computer. When translators were faced with an English term, they could ask the computer for a Vietnamese equivalent. If no exact equivalent were in the memory, the computer could easily be programmed to give equivalents of related English words or terms. The translator could enter a suggested new equivalent if none existed. The advantage of the computer system would be its immediacy—any contribution by one translator would be available to others within seconds.

Such a dictionary-computer system was a far less ambitious project than a fully operational computer translation system. We cautioned against acceptance of a full system because of our feeling (imprecise, to be sure) that the necessary basic linguistic work, described in Toma's chapter for the Russian system, had not been done, and that it would perhaps be more difficult to do in the Vietnamese case. At one task force meeting I remember a young lieutenant saying, "I talked to (a contractor requesting a large contract for a machine translation system, English to Vietnamese), and he said that it would be operational in 6 months." Our response was that 6 months had been a constant for the last 10 years—since 1960 claims have been made that such and such a system would be ready in 6 months.

What final decisions were made? No fully operational, practical, and successful machine system was established, probably because the type of preliminary analysis Toma describes in his chapter was not done. Further, a computer simply cannot do the type of creative coining and "explaining around" of complex English language technical terms, as can humans, like "rotation measuring device" and "by-pass valve," described previously. Also, with the one experimental system that was set up, administrators were not convinced that the output was of sufficiently high quality. Estimates of postediting costs, that is, costs for editing the machine-produced Vietnamese so that it would be usable, were never significantly less than the costs of a direct human translation from English to Vietnamese. The final operations to solve the translation problem actually consisted of a variety of methods. Dictionaries were constructed with and without the use of computers. Vietnamese personnel were given instruction in English so that they could use the English language documents. Any actual translation that was undertaken was done by humans. We never discovered exactly how often our quality-control translation assessment methods were used, but we think that use was infrequent because of their cost and time-consuming nature. Even back-translation was rarely used, the argument being that a bilingual should be assigned to the backlog of *translations* requested by various people rather than to *back-translation* to check the quality of other work, given the volume of material to be processed.

The conclusion made by Toma based on his experiences with his system is the same as my conclusion based on an analysis of my experiences in Washington, D.C. There are no secrets to success in translation of any kind—hard work is the needed input. Toma describes the work necessary for the linguistic analysis that is needed prior to an operational machine translation system. I hope I was able to convey the hard work needed to assess translation quality, and the differences in performance when seemingly good translations are actually compared (71% vs. 11% error-free performance in our helicopter maintenance task). Certainly Lila Ray is successful in describing the careful analysis needed for successful translation of poetry, as are D. Seleskovitch and W. Wilss for the successful training of interpreters, and R. Kassühlke for translators who have the task of communicating ideas in the Bible to people unfamiliar with the background of the ideas.

Translation as a Research Tool

The most careful and formal checks on translation quality have been designed (and used) for empirical research in the social and behavioral sciences. A survey researcher may want to ask the same set of questions in two or more cultures, and members of the cultures may speak different languages. Let us use some questions about people's responsibility during election time as example of the survey's content. If the people in the research study speak different languages, and if the researcher wants to ask the same set of questions (an important decision step, because the procedure Triandis outlines in his chapter does not demand that the same questions be asked), then a translation between languages is necessary. Obviously, if the researcher obtains different results, he wants to be sure that they are based on respondents' feelings about responsibility during elections, not on differences in the original language form of the questionnaire and its translation. In cross-cultural work (or the comparison of behavior across cultures), there have long been pleas from psychologists, sociologists, and anthropologists alike (e.g., Goodenough, 1926; Bartlett, 1937) that the most careful precautions be taken during the stage of research when instruments are developed. Instruments include questionnaires or tests—these often demand translation —hence the concern with assuring equivalent versions in the languages of the cultures under study.

Procedures for quality checks when instruments are translated have been developed by a number of behavioral scientists (e.g., Werner and Campbell, 1970; Prince and Mombour, 1967; Brislin, Lonner, and Thorndike, 1973). Procedures when translation is *not* to be a major method have been developed by Triandis, and these are described in his chapter. Triandis rightly points out that by defining exactly where translation is and is not needed, and what it can and cannot do, then our analysis of the research process is sharpened. Because recent treatments of cross-cultural research methods have contrasted the procedures suggested by Brislin and Triandis (e.g., Triandis et al., 1972; Brislin, 1975), I will briefly describe procedures that can be used when a researcher decides that translation is needed. Further, even Triandis recognizes the necessity of some translation for research purposes, as in the instructions to respondents for answering questions, or as a help in putting people who speak different languages in the same frame of mind (e.g., frank, open, free to admit that they don't know certain answers) before answering any questions. The procedures are detailed without elaboration on how they were developed, but references are given to places where such information can be found.

Translation Methods

There are four basic translation methods that can be combined for the special needs of any one research project.

1. Back-translation, as discussed previously.

2. The bilingual technique, in which bilinguals take the same test, or different groups take different halves of a test, in the two languages they know. Items yielding discrepent responses, or differing frequency of responses, can be easily identified. The advantage of the technique is its preciseness and the potential for using sophisticated statistics and test concepts such as split-half reliability assessment. The disadvantage is that the research instrument is being developed on the basis of responses from an atypical group, bilinguals (see Anderson's chapter for more information on this point).

3. The committee approach, in which a group of bilinguals translates from the source to the target language. The mistakes of one member can be caught by others on the committee. The weakness of the method is that committee members may not criticize one another, and may even unify against the researcher (again, see Anderson).

4. Pretest procedures: After a translation is completed, it should be field tested to ensure that people will comprehend all material to which they will be expected to respond. There is no weakness per se with this method. Indeed, all translated material should be field tested. But, of course, the technique will only be good as the interviewers doing the pretesting (e.g., see Frey, 1970; Brislin, Lonner, and Thorndike, 1973).

Any of these methods can be used if the strengths and weaknesses of each are recognized and if steps are taken to accentuate the former and eliminate the latter. No matter which technique is chosen, there has to be a starting point, and this is usually some material in one of the languages to be used in the cross-cultural study. The material can be questionnaires, instructions to respondents, test items, and so forth. English will be used as an example only because more analysis for cross-cultural research has been done on English than on any other language. Guidelines have been formulated for writing translatable English, that is, English that is easier to translate than corresponding material in which these suggestions are not followed. These rules were developed by giving a wide variety of English-language materials to bilinguals competent in English and in a variety of other languages, and then determining successes and failures in their translation efforts (described more fully in Brislin, Lonner, and Thorndike, 1973).

The suggested rules are as follows:

1. Use short, simple sentences of less than 16 words.

2. Employ the active rather than the passive words.

3. Repeat nouns instead of using pronouns.

4. Avoid metaphor and colloquialisms. Such phrases are least likely to have equivalents in the target language.

5. Avoid the subjunctive mood (e.g., verb forms with could, would).

6. Add sentences that provide context for key ideas. Reword key phrases to provide redundancy. This rule suggests that longer items and questions be used than in single-country research.

7. Avoid adverbs and prepositions telling where or when (e.g., frequent, beyond, upper).

8. Avoid possessive forms wherever possible.

9. Use specific rather than general terms (e.g., the specific animal such as cows, chickens, pigs, rather than the general term, livestock).

10. Avoid words indicating vagueness regarding some event or thing (e.g., probably, frequently).

11. Use wording familiar to the translators wherever possible (see the chapter by Seleskovitch).

12. Avoid sentences with two different verbs if the verbs suggest two different actions.

If these suggestions are followed the next step would be to translate the material into another language. Let us assume that a questionnaire is to be translated. If the back-translation technique is used it has the additional advantage of "decentering" the questionnaire away from the original language form. Decentering is a translation concept first outlined by Werner and Campbell (1970), and it refers to a process by which one set of materials is *not* translated with as little change as possible into another language. Rather, material in one language is changed so that there will be a smooth, natural-sounding version in the second language. The result of decentering contrasts with the awkward, stilted versions common when material in one language is taken as the final content that must be translated with minimal change into another language. Decentering means that the research project is not centered around any one culture or language. Instead, the idiosyncrasies of each language under study contribute to the final version of the questionnaire.

Here is how the decentering procedure works in actual practice (Brislin, Lonner, and Thorndike, 1973, pp. 38–39). An original-language version of a question or test item such as the following is given to a translator. This item is from the Marlowe-Crowne Social Desirability scale (Crowne and Marlowe, 1964), and respondents would answer true or false as the item applies to them.

"I don't find it particularly difficult to get along with loudmouthed, obnoxious people."

In a research project I had this translated into Chamorro, the native language of Guam and the Marianas Islands, and then back-translated into English. The terms particularly and obnoxious were not in the backtranslation, and the bilinguals explained that there were no good Chamorro equivalents. The first back-translated version was given to another bilingual (not the original version, as above). The decentering process has started as the nature of the Chamorro language is determining the decisions made about the English language version. In the second back-translation get along with was replaced by talk with. The bilinguals pointing out that the Chamorro term for the latter would be more understandable to the projected population of respondents. Another translation and back-translation showed word-for-word equivalence (this is probably not a necessary criterion in all cases), and the final version was:

"It is not hard for me to talk with people who have a big mouth."

This is the version subsequently used for the cross-cultural study comparing English-speaking and Chamorro-speaking people. This version led to a good Chamorro translation, the original version did not, and hence the revised version was used. The decentering process determines the changes that must be made—a combination of examining the back-translated versions and discussions with translators will lead the researcher to the best choice for an original language wording that will be best for obtaining reliable and valid research results.

In many cases, of course, use of the rules for writing translatable English and application of the decentering procedure will help formulate a revised version that is more easily understandable to speakers of English than if these aids were not used. Designers of questionnaires and tests are constantly looking for ways to write questions or statements that are easily understandable. The decentering procedure may help.

Other original and revised items were as follows:

Original: I like to gossip at times.
Revised: I sometimes like to talk about other people's business.
Original: I sometimes think when people have a misfortune they only got what they deserved.
Revised: Sometimes I have thought that if people have hardships it's their own fault.

Another by-product of back translation and decentering is that research ideas may be generated by the results of the translation efforts. For instance, in the item above gossip did not translate well because Chamorro has terms for male gossip and female gossip, but the sex is not specified in this item. Phillips (1960, p. 302) could not have the sentence stem, "Sometimes a good quarrel is necessary because. . . ." translated into the Thai language. "After much discussion the translators decided that, although it was conceivable that an American might enjoy a quarrel for its cathartic effect, the notion would be incomprehensible to a Thai." Such results can suggest fruitful lines for further study.

The decentering procedure can be viewed as part of a larger cross-cultural research strategy involving the emic-etic distinction, which is also central to the Triandis approach. The emic approach refers to the practice of designing research instruments that inquire into issues central to *each* culture under study. The term comes from "phonemic" analysis in linguistics as phonemics refers to the analysis of sounds meaningful in any one language. The etic approach refers to the search for instruments that inquire into issues general across cultures and hence central to theory building. The term comes from "phonetic" analysis in linguistics, which refers to creating a system that can analyze any meaningful sound in any language. Both the emic and etic approaches are necessary for good cross-cultural research, because behavioral scientists want to study meaningful, important behavior in each and every culture in a study, but they also want to make theoretical generalizations across cultures. As an example, an etic analysis might document the nature of affiliation and achievement. In the United States, these are often separate needs that can exist at any one point in time independent of each other. However, in Polynesian cultures they are very often tied together, and to obtain the ends of achievement, such as getting a hard job done, a person has to work through the affiliation need. In other words, a person will work for another (achievement) only when he likes the other (affiliation). In this case, the achievement and affiliation needs are etics, but the way in which they combine in various cultures are emics.

The methods for obtaining emic and etic concepts differ in the techniques covered in this chapter and in the Triandis chapter. Using the decentering approach, etic concepts would be those that "survive" the translation–back-translation procedure because terms would have to be readily available in both languages if the concepts are to survive. Emic concepts would be those that are "lost," because after a concept is described in one language, losing it means that no equivalent could readily be found in the other language(s) that are part of the research study. Etic and emic concepts would then be interrelated through correlational techniques, as in the example above, where it was pointed out that achievement and affilia-

tion are related to each other in Pacific societies, but not necessarily in the United States.

In the Triandis procedure different questions are written for
each culture in the study, questions meant to tap meaningful
dimensions in each culture. This is a laudable goal, and it
means that questions written in one language are not translated into another language—not even the type of decentering
translation already described. Analysis of the results, and decisions on emic-etic distinctions, come after the data from many
respondents are collected and after complex statistical
manipulations are applied, usually factor analysis in Triandis'
own work. Factor analysis has been put forth as a tool that can
summarize large amounts of data, and results are reported as
underlying dimensions (or factors, labeled by the investigator)
that best describe the data in a parsimonious way. My misgiv-
ings about this approach are that a researcher risks uninterpre-
table results if the factor analysis does not yield clear output
that can placed in an emic-etic framework. In addition, researchers using factor analysis are placing the outcome of their
research projects onto a technique about which methodological specialists continue to have disagreements as to proper use
and misuse (e.g., Armstrong and Soelberg, 1968; Ray, 1973;
Dziuban and Shirkey, 1974). Too often (not in the Triandis
research program) all kinds of information are fed into a computer in the hopes of obtaining interpretable results. In the
words of two specialists (note the similarity to the reasons behind the development of machine translation): "It has become
common practice for researchers to report in professional journals the results of factor and component analyses of various
correlation matrices. Undoubtedly this is, at least in part, due
to the accessibility of computer programs that perform these
tasks. . . . Seldom, however, is evidence provided that the
sample correlation matrices at hand are appropriate for factor-
analytic methods" (Dziuban and Shirkey, 1974, p. 358).

There is no substitute for careful thought about what are the
best, most profitable types of information to collect, the thinking to be done long before data are collected and analyzed. As
a final comment on the Triandis procedure, it should be
pointed out that the final results of any factor analysis of responses to different-language questionnaires have to be translated so that findings can be communicated to people in the

cultures under study and to readers of professional journals everywhere. Hence knowledge of translation methods is necessary at the "reporting of results" phase of the Triandis procedure.

I like to think of the procedures reviewed here and in the Triandis chapter as providing a smorgasbord for researchers. According to the special needs of their project, researchers can consider the advantages and disadvantages of the various techniques and proceed accordingly.

The Special Role of the Translator and Interpreter

There are differences, I believe, in feelings about translators and interpreters, on the part of the general public, in the United States and Europe. In the United States one reaction centers around the translator as a rather low-status individual. The image is of a middle-aged person in a shabby jacket who speaks English with a noticeable accent, and who is probably an immigrant to the United States. Because so many practical translation principles were formulated on the basis of experiences with Bible translation (see the chapter by Kassühlke), another image is that of a Bible-quoting evangelist who may try to convert anyone wishing to consult about translation. A third image that surrounds the interpreter is that such a person is just a mimic—a "bookkeeper" who maintains records and summarizes them, rather than the "executive" who creates the records. Such a "faithful echo" role is incompatible with the values of independence and achievement prevalent in the United States. Of course, all these images are nonsense, as demonstrated by the high status afforded to translators and interpreters in Europe. There, people in these professions are well paid, and there are fine schools that people wishing to become translators or interpreters can attend. Similarly, the skills demanded of a good translator or interpreter as outlined by Seleskovitch should diminish any unfavorable stereotypes.

Anderson also covers the unique qualities and the special social role of the interpreter, skillfully using concepts drawn from sociological theory. Anderson once told me that the stimulus for this treatment on the social role of the interpreter occurred at a professional meeting of sociologists. Anderson was expanding on some of the ideas he had formulated (Anderson, 1967) on the measurement of the translator's output. After his presentation someone in the audience asked why he had not analyzed the role of the translator, because this would be the type of contribution a sociologist could make. Anderson thought about the challenge, and his analysis forms the bulk of his chapter.

Another possible way to obtain insight into the interpreter's role is to do an analysis based on power relations, drawing from a framework established by a psychologist (French, 1956). Assume that person *B* is an individual who needs to communicate with (hence he will also be called the communicator person *C*, but he cannot speak *C*'s language. Person *B* then has to use an interpreter, person *A*, and *B* is then dependent on *A*. Person *A* has a good deal of power over *B*, especially if *B* must communicate with person *C* over an important matter of economics, politics, and so forth. Power is defined by French (1956, p. 183) as "the maximum force that person A can induce on B minus the maximum resisting force which B can mobilize in the opposite direction." It is important to note that this definition applies only to specific, concrete situations, such as the total time taken up by the negotiations between *B* and *C*. Outside the situation in which *B* needs an interpreter, person *A* might have no power at all.

There are five types of interpersonal power that are based on the relationship between *A* and *B*. In French's words (1956, pp. 183–184) these are: "attraction power based on B's liking for A, expert power based on B's perception that A has superior knowledge and information, reward power based on A's ability to mediate rewards for B, coercive power based on A's ability to mediate punishments for B, and legitimate power based on B's belief that A has a right to prescribe his behavior or opinions."

All five are applicable to the role of the interpreter, although some are probably more common in practice than others. Attraction power would occur when the person needing translation help likes his interpreter as a person, above and beyond a liking based on the interpreter's special skills. While working in Washington, D.C. I became acquainted with the person Charles De Gaulle used as an interpreter when visiting the United States. Reportedly, if De Gaulle knew that he would be visiting only Washington, D.C. and not traveling extensively elsewhere, he would *not* bring an interpreter from France, because he knew that he could call on this person in the United States, because they were friends. Expert power is the most obvious attribute held by the interpreter, as his special skills in language are needed by monolingual people wanting to communicate with others who speak various languages. Reward power will likewise be frequent. French's use of the word mediate is well chosen since the interpreter may not have any rewards himself in the form of economic help or political influence, but he can mediate these by skillfully interpreting the wishes of one person (*B*, in the shorthand introduced above) to another (person *C*).

Coercive power is a contrast to reward power, and it refers to situations in which the interpreter can mediate punishments. The clearest case probably is the situation in which an interpreter can make communicators angry at each other by doing a poor job of interpreting their desires and feelings to each other. A well-published recent case occurred during negotiations between Richard Nixon, in his role as President of the United States, and the Emperor of Japan. Nixon asked a question about a trade policy. The Emperor's response was interpreted to Nixon as "I'll think about it." Nixon took this response as a yes, but the Emperor meant it as a polite no. Unpleasant feelings followed when the differing interpretations became clear. Anderson also reviewed a communicator-interpreter relation that could be classified "reward power" if it succeeded, and "coercive power" if it failed. In his chapter he tells of an army officer, stationed outside his own country, who wanted what he felt was a certain desirable behavior on the part of the host country army. The interpreter was the only person who could communicate the officer's desire, and he had to choose the best way to do so. If the interpreter succeeded, the officer would be pleased; if the interpreter failed, the officer might be the target of hostile feelings from the host country army.

Legitimate power may be more common than would be considered at first glance. If the communicator realizes that there are cross-cultural differences in the way that people discuss differing viewpoints and make decisions, he may call upon the interpreter (who ideally knows both the languages and the cultural practices of both parties in the negotiation) to make suggestions regarding the best way to present a certain point of view. As an example, assume that the interpreter is to accompany a communicator from the United States to a meeting where there will be several Japanese businessmen. In Japan, it is improper to disagree with another person in public—of course, in the United States it is perfectly proper to disagree tactfully with another person whether or not an audience is present. In Japan, people have their disagreements in private, away from anyone else, and meetings of more than six people are really a formality where ideas already agreed on are presented. Similarly, it is rare that a new idea not previously discussed in private meetings would be brought up in a public meeting. A knowledge of such methods of individual and group decision making is more important than a knowledge of the Japanese language. A sensitive and intelligent communicator will realize that there may be differences in negotiation styles in the United States as contrasted with Japan, will ask his interpreter about them, and will behave accordingly (Paul Pedersen and I have written about orientation programs to introduce such cross-cultural interaction skills: Brislin and Pedersen, 1976). Such a communicator-interpreter relation would then fulfill the qualities under French's description of legitimate power.

Perhaps I can summarize the desirability of more research being done on the role of the interpreter by repeating two anecdotes I have heard recently. One is from the television show *The Jeffersons,* in which one of the characters is an eccentric Englishman named Bentley who is employed as an interpreter by the United Nations. In one episode of the show he rushed out of the Jeffersons' apartment saying, "I have to get down to the U.N. The Arabs and Israelis are debating, and I have to tell them what they are fighting about."

My second anecdote concerns an actual state of affairs reported to me by lawyers in Honolulu. Because there are so many monolingual speakers of such languages as Samoan, Ilocano, and Cantonese in Hawaii, interpreters are provided for negotiations between defendants (and/or their lawyers) and the judge. Lawyers have told me that a problem has arisen because the interpreters are not behaving as a "faithful echo" of the defendant but rather are presenting the communication as they (the interpreters) feel will be most acceptable to the judge. Since no one else in the courtroom can understand both the language of the defendant and English, there is no one to check on the interpreter.

In her chapter Seleskovitch describes how the interpreter must be sensitive to the nuances of all aspects of a communication situation so as to deliver fully the total message from one person to another. Her example of the person coming home from a safari and showing pictures to his friends is excellent. The meanings conveyed by each picture to the safari-alumnus and to his audience are vastly different. Yet, it is quite possible that an interpreter could be asked to act as a go-between if the picture shower and the audience speak different languages. This is a large task to be sure, and Seleskovitch is very skillful at showing how much of the total content of the communication is conveyed by aspects of the social situation above and beyond the words chosen for use. Kassühlke gives examples of how the meanings of passages in the Bible are dependent on the historical setting that provides the background for the passage.

There is a recent study area in the social and behavioral sciences that is devoted to just these aspects of communication in social settings. It is called sociolinguistics, and it has been described in a number of places (Fishman, 1968; Ervin-Tripp, 1969; Gumperz and Hymes, 1972). The following collection of short quotes from Ervin-Tripp, (1969, p. 92) may help explain the admittedly diverse new field.

During the past few years the systematic study of the relation of linguistic form and social meaning has greatly accelerated. The formal recognition of a field of sociolinguistics has been marked in the United States by courses, programs, seminars, and textbooks. . . . Many of the central figures in the development of sociolinguistics are regarded as linguists and have developed their sociolinguistic concepts because they found social features continually central to linguistic descriptions. . . . Sociolinguistics [includes] studies of the components of face-to-face interaction as they bear on, or are affected by, the formal structure of speech. These components may include the personnel, the situation, the function of the interaction, the topic and message, and the channel. As Fishman has pointed out, sociolinguistics is thus distinct from "communication." It is concerned with *characteristics of the code* and their relationship to characteristics of the communicators or the communication situation, rather than with message or communication functions and processes alone (1967, p. 590).

Although not using the term "sociolinguistics," Seleskovitch gives us a number of good examples of such meaning beyond the actual words used, and an interpreter has to be able to process these bases of additional meaning. Perhaps another example will be helpful. I recently had a discussion with a colleague about the language exams that were commonly required as part of any Ph.D. program (less frequently now than 10 years ago). He discussed the difficulty of one that he had to take in German, pointing out that no dictionary was allowed and that there was no hint as to the content area of the exam at any time before the test administrator actually handed the test taker a passage to be translated. My colleague then said, "I was lucky to recognize the passage as a treatment on the inheritance of syphilis, part of a discussion of Henrik Ibsen's play, 'Ghosts.'" It struck me later that my colleague had insulted me just a little by using the expanded description, "Henrik Ibsen's play, 'Ghosts.'" I happen to know the play, have seen a production of it, have read some critical commentary about it, and so forth. If my colleague wanted to, in effect, compliment me he simply would have said ". . . Ibsen's 'Ghosts.'" By using the expanded form he was assuming that I did not know much about the piece of literature. The point, following Seleskovitch's arguments, is that this mild insult would have to be translated in addition to the actual words of the content-oriented part of the message concerning syphilis and "Ghosts." On the other hand, again following Seleskovitch, it is quite conceivable that an interpreter could decide that the additional meaning shown by the difference between the expanded form and the shortened form is not important enough to convey as part of the translation.

Of course, any communication situation involves feelings and emotions as well as actual message content (or factual information conveyed). In studying expressive communication Mehrabian, (1971; discussion here follows that of Zimbardo and Ruch, 1975, p. 161) analyzed three channels for conveying emotion and feeling: verbal (actual words and sentences), vocal (tone and changes of intonation, e.g.), and facial (muscle movements in the face). After studying a large number of encounters between people, Mehrabian suggested a tentative equation of the importance of each of the channels to the overall interpretation of the message: Total feeling = 7 percent verbal feelings + 38 percent vocal feeling + 55 percent facial feeling. It appears from this summary equation that people primarily trust the face in interpreting the messages of another and that the actual words play a secondary role. There may be quibbles with Mehrabian's exact estimates for each channel, but certainly the point that vocal and facial signals communicate a great deal of emotion and feeling seems justified.

When people speak the same language they know what facial signals go with what words, and so can interpret the *interaction* between these two signals. But when a communicator interacts with another person who speaks a different language, the other person might be able to study the communicator's facial cues but will *not* be able to associate these facial cues with exact words and sentences. Hence more mistakes of attribution of intent will be made in such a situation, unless there is a good interpreter who can understand and communicate the entire meaning contained in the message. Such total communication, as Seleskovitch points out, is impossible even when monolinguals interact. In actual practice good interpreters will keep communication at a maximum level, conveying as much of the message as possible. Seleskovitch's contribution is that she points out the difficulties of this role but at the same time explains precisely what the job of the interpreter is, and how certain types of educational experiences can increase the level of desirable skills found in good interpreters.

My guess is that more general background experiences will lead certain people to become potentially good interpreters. Recent research (Lambert, 1974; Ben-Zeev, 1972) has shown that bilinguals possess the trait psychologists have labeled "cognitive flexibility" to a greater degree than their monolingual counterparts. This means that bilinguals, in solving a problem, can look at it from a number of different points of view, switching quickly from one possible approach to another, and they can suggest more novel, creative solutions to the problem. Such a benefit associated with bilingualism is probably because knowing two languages and the cultures associated with the languages (in contrast to monolinguals who know only one), bilinguals know at least two systems or two ways of looking at the world. Recall the example of the Japanese and American approaches to decision making in groups —a Japanese-English bilingual would know both approaches and thus would have more knowledge from which to draw in a problem involving the assignment of individuals to decision-making tasks. In general, then, a bilingual can draw on a wider variety of input, learned from experiences with at least two systems, in problem-solving activities.

Another type of experience that would encourage flexibility and would also lead to a wide background of knowledge, both necessary for a good interpreter, is overseas study or travel. A number of researchers (Bochner, 1973; Brislin and Van Buren, 1974; Useem and Useem, 1968) have found that people who live outside their home country for long periods of time learn a good deal about themselves because they are inevitably challenged in the other culture. The types of behavior that fit well into their home culture do not work as well in the other culture, leading to culture shock and forcing the person to reexamine the basis of the behavior and the nature of how it fits different situations. Thus the person learns that certain behaviors fit certain situations only, and this would encourage a more mentally flexible approach to problem solving. A less flexible approach would be the belief that one behavior is always right for every situation. The Japanese-American contrast in decision-making styles could be cited again, but another example may be helpful. In Greece (Triandis et al., 1972) visitors from another country may find that shortly after their arrival, Greek acquaintances whom they have just met may start asking questions about salary earned, religious views, and even preferences regarding members of the opposite sex. Many people, from the United States, for example, would be insulted by such questions and would consider the Greeks boorish and overly

personal for asking such questions after only a short acquaint-
ance. The key, however, is that Greeks define an in-group
differently than people in the United States. In the latter, the
in-group consists only of people an individual knows well, for
instance, family and friends known for a long period of time.
In Greece, the in-group consists of family, close friends, *and*
visitors to the country. Personal questions are quite appropriate among members of the in-group, and Greeks would not
consider themselves rude in asking them.

My argument is that a person who has gone through such
intercultural experiences will be more flexible, possibly more
aware of subtle communication variables, and will have more
knowledge on which to draw in the role of interpreter.
Bochner (1973), in fact, has labeled people with intercultural
experiences as mediating men (perhaps mediating persons
would be better) because they can act as a link between monocultural people from their own country and monocultural people from the country in which they lived. In addition, mediating persons will be sensitive in a general way to many potential
misunderstandings in cross-cultural interaction, and they will
be able to contribute to increased communication in any mul-
ticultural situation, not just communication between people
from the two specific countries they know. Certainly the description of the interpreter provided by Seleskovitch fits this
concept of mediating persons well.

The Translation of Poetry and Other Literary Forms

Lila Ray, a successful translator who has often been commis-
sioned to translate poetry written in various Indian languages,
has detailed the steps she takes in translating from one language to another. She has given us some of the specific techniques she uses, quite a contribution on her part because, as
she rightly points out, many translators guard their techniques
like the secrets of a snake charmer. Her analysis of the special
task faced by the translator of poetry further sharpens our
understanding of the skills demanded of a good translator or
interpreter.

When we compare the translation of poetry and creative
literature with other forms of writing, we must deal with such

added dimensions as the more frequent use of metaphor, irony, alliteration to achieve a purpose, onomatopoeia, and so forth. The starkest example of the absence of such literary devices is in technical material, such as the maintenance manuals studied as part of our work on technical translation, covered earlier. It is probably no accident that the one example of success in machine translation, as reported in Toma's chapter, is in the area of technical translation, because any information conveyed is almost always in the words themselves, *not* through feelings and emotions conveyed by the words. As another example of such material, consider this:

The power train is a system of shafts and gearboxes through which the engine drives main rotor, tail rotor, and accessories such as DC generator and hydraulic pump. (from UH-1H Helicopter manual, as used by Sinaiko and Brislin, 1970)

Then contrast this with a passage from the Bible; the original has been translated into 1077 languages as of 1970 (Nida, 1972):

As it is written in the prophets, Behold, I send my messenger before thy face, which shall prepare the way for thee.
The voice of one crying in the wilderness, Prepare ye the way of the Lord, make his paths straight. (Mark 1:2–3)

Given that these are dictionary aids of equal usefulness, the latter passage is harder to translate (despite the more unfamiliar words of the technical passage) because of the difficulty of finding equivalents for such symbolic language as voice crying in the wilderness and make his paths straight, (or, more precisely, for these images in the original language used by Mark). Other examples can be found in the chapter by Kassühlke. Once technical words are coined and are available in a dictionary, technical translation is much more straightforward than the translation of literature.

The quality of technical translation is also easier to measure, since any criterion of quality centers around amount of information conveyed. Measurement specialists in the fields of psychology and education have suggested good techniques for measuring the amount of information conveyed in a passage, and several have been covered previously in this chapter. Literature, on the other hand, conveys feelings, emotion, and affect as well as information, and there is not the range of devices available to measure such variables. Indeed, many specialists in literature and the humanities shun any attempt to measure these variables, pointing out its impossibility and objecting to the concept that these affective qualities can be measured precisely. Perhaps their feelings is that such measurement belittles the creative achievement shown by the author of a piece of literature. This difference of opinion between empiricists (including measurement specialists) and humanists has long been a stumbling block hampering cross-fertilization between these two approaches to understanding literature, and also in understanding the nature of translation.

An attempt has been made in recent years at measuring the affective qualities of human communication, however, and I feel that the techniques developed are especially applicable to the measurement of variables *beyond the information* that is contained in literature. The advance has been made by Charles Osgood and his colleagues who have been interested in measuring the connotations of words and concepts. Their most influential publication was entitled *The Measurement of Meaning* (1957). A recent summary statement of the approach is available (Osgood, 1971). Certainly connotation and meaning are central to literature, hence its potential applicability to the measurement of translation. After painstaking analysis Osgood concluded that the connotation of words and concepts can be analyzed, and summarized, according to three dimensions, and that each of these dimensions can be measured by a series of seven-point scales associated with each dimension. The three dimensions are evaluation, potency, and activity, and examples of scales for measuring each are as follows:

Evaluation

Good	_	_	_	_	Bad
Unfavorable	_	_	_	_	Favorable
Dislike	_	_	_	_	Like

Potency

Strong	_	_	_	_	Weak
Soft	_	_	_	_	Hard

                                  Big _ _ _ _ Little
Activity

                                  Fast _ _ _ _ Slow
                                  Quiet _ _ _ _ Noisy
                                  Alive _ _ _ _ Dead

In actual application of the measurement technique, called the semantic differential, people would be asked to think of a concept, such as beauty, and rate it on the scales. On the strong-weak scale, for instance, they would check at place (a) if they felt that it was a strong concept, place (b) if very strong, place (c) if weak, and so forth.

$$\text{strong}\ \underline{\overset{(b)}{7}}\ \underline{\overset{(a)}{6}}\ \overline{\ \ }\ \overline{\ \ }\ \overline{\ \ }\ \underline{\overset{(c)}{2}}\ \overline{\ \ }\ \text{weak}$$
$$\qquad\qquad 7\quad 6\quad 5\quad 4\quad 3\quad 2\quad 1$$

By numbering the "strong" end of the bipolar scale with a 7 and the "weak" end with a 1, a seven-point scale results. The numbers can then be subjected to statistical manipulation both simple and complex, a simple and common manipulation consisting of adding the number checked on this scale to the number checked on other scales, such as the hard-soft scale.

Of course, when people rate beauty on such dimensions as hard-soft or strong-weak, they are indicating what the concept connotes to them. Osgood has found that people are quite good at indicating connotation in this way. They may perhaps find the task a bit strange at first, but are quite willing to engage in this form of metaphorical thinking after only a few minutes of practice. An especially impressive body of research supervised by Osgood (1965) has shown that people from many different countries (over 30 languages have been studied) scattered all over the world use these three dimensions of evaluation (the most important or central aspect of connotation), potency, and activity when explaining the meaning of concepts. These dimensions have been posited as a cultural universal, employed by people everywhere. Scales have been developed in over 30 languages using a similar procedure to that of Triandis, reviewed earlier in this chapter. Some examples of English and French scales for the evaluative dimension are:

English	*French*
Likeable-repugnant	Sympathique-antipathique
Happy-sad	Gai-triste
Nice-awful	Gentil-mechant

These are not exact translation equivalents, but there is an "evaluative feeling tone" (Osgood, 1965, p. 102) that is common to the English and French scales, and it is the total feeling tone that would be used in comparison of meaning across cultures. Further information on, and additional references to, the cross-cultural use of the semantic differential can be found in Brislin, Lonner, and Thorndike (1973, pp. 243–245).

My argument is that because poetry, as Lila Ray explains, and literature in general deal with affect, connotation, metaphor, emotion, and so forth, then the semantic differential technique can be used. In its application, some people would read an original language passage and some would read the translated version. They then would complete the scales according to what they feel about the poem or its translation, using scales in the original language or in the language to which the original was translated. Scales are presently available for over 30 languages. Scores across the scales should be similar for readers who see the original version as compared to readers who see the translated version. If the technique were used as a method to pinpoint difficulties during the development of a translation, then individual scales could be compared. It would be very helpful information, for instance, if it were known that there were problems with the ratings of, say, warm-cold in comparing the original-version ratings with the translation ratings, but that all other scales "checked out" as to connotated meaning. The translator could then work on the warm-cold dimension in developing a subsequent version, and then this revised version would be subjected to additional testing. The technique is flexible enough so that different scales can be used if translators would like to check out various aspects they feel should be in the translation because they are in the original. In other words, scales can be made up for ad-hoc reasons. Perhaps the following scales (made up by this writer) could be used for a given piece of literature:

Ironic _ _ _ _	Not ironic
Motivated me to read fast _ _ _ _	Motivated me to read slowly
Encourages me to read other works by the author _ _ _ _	Does not encourage me to read other works by the author

It seems to me that this would be a useful aid to translators of literature and would help them, rather than insult them, in their job. Almost all literature is written for people other than the author alone, and translators also work so as to communicate to a large number of people. A technique is now available to compare audience reaction (I know this sounds a little like a television-rating term) to original and translated versions by testing the reactions of a sample of people who might read the literature. It is extremely difficult to translate literature from one language to another, and if behavioral scientists have developed a technique that can help, it should be made available to translation specialists, and this has been my goal in presenting it.

The Future

There are many indications that interest in and research on translation will continue into the future. Interdisciplinary barriers across specialities are breaking down, encouraging collaboration among linguists, psychologists, humanists, educators, anthropologists, and representatives of other disciplines. The current trends in research on learning and memory, and the development of the information theory approach to human communication, encourage research on the activities of good translators, because these people combine all these elements in their work. The increase in contact across peoples from various cultural backgrounds, as in overseas education, multinational corporations, and diplomatic negotiations, will create a great demand for as much knowledge about the nature of translation as possible. Recent legislation concerned with minority group recognition, as in the development of bilingual education programs, provides another example. One of the purposes of such programs is to encourage maintenance of languages spoken by small numbers of people, and thus there will be a demand for the translation of educational materials. Translation is an exciting area in which to work, as the authors of the following chapters demonstrate, both through their obvious enthusiasm and through their scholarly contributions.

REFERENCES

Anderson, R. On the comparability of meaningful stimuli in cross-cultural research. *Sociometry,* 1967, 30, 124–136.

Armstrong, J., and Soelberg, P. On the interpretation of factor analysis. *Psychological Bulletin,* 1968, *70,* 361–364.

Barik, H. A description of various types of omissions, additions and errors encountered in simultaneous interpretation. *Meta,* 1971, *16,* 199–210.

Bartlett, F. Psychological methods and anthropological problems. *Africa,* 1937, *10,* 401–419.

Ben-Zeev, S. The influence of bilingualism on cognitive development and cognitive strategy. PhD dissertation, University of Chicago, 1972.

Bochner, S. The mediating man and cultural diversity. In R. Brislin, Ed., *Topics in Culture Learning,* Vol. 1. Honolulu, Hawaii: East-West Culture Learning Institute, 1973, pp. 23–37.

Brislin, R. Back-translation for cross-cultural research. *Journal of Cross-Cultural Psychology,* 1970, *1,* 185–216.

Brislin, R. Cross-cultural methods of possible relevance for other forms of comparative research. Paper delivered at the meetings of the American Psychological Association, August, 1975.

Brislin, R., and Van Buren, H. Can they go home again? *International Educational and Cultural Exchange,* 1974, *9*(4), 19–24.

Brislin, R., and Pedersen, P. *Cross-Cultural Orientation Programs.* New York: Gardner Press, 1976.

Brislin, R., Lonner, W., and Thorndike, R. *Cross-Cultural Research Methods.* New York: John Wiley, 1973.

Campbell, D. A cooperative multinational opinion sample exchange. *Journal of Social Issues,* 1968, *24,* 245–258.

Casagrande, J. The ends of translation. *International Journal of American Linguistics,* 1954, *20,* 335–340.

Chapanis, A. *Man-machine engineering.* Belmint, Calif.: Wadsworth, 1965.

Cofer, C. Constructive processes in memory. *American Scientist,* 1973, *61,* 537–543.

Crowne, D., and Marlowe, D. *The approval motive.* New York: John Wiley, 1964.

Dziuban, C., and Shirkey, E. When is a correlation matrix appropriate for factor analysis? some decision rules. *Psychological Bulletin,* 1974, *81,* 358–361.

Ervin-Tripp, S. Sociolinguistics. In L. Berkowitz, Ed. *Advances in Experimental Social Psychology,* Vol. 4. New York: Academic Press, 1969, pp. 91–165.

Fishman, J. Review of J. Hertzler: A sociology of language. *Language*, 1967, *43*, 586–604.

Fishman, J. *Readings in the sociology of language.* The Hague: Mouton, 1968.

French, J. A formal theory of social power. *Psychological Review*, 1956, *63*, 181–194.

Frey, F. Cross-cultural survey research in political science. In R. Holt and J. Turner, Eds., *The methodology of comparative research.* New York: The Free Press, 1970, pp. 173–264.

Goodenough, F. Racial differences in the intelligence of school children. *Journal of experimental psychology*, 1926, *9*, 388–397.

Gumperz, J., and Hymes, D., Eds., *Directions in sociolinguistics: the ethnography of communication.* New York: Holt, Rinehart, and Winston, 1972.

Janis, I. *Victims of groupthink: a psychological study of foreign policy decisions and fiascoes.* Boston: Houghton-Mifflin, 1972.

Lambert, W. Culture and language as factors in learning and education. In the *Fifth Western Symposium on Learning.* Bellingham, Washington: Western Washington State College, 1974, pp. 91–122.

Longacre, R. Items in context—their bearing on translation theory. *Language*, 1958, *34*, 482–491.

Mehrabian, A. *Silent messages.* Belmont, Calif.: Wadsworth, 1971.

Miller, G. What is information measurement? *American Psychologist*, 1953, *9*, 3–11.

Nida, E., Ed., *The book of a thousand tongues.* New York: United Bible Societies, 1972.

Osgood, C., Cross-cultural comparability in attitude measurement via multilingual semantic differentials. In I. Steiner and M. Fishbein, Eds., *Current studies in social psychology*, New York: Holt, Rinehart, and Winston, 1965, pp. 95–106.

Osgood, C. Exploration in semantic space: a personal diary. *Journal of Social Issues*, 1971, *27*(4), 5–64.

Osgood, C., Suci, G., and Tannenbaum, P. *The measurement of meaning.* Urbana, Ill.: University of Illinois Press, 1957.

Phillips, H. Problems of translation and meaning in field work. *Human Organization*, 1960, *18*(4), 184–192.

Pierce, J. et al. "Language and machines," National Academy of Sciences, Washington, D.C., 1966.

Ray, J. Factor analysis and attitude scales. *The Australian and New Zealand Journal of Sociology*, 1973, *9*(3), 11–13.

Richards, I. Toward a theory of translation. *Studies in Chinese thought.*

American Anthropological Association, 1953, volume 55, memoir 75. Chicago: University of Chicago Press.

Sinaiko, H. Teleconferencing: preliminary experiments. Research Paper P-108. Arlington, Va.: Institute for Defense Analyses, 1963.

Sinaiko, H., and Brislin, R. Experiments in language translation: technical English to Vietnamese. Research Paper P-634. Arlington, Va.: Institute for Defense Analyses, 1970.

Sinaiko, H., and Brislin, R. Evaluating language translations: experiments on three assessment methods. *Journal of Applied Psychology*, 1973, *57*, 328–334.

Thorndike, E., and Lorge, I. *The teacher's word book of 30,000 words.* New York: Bureau of Publications, Teachers College, Columbia University, 1944.

Triandis, H., et al. *The analysis of subjective culture.* New York: John Wiley, 1972.

Useem, J., and Useem, R. American-educated Indians and Americans in India: a comparison of two modernizing roles. *Journal of Social Issues*, 1968, *24*(4), 143–158.

Werner, O., and Campbell, D. Translating, working through interpreters, and the problem of decentering. In R. Naroll and R. Cohen, Eds., *A handbook of method in cultural anthropology.* New York: American Museum of Natural History, 1970, pp. 398–420.

Wickert, F. An adventure in psychological testing abroad. *American Psychologist*, 1957, *5*, 86–88.

Zimbardo, P., and Ruch, F. *Psychology and life*, ninth edition. Glenview, Ill.: Scott, Foresman, and Co., 1975.

PART 1

The Language Sciences

CHAPTER 1

A Framework for
the Analysis and Evaluation of
Theories of Translation

EUGENE A. NIDA

THE PURPOSES OF TRANSLATION are so diverse, the texts so different, and the receptors so varied that one can readily understand how and why many distinct formulations of principles and practices of translation have been proposed. All who have written seriously on translating agree that translators should know both the source and the receptor languages, should be familiar with the subject matter, and should have some facility of expression in the receptor language. Beyond these basic requirements there is little agreement on what constitutes legitimate translating and how the science of linguistics, or even the knowledge of language structures, can and should be applied.[1] For a better understanding of the causes of this lack of agreement and in order to construct a framework for the analysis and evaluation of the various theories of translation, it is essential to review briefly the relations between the source, the message, and the receptors in the communication process, and also the function of the medium of communication which is employed.

In an analysis of the types of interlingual communication involved in translating, one must describe the role of the source as a combination of the intents of the primary source, the author, and of the secondary source, the translator himself.[2] The message must be described in terms of both form and content, and the receptors must be viewed from the perspective of their monolingual comprehension of the translated text. As for the medium, it must be considered primarily in terms of the basic differences between oral and written communication, usually referred to as interpreting and translating. At the same time one must consider the various purposes involved in communication, causing it to be expressive, informative, imperative, provocative, and so on. In most situations, of course, several purposes operate conjointly and often in different types of configurations, reflecting diverse emphases.[3] For example, in informative communication, the focus is primarily on the message, in expressive communication it is on the source; and in imperative communication it is on the response of the receptors. Accordingly, these purposes are best described in their relation to the three basic elements in communication with which each one is characteristically associated.

After treating the communication factors of message, source, receptors, and medium, brief consideration must be given to some of the practical and theoretical issues that have arisen in the development of translation theory: (1) the limits of translatability, (2) evaluation of translations, and (3) translating as an art, a skill, or a science. The final section of this chapter is devoted to the analysis of the various theories, in terms of the principal bases involved, namely, philogical, linguistic, and sociolinguistic.

In discussing the various theories of translation it is important to recognize that these theories are seldom developed in a comprehensive form.[4] In most cases the theories are far more implicit than explicit. Nevertheless, the largely implicit formulations must be treated as theories of translation, because the stated principles or rules for translating rest on important underlying considerations and reflect corresponding theories.

The Role of the Message

Traditionally, the role of the message, especially in terms of cognitive equivalence, has been the dominant element in discussions of translating. In fact, the emphasis on correspondence in content has been so strong that features of form have often been seriously slighted. Equivalence in content is so basic to certain types of scientific documents that relatively crude machine translations have gained a fairly wide acceptance. In reality, however, content cannot be divorced completely from form. Form and content often constitute an inseparable bond, as in the case of religious texts, in which concepts are often closely related to particular words or other verbal formulas. Wherever strong beliefs in word magic or verbal inspiration are associated with a text, the form of the message nearly always holds a dominant role, and the meaning of the surface content is frequently sacrificed for the sake of preserving the hidden significance which is thought to lie in the form.

Problems of Content

In treating the content of a message, one must often distinguish clearly between the discourse itself and its temporal-spatial setting. That is to say, what happened in a narrative may constitute one series of problems, but the cultural setting of the narrative itself may introduce quite a different series of difficulties. When the circumstantial setting of a source-language text is widely divergent from any corresponding setting in a receptor language, serious problems may be involved in providing a meaningful equivalent text. In such cases the translator may be forced to choose between the less comprehensible cultural setting of the source language and the more intelligible but anachronistic setting of the receptor language. In translating the Greek classics, for example, the translator must decide whether to preserve as much as possible the unique cultural features of Ancient Greece and thus attempt to transport the reader back in time to the setting of the original communication, or to provide a new cultural setting for the corresponding cognitive content. If there is great concern for the historical setting of a text and the historicity of the events involved, the translator obviously feels compelled to emphasize the unique historical setting and usually explains in appended notes such features of the source culture as are entirely unknown in the receptor culture. But if historicity is not regarded as an important factor, a translator often feels quite justified in modernizing the setting—usually with the intention of highlighting the present-day relevance of the message. This is sometimes done in quite radical ways, as, for example, in the Cotton Patch Version of the Gospels by Clarence Jordan (1969), in which Jerusalem becomes Atlanta, the Temple is referred to as First Church, and Peter, son of John, becomes Rock Johnson. But even when the translator strives to avoid the introduction of features of the receptor language, he may find it impossible to omit them altogether. In the Thai language, for example, it is impossible to talk about anyone without reflecting, simply in the use of pronouns, a number of the different classes that exist in Thai society, only some of which may have identifiable equivalences in a Western culture.

Two dimensions that are directly relevant to the content of the setting are time and culture. When the temporal distance is great, there are almost always considerable cultural differences, as between Ancient Rome and present-day Italy. But even when two settings are contemporaneous, they may have great cultural distances. For example, the problems of translating the content of Navajo healing songs into present-day English are much greater than the difficulties encountered in translating Homer's Illiad into modern English. Some translators have concluded that an attempt to bridge a wide time-cultural span requires not simply a translation but a kind of running commentary, the modern equivalent of an ancient Hebrew targum. Most translators, however, prefer to avoid the inevitable anachronisms and distortions that a targumlike translation involves, preferring to retain the cultural features of the source-language text in the text of the translation and to attempt an explanation of their significance in appended notes.

The degree to which the foreign cultural setting is preserved in a translation depends in large measure on the extent to which the imperative function of the translation is in focus. If its purpose is to promote particular types of behavior by the receptors within their own cultural context, the translator often feels justified in altering the cultural features of original setting. But if its purpose is to make the receptors understand what happened at a particular time in history or in another culture, the translator generally feels obligated to preserve as much of the original cultural setting as possible. In the translation of scientific articles, the factors of time-culture setting are usually so important that one cannot afford to introduce cultural adjustments, except by way of supplementary notes. In translating business letters, however, sensitive translators often make radical adjustments in certain aspects of the content so as to make the message more acceptable to the receptors, for it is readily appreciated that the forms of accepted business etiquette differ widely in various parts of the world. One should not assume, however, that any and every part of a text in a particular category (e.g., the business letter) is equally subject to alteration. In certain parts of the translation even the very form of the original text may have to be followed very closely.

Problems of Form

Though the difficulties related to the adequate reproduction of content are often acute, they generally do not constitute as complex and intractible a series of problems as the particular formal features of language employed in a message. One can much more easily analyze and describe the cognitive equivalences of content than the formal equivalences of language. That is to say, the componential features of cognitive meaning can be more readily transferred and, if necessary, redistributed from source to receptor language than the corresponding features of discourse structure. The latter include, not only the traditionally described rhetorical elements of style, but also the more complex structures of paragraph, episode, section, chapter, and the like. In fact, for many of these higher-level structures there are as yet no established metalinguistic terms. The various genres have been described for a number of languages, but little has been done in determining their function and hence the corresponding equivalences between possible source and receptor languages.

The formal linguistic features become all the more important as the text under consideration contains more and more highly specialized stylistic features. Furthermore, the greater the significance of the form for the comprehension and appreciation of the message, the more difficult it is to find appropriate formal equivalences in the receptor language. That is to say, it is in proportion as the original author has exploited the distinctive rhetorical resources of the source language to communicate his message, so is it correspondingly difficult for the translator to reflect these features in the receptor language, for that has its own distinctive and perhaps very different rhetorical devices. "The most convincing criterion of the quality of a work is the fact that it can only be translated with difficulty, for if it passes readily into another language without losing its essence, then it must have no particular essence or at least not one of the rarest" (O'Brien, 1959).

If the term *meaning* is to be understood in its broader sense of any conceptual components communicated by a text, the formal features of a message must certainly be regarded as having meaning. The fact that the book of Job is in the form of an elaborate dramatic didactic poem is itself an indication that one should not interpret the text as a recording of a bedside conversation, but as a highly formal probe into existential mysteries, in which the prologue and the epilogue simply provide the rhetorical setting and not the *raison d'être* of the dialogue.

As the formal features of a text become more highly specialized (that is, distinctive of the source language in question), the more difficult it is to approximate the form and the more unlikely it is that even a formal equivalence will carry anything like the same significance for receptor-language readers. This fact is conspicuously evident in attempts to translate *hayku* from Japanese to English. Even if one succeeds in reproducing a relatively satisfactory content equivalent of the seventeen-syllable original, the average English-speaking person will have much less appreciation for *hayku* as a literary form than would a correspondingly literate individual in Japan.

This fundamental problem of equivalences of literary genres has concerned a number of translators and linguists involved in issues of translation theory and practice. The volume on *The Nature of Translation* (Holmes, 1970) has an excellent series of articles dealing especially with the issue of literary translation. The same concerns are typical of a similar volume edited by Brower (1959). Levý (1969) has proposed a complete theory of literary translation based primarily on a classification of literary genres, and Petöfi (1971, 1972) has elaborated a complex system for the description of various discourse types.[5]

The principal difficulties with literary genres are not their formal features—many of which can be satisfactorily reproduced—but their lack of functional equivalence within the respective communication structures of source and receptor languages. It was quite appropriate for ancient Hebrew prophets to pronounce ultimatums in poetic form, but in present-day English a corresponding poetic form would suggest to many persons something rather trivial and/or nonhistorical. Rieu (1953) chose to translate the Iliad and Odyssey into English prose rather than into poetry, not because English lacks poetic structures, but because epic poetry is no longer a common literary form in English, whereas epic prose still is. Epic poetry strikes many present-day English readers as quaint and artificial, but Rieu's vigorous prose is entertainingly vivid and up-to-date.

The extent to which formal features of a text are retained in translation depends in large measure on the extent to which information concerning such forms are relevant to either the text or the receptors. For example, one of the principal purposes in translating and publishing certain literary and ethnographic texts is to communicate to receptors something of the formal features of these texts. Persons who wish to study medieval French literature, without learning medieval French, want translations that reflect as many as possible of the distinctive features of the original texts. Rather than adjusting the texts to modern idiom and form and placing information as to their formal features in footnotes, translators usually produce a close literal translation and give explanations of the meaning in the footnotes. Even more literal renderings are often demanded of ethnographic texts, especially in instances in which linguists want to analyze some of the formal syntactic features as well as some of the rhetorical devices.

If the form of the original text must be in focus, there are a number of features of format that may highlight the formal elements. A strictly interlinear translation is perhaps the most extreme adaptation to the formal features of a source-language text. Early translations of Chinese Buddhist texts into Japanese were even more formal, in the sense that the Chinese characters were all retained, but the order of the corresponding words in Japanese (which employed the same *kanji* characters) was simply marked by numerals.

Because strictly interlinear translations are often quite unintelligible, publishers often add a more-or-less literal translation in a parallel column or on a facing page.

The pros and cons for attempting to reveal formal structures through translations have been aired extensively. Fitts (1959) has insisted on the validity of using literal translations as a means of representing the genius of foreign-language poetry, while in the same volume on translation theory and practice Matthews (1959) insists that "to translate a poem whole is to compose another poem," and he objects strongly to the printing of verse translations facing their models, contending that "the life is knocked out of translated poems by the kind of misreading they get under these circumstances."

Attempts to reflect the formal features of the source-language text are generally of three types: (1) a concordant translation, which insofar as possible reproduces each word (and even in some cases each grammatical form) of the source language by a single corresponding lexical item or grammatical form of the receptor language; (2) a more-or-less literal translation, with footnotes to explain otherwise obscure or meaningless expressions and to call attention to rhetorical specialities (e.g., literary allusions, plays on words, rhyme, alliteration, acrostic series, hendiadys, and chiasmus); and (3) nonliteral translations, with footnotes referring to various formal features.

The so-called rhetorical features of language are presumably employed by authors for the sake of impact and aesthetic appeal. That is to say, the purposes relate both to the author's intent and to the receptor's response. But these formal features also communicate information about the author and his attitudes toward the text. If the rhetorical devices appear to be in keeping with the content, the communication is regarded as effective, but if the rhetorical devices are "overdone" (as is characteristic of so-called purple prose), the author is judged as being artificial or the communication is thought to be in some degree ironic. Rhetorical features do not have meanings in and of themselves, but insofar as they match certain expectancies on the part of receptors, they are judged as meaningful indices of the author's (and correspondingly of the translator's) ability in the use of language and his attitude toward the subject matter of the text.

There are many formal features of language that are not rhetorical, but rather are role related. They do not signal information about the structure of the discourse, but about the roles of those who participate in the discourse or about the settings in which the discourse takes place. Dialect differences are typical of such role-related formal features. In some instances a translator is even required to represent certain idiosyncratic features, such as stuttering, lisping, high frequency of certain exclamations, a tendency to scatological vocabulary—all of which may cause considerable difficulties in finding adequate receptor-language parallels. More frequently the dialect forms used by writers are either horizontal (geographical) or vertical (socioeconomic) dialects, and rarely do authors or translators consistently represent all the details of such dialects, but at least certain easily recognized features are selected that serve to signal the type of dialect being used. A form such as you all is supposed to typify Southern American English, and boid 'bird' and goil 'girl' are supposed to represent the Lower East Side of New York City. The problem for the translator is to find in a foreign language a dialect with approximately the same status and connotations. Rarely is the dialect match fully successful, for the values associated with a particular dialect are often highly specific.

The use of archaic or obsolescent language in translation to reflect an old-fashioned dialect usage in the source-language text is another important technique for representing certain aspects of formal correspondence. The use of such a technique is, however, very different from the attempt to use archaic language throughout a translation simply because the text of the source-language was written some centuries ago. Trying to reflect the antiquity of a source-language text by archaic receptor-language vocabulary of grammatical forms is actually a violation of the source-language discourse, unless the original text itself contains intentionally archaic forms as a means of providing an archaic flavor. In some cases receptors have come to associate archaic forms with ancient documents. Hence there are persons who insist that any translation of the Bible must sound old-fashioned simply because the patriarchs and the apostles lived many centuries ago.

Closely related to the archaizing of formal features is the tendency to intentional obscurantism and mystification in texts. Attempts to translate cabalistic writings or the musings of the mystics into completely clear present-day language are almost certainly doomed to failure. In fact, making clear what is intentionally obscure in the original text is a violation of the intent of the author and of the spirit of the text.

One type of dialect distinction particularly difficult to represent in translation is that of the sexes, that is, men's versus women's usage. It is not always easy to find satisfactory equivalents for typical English feminine expressions as mercy me, goodness gracious, dearie no, and you can't imagine. Though in some languages there are radical differences between the forms of women's and men's speech, in general the distinctions are very subtle. They do, however, signal important aspects of participant roles. As is often the case, conformance to expected norms goes almost unnoticed by receptors, but violation of the norms produces shock, as when typical female speech is attributed to a man. The reader can only conclude that either the translator missed the point or that the author was trying to characterize the man in question as being effeminate.

In addition to the various types of dialects used by participants in discourse, there is also a variety of levels of usage which primarily reflect differences of psychological distance between participants in the communication setting. These levels (or registers) of language have been variously described in terms of graded series and are designated by such terms as frozen, formal, consultative, informal, casual, and intimate (Joos, 1962; Catford, 1965). It is also possible to describe a so-called common language (Wonderly, 1968), a type of language overlapping other levels, such as might be used, for example, when an astrophysicist and his gardener communicate with each other.

The frozen level of discourse consists essentially in formalized phrases and set patterns of expression, such as those that are typical of liturgical performances, whether they be enacted in the pulpit or on the political platform. In a sense frozen discourse may be described as representing the greatest psychological distance between source and receptors. Since both the form and content of the message are largely redundant, there is little or no conscious encoding or decoding; except for the paralinguistic aspects of the communication, there is very little psychological identification between the source and the receptors.

In formal discourse there is likewise considerable psychological distance between the source and receptors, but both form and content are much less redundant. The use of formal language seems to be dictated primarily by the desire of the source to emphasize the importance of his subject matter or the superiority of his intellectual status. At any rate, formal discourse generally represents a considerable psychological distance between source and receptors. On the consultative level the participants are presumably unknown to each other, but the desire for clarity of communication reduces the psychological distance and normally results in the elimination of either frozen formulas or formal aloofness. On the informal level the participants are presumably known to one another and have no desire to maintain psychological distance. They can relax the linguistic barriers and use more common forms of language. In English the use of the elided forms he'd and we'd (for he would and we would) is typical of the shift from consultative to informal speech. Casual speech may be described simply as a more informal level, the type of speech one employs at a party beside the swimming pool, whereas the informal level would be more appropriate at a dinner party. The intimate level is restricted to communication between intimate friends or members of the same family. They use highly elliptical expressions because they share a large amount of background information, and they employ many terms with highly specialized meanings, because their common experiences provide a basis for references which only they can understand and appreciate.

Topic-related forms of language are closely related to levels of language, but in certain important respects they also differ from levels. For example, the types of language that are typical of scientific discourse, religious discussion, government pronouncements, and committee reports are strikingly different, not only in vocabulary and certain frozen formulas, but in the order and arrangement of information, the extent of verbal padding, and the amount of apparent intentional ambiguity. It is also possible to describe topic-related forms of language as being role-related, because those who are proficient in the use of such language are normally professionals in their respective fields and thus are using language forms that correspond to their roles. The expectancies that receptors have for the forms of language which are supposed to correspond to various role-topic contexts are very strong. Thus there is quite a shock for the receptors when a theologian writes like a scientist (as in the case of John A. T. Robinson's book *Honest to God*) or when a scientist uses language typical of theologians (as in the case of Teilhard de Chardin's *Hymne de l'univers*).

What is perhaps even more surprising is the fact that in almost all so-called world languages, representing a highly heterogeneous set of roles and specializations of information, there are a surprising number of corresponding sets of formal differences, so that diverse role-related levels of language can be suggested, even if they are not fully imitated. Skillful translators have been amazingly adept at finding means for such correlations. Even in the case of translations into so-called primitive languages, it has been possible to reproduce the equivalents of several diverse literary genres, as has been well illustrated by the number of excellent translations of the Bible into minor languages.[6]

The Role of the Translator

In addition to competence and skill in verbal communication, a translator must have at least three other characteristics if he is to excel in his work. First, he needs to have a sincere admiration for the formal features of the work to be translated, for without this he is unlikely to possess either the patience or the insights necessary to reproduce a fully adequate equivalent. Second, he should have a respect for the content of the text, or he is likely to shortchange the message. Third, he must be willing to express his own creativity through someone else's creation. These qualities may also involve the translator in certain serious liabilities. For example, his admiration for the form of the original text may induce him to reproduce a disproportionate amount of that form or to feel compelled to weight down the text with numerous superfluous notes. He may also be too easily tempted to reveal his mastery of the text by introducing various formal subtleties, which may be pleasing to the receptor who also knows the language of the source text (in which case he really does not need a translation) but misleading to receptors unacquainted with the source language. This is one of the serious criticisms that can be brought against the translation of the Pentateuch by Buber and Rosenzweig (1930), a remarkably effective translation for persons who are already familiar with the Hebrew original, but often misleading or obscure for others.

Too much identification with the original text can lead to a tendency to try to improve on it by correcting its apparent inaccuracies and glossing over its stylistic weaknesses and failures. A tendency to alter the meaning of the text to fit the translator's own presuppositions is too often found in translations made by those who most firmly declare their identification with the original message.[7]

Though these attitudes of translators may at first seem to be unrelated to a framework for the analysis and evaluation of theories of translation, they do in fact have a great deal to do with the development of various theories and with the promulgation and justification of related principles of translation. They are also involved in the setting of standards and in the development of expectancies on the part of receptors.

The Role of Receptors

The role of receptors in the development of principles and practices of translation is far more important than has often been thought to be the case. The fact that some persons have often spoken of the receptors as the "target" of translating indicates how oblivious these persons are to the role of those who are expected to receive and decode the communication.

The role of receptors in the translation process should be viewed from two related perspectives: (1) the reaction which a particular translation produces in receptors and (2) the expectations which receptors have as to what constitutes legitimate translating.

If the translator is merely concerned with entertaining the receptors or with enriching their knowledge, he is likely to have a much freer attitude toward modifying the form and content of the underlying text. If, however, the translator hopes through a translation to change the behavior or value system of the receptors, he will no doubt pay much more attention to factors of clarity and impact in which the imperative force of the message is clearly signaled.

Translators often differ as to the extent to which they regard a particular text as being applicable to the behavior of particular receptors. For example, some Bible translators insist that all the Bible is directly applicable to any and all receptors, whereas other translators regard only certain portions of the Bible as applicable. These differences of hermeneutical viewpoint become extremely important in the selection of various formal devices to heighten the impact and to suggest the present-day relevance of the Bible.

The expectancies of receptors as to the validity of certain types of translation are crucial for determining the probabilities for the acceptance or rejection of a translation. Cary (1959, 1963) has described in a charming and effective way the manner in which matters of taste differ in successive periods of history, and Nida (1959) has outlined some of the major differences in attitudes toward literal and free translations (especially as these relate to Bible translating) during several centuries in Western Europe. Although literary critics often appear to dictate canons of acceptability in translating, the response of the book-buying public is ultimately more important, at least in a so-called free society.

In the past the role of the literary critic was often regarded as determinative with respect to the adequacy of a translation, since he was presumably in the best position to judge whether the translator had been faithful to both the content and the form of the original. In recent years, however, the role of the average receptor has become far more important in judging the validity of various translations. Oller and others (1972) and Nida and Taber (1969) have indicated how the cloze technique can be applied to testing the relative accuracy of translated texts. Alverson (1969) and Brislin (1970) have discussed back-translating by receptors as a basis for judging correctness of content. The traditional practice of direct questioning of receptors as to content is still valid, but an even better way of judging the adequacy of a translation is to record the ways in which receptors relate to other persons the content of what they have read. The alterations these receptors make in both form and content can be very significant, especially if two or more receptors introduce similar alterations. Another technique for analyzing the naturalness of certain formal features is to record the oral reading of a text by several receptors. If two or more relatively competent readers stumble, hesitate, or alter a text at the same point, one can be reasonably sure that at that point some serious problem of formal structure occurs.

These various techniques for checking translations on the basis of receptor reactions simply highlight the increased importance being attached to the role of receptors in the translation process. A translator who cannot properly anticipate the reactions of his prospective audience is doomed to be less than successful.

The Role of the Medium of Communication

The form of interlingual communication is greatly influenced by its oral or written medium. Oral texts also differ extensively, depending on the number and types of accompanying constraints. Simultaneous interpreting demands that one get across the gist of the message, often with minimal regard for the stylistic features of the original utterance. When two languages are closely related, for example, Cantonese and Mandarin, it is possible for a simultaneous interpreter to remain not more than one second behind the speaker and to convey a high percentage of the formal structures of the source text. With sequential interpreting, for example, a sentence or brief paragraph at a time, the receptor-language utterance is supposed to reflect a much greater refinement in stylistic coherence than in the case in simultaneous translating. In those rare situations in which interpreters are able to reproduce entire speeches with almost complete sentence-for-sentence correspondence, there may be a high degree of formal adaptation and equivalence.[8]

The influence of the oral medium of communication must be

noted not only in interpreting but also in the oral production of texts, especially in those situations in which there may be a number of extralinguistic constraints. For example, in translating songs, various extralinguistic factors serve as constraints on the form of the receptor-language text, such as the number of syllables, relation of accented and nonaccented syllables to corresponding stressed notes of music, patterns of rhyming, length of syllables, and the tones of syllables in the case of tonal languages. The greater the number of such constraints, the greater the need for alteration of content in order to fit the words to the musical score.

Translations designed for stage production also require a number of adjustments in form and content in order to make them effective. What might be quite satisfactory in written form may fall flat when uttered in a dramatic performance.

One of the most rigid sets of constraints in translation occurs in the case of synchronization of cinema dialogue. Not only must the corresponding expressions be pronounceable within approximately the same time span, but the movement of the lips must be closely matched.

In the same way that written communications generally differ from oral communications in conceptual compactness, grammatical correctness, and structural cohesiveness, so also are written translations expected to differ from oral ones. There may, however, be intentional deviation from this expectancy in order to respond to certain more pressing demands. For example, a group of students in one country of Latin America wished to reproduce in a printed flyer a selection from one of the Old Testament prophets dealing with the issues of social justice. In place of a well-constructed translation in traditional biblical language, they chose to produce an extemporaneous type of translation, poorly mimeographed on cheap paper. The production had considerable success, because it closely paralleled in form and content the types of revolutionary documents students were eager to read.

Basic Issues as to the Nature of Translating

In view of the different purposes of translating and the large number of diverse influences that affect both the principles and practices of translating, it is no wonder that several important issues have arisen over the fundamental nature of translation. These issues have centered primarily around three questions: (1) Is translation possible? (2) What is the best translation? (3) Is translating an art, a skill, or a science? Only in the light of these issues can one consider satisfactorily the various underlying theories of translation.

Is Translation Possible?

A number of linguists and philologists have discussed the question of translatability. Mounin (1963) has dedicated essentially an entire volume to this issue and has discussed its pros and cons with excellent critical insight. House (1973) describes in detail certain formal features that cannot be directly translated, for example, puns, metalanguage, certain types of literary allusions, and some sociolinguistic dialects. Irmen (1970) takes a more optimistic view on translatability, because all languages are presumably built up from the same elementary units and all appear to have many of the same rhetorical devices, such as irony, hyperbole, and litotes. Certainly the most charming discussion of this issue is found in Güttinger's delightful volume *Zielsprache* (1963), in which he points out that philologists generally contend that translation is impossible, whereas authors are not only pleased but anxious to have their works translated. Even some of the same philologists who insist on untranslatability want their own works translated!

The question of untranslatability has too often been discussed in terms of absolute rather than relative equivalence. If one is to insist that translation must involve no loss of information whatsoever, then obviously not only translating but all communication is impossible. No communication, whether intralingual, interlingual, or intersemiotic, can occur without some loss of information. Even among experts discussing a subject within their own fields of specialization, it is unlikely that comprehension rises above the 80 percent level. Loss of information is a part of any communication process, and hence the fact that some loss occurs in translation should not be surprising, nor should it constitute a basis for questioning the legitimacy of translating.

The extent to which the meaning of a text is translatable

depends in large measure on one's definition or concept of meaning. Catford (1965) is quite right in insisting that in a strict sense the meaning of any unit of language can only be described in terms of the sets of contrasts within that language. Therefore, there can be no identity of meaning between languages. On the other hand, as Katharina Reiss (1971) has indicated, there are certain areas in which practical and functional equivalences can be attained, and these can be best identified through a linguistic approach to the structures of the respective languages. Such a position differs radically from the contentions of Burton Raffel (1971, p. 103) who insists that "linguistic knowledge is not the best nor even a good road toward successful translation."

Although in translating one cannot count on an identity of semantic structures *(Bedeutung)*, there is a sense in which equivalences can be found on the level of referential function *(Bezeichnung)*. This means that there can be substantial agreement on the pragmatic level. This dependence on referential function means that one must look to the nonlinguistic world for many of the answers to problems of translational equivalence. It is precisely such need for nonlinguistic data which means that translating involves not only linguistic evidence but encyclopedic knowledge as well. This is precisely the point made by Revzin and Rozencveyg (1964) and commented on by Balcerzan (1970) as one of the principal reasons for the failure of machine translation.

What is the Best Translation?

When the question of the superiority of one translation over another is raised, the answer should be looked for in the answer to another question, "Best for whom?" The relative adequacy of different translations of the same text can only be determined in terms of the extent to which each translation successfully fulfills the purpose for which it was intended. In other words, the relative validity of each translation is seen in the degree to which the receptors are able to respond to its message (in terms of both form and content) in comparison with (1) what the original author evidently intended would be the response of the original audience and (2) how that audience did, in fact, respond. The responses can, of course, never be identical, for interlingual communication always implies some differences in cultural setting, with accompanying diversities in value systems, conceptual presuppositions, and historical antecedents.

The ultimate validation of a translation can never be a purely linguistic undertaking. In fact, as has already been noted in the description of the influences that bear on the translating, the underlying principles for determining the adequacy of a translation are largely sociolinguistic. That is why Reiss (1972, p. 115) insists on subjective evaluation in translating, and for the same reason Neubert (1969) has emphasized the 'situation context' for evaluating the appropriateness of a translation. In essence, this means that translation cannot be viewed merely as a linguistic undertaking but as essentially an aspect of a larger domain, namely, that of communication.

Is Translating an Art, a Skill, or a Science?

Cary (1959) was convinced that translation is an art. One can appreciate Cary's position, for he not only concentrated his genius on literary works, but he demonstrated unusual aesthetic creativity in his translating. Cary's good friend and colleague, Jumpelt (1961), while fully appreciating Cary's concern for the translation of literary works, treated translating more as a science. Jumpelt's position is likewise entirely explicable, because his area of specialization has been technical and scientific documents.

"Is translating an art, a skill, or a science?" is a question wrongly phrased. The issue is not one of alternative but of supplementary factors. A satisfactory translation of an artistic literary work obviously requires a corresponding artistic ability on the part of the translator. The pleasing use of words demands aesthetic sensitivity in the same way that the pleasing arrangement of colors or of three-dimensional space requires aesthetic competence. But competence in translating is not solely an innate ability. To a considerable extent it can be taught and improved, so that translating can also be regarded as a skill. The mural artist may exhibit artistic ability in the composition and also may acquire skill in the application of paint to canvass. Similarly, the translator may exhibit artistic ability in his choice of an appropriate form in a receptor language to recast, let us say, a sonnet, and at the same time demonstrate skill in his arrangement of the rhythmic units.

Whether translating is to be regarded as a science depends on the meaning given to translating. If by translating one refers only to the actual process of reproducing the message of language *A* to the forms required by language *B*, then it is not a science. However, the activity involved in such interlingual communication can certainly be made the subject of scientific inquiry. An act of verbal communication is not science, but speech itself may become the object of scientific analysis, description, and explanation. Whether the composer of music is better qualified for his work by studying the science of tonal harmonics is open to question, but if he has the task of teaching others something about the fundamentals of music composition, then some knowledge of the science of tonal harmonics is surely important. Precisely for this same type of reason, institutes designed to train translators and interpreters are increasingly emphasizing the scientific aspects of interlingual communication.[9]

This emphasis on the scientific basis for translating and interpreting results from the fact that most students can progress more rapidly in the acquisition of translating skills if they have a satisfactory understanding of the scientific basis for effective interlingual communication. Mere competence in a second language does not in itself indicate significant ability in translating into or from that language. Furthermore, even literary competence in a language does not necessarily carry with it adequacy as a translator. Maillot (1974) makes some interesting observations about the serious faults of André Gide as a translator of English into French. His translation of one of Conrad's sea stories contains a striking number of typical translational errors.

Theories of Translation

Because translation is an activity involving language, there is a sense in which any and all theories of translation are linguistic. There are, however, three quite different ways in which the principles and procedures of translation have been formulated and defended. These diverse approaches to the problems of translating are essentially matters of different perspectives or foci. If the focus of attention is on particular texts (and especially if these are of a so-called literary quality), the underlying theory of translation is generally best regarded as philological.[10] If, however, the focus of attention is on the correspondences in language form and content, that is, on the structural differences between the source and receptor languages, the corresponding theory may be regarded as linguistic. Finally, if the focus is on translation as a part of an actual communication process, the most appropriate designation for the related theories is sociolinguistic. In actual practice, of course, there is a considerable degree of overlap both in the formulation of principles and in the corresponding recommendations on procedures.

The Philological Theories of Translation

The philological theories of translation have been concerned primarily with so-called literary texts. These are regarded as being sufficiently important to warrant special study and as having a sufficiently complex history (both in their development and in their subsequent interpretation) to require attention to the circumstances of production and transmission, if the form and content are to be adequately understood and appreciated, and if their translation is to be satisfactorily carried out.

The philological theories of translation are, of course, based on a philological approach to literary analysis. They simply go one step further; in place of treating the form in which the text was first composed, they deal with corresponding structures in the source and receptor languages and attempt to evaluate their equivalences.

In view of the significance of literary texts for the philological theories of translation, one can readily understand how and why problems of equivalence of literary genres between source and receptor languages become so important. Moreover, the mere existence of similar genres in the source and receptor languages is not the primary consideration. The more important issue is the functional correspondence of such genres. Philological theories of translation are normally concerned with all kinds of stylistic features and rhetorical devices. A number of scholars are increasingly interested in many of the larger structural units of discourse, in terms of hierarchical structures, dependency relations, and semantic interpretations.

In certain respects the philological approach to translation may also be said to deal with deep structures. For example, it is not enough for the philologist to describe the principal episodes of a narrative. It is more important to understand these in terms of their underlying structures, for example, violence-revenge or attack-capture-escape-retaliation. In another sense philological analysis must deal with the deep structure of symbolic levels. Parables are noted for their multilevel symbolic structures, so that a parable such as the story of the prodigal son must be understood on several levels: (1) freedom to waste one's heritage without losing one's sonship, (2) the callousness of legalism, and (3) the joyful forgiveness of divine love. Without an adequate appreciation of certain of these factors the translator can make a number of serious mistakes, especially when certain types of acts have quite different symbolic meanings in other cultures. Among the Ifugao of the Philippines the dividing of property in the parable of the prodigal son seems quite natural, because the Ifugao parents normally divide their property when their children get married. But in some societies readers of this story almost unanimously place on the father the blame for the younger son's failure. They reason that the father should have known his son well enough to know what he would do, and, therefore, he should have refused to give him the money which he would see wasted. The translator cannot, of course, recast the story, but he needs to be aware of the probable differences in interpretation and thus suggest by way of footnotes the information that is necessary for an adequate understanding of the underlying symbolism of the story.

Prior to World War II practically all attempts to formulate theories of translation were based essentially on philological comparisons of texts. Traditional lists of rules (or advice) for translators are all based on fundamentally philological view-points.[11] Belloc's (1931) insightful treatment of translation represents this philological approach, and the volume *Quality in Translation* (Cary and Jumpelt, 1963), containing the papers of the Third International Congress of the International Federation of Translators, is likewise essentially philological in outlook, even as most of the articles in *Babel* (the journal of the same organization) have continued to be. Even the book *On Translation* (Brower, 1959) is largely philological in orientation. Fedorov (1958, 1968) protested strongly against the domination of philology and its methodology in translation theory, with the result that many people began to recognize the necessity of a more linguistic orientation for translation theory and practice. Fedorov's proposals, however, did not please the linguists, for in general they felt that he had not gone far enough, nor did his suggestions find favor with the philologists, for they insisted that he had departed too radically from proven tradition. Levý's work (1969) marks a decisive step in the direction of introducing sound linguistic principles into a theory of literary translating.

Linguistic Theories of Translation

Linguistic theories of translation are based on a comparison of the linguistic structures of source and receptor texts rather than on a comparison of literary genres and stylistic features. The development of these theories can be attributed to two principal factors: (1) the application of the rapidly expanding science of linguistics to several different areas of intellectual activity, for example, language learning, cognitive anthropology, semiotics, and the teaching of skills in translating and interpreting, and (2) machine translation.

The fact that linguists have been able to provide a number of important insights into the nature of meaning (an area traditionally reserved for philosophers and logicians) has helped to stimulate interest in a linguistic approach to translational problems. The works of Hjelmslev (1953), Greimas (1966), Pottier (1970), and Coseriu (1970a, b), have been especially important in this respect. The increasing influence of linguistics on translation principles and procedures is also clearly seen in the types of articles appearing in *Meta* and the increase of linguistically oriented articles in *Babel*.

Machine translating has provided an especially important motivation for basing translation procedures on linguistic analyses and for a rigorous description of the related structures of source and receptor languages. It was quite impossible to instruct a machine how to translate even simple texts unless the programming was based on detailed linguistic analyses and descriptions. The work of Yngve (1954, 1957, 1958), Tosh (1969), and Oettinger (1959) are all clearly linguistic in orientation, and the later summaries of successes and failures, for example, Wilss (1970) and Gross (1972), only make sense in terms of the linguistic framework in which attempts at machine translation were undertaken. Although machine translation has had only limited success (Peter Toma of LATSEC seems to be the only one who has developed a commercially profitable system), it has contributed enormously to the development of linguistic theories of nonmechanical translation.

The principal differences between various linguistic theories (or semitheories) of translation lie in the extent to which the focus is on surface structures or corresponding deep structures. Theories based on surface-structure comparisons involve the use of more-or-less elaborate sets of rules for matching roughly corresponding structures, for example, the manner in which actives in language *A* correspond to passives in language *B*, the relations between nominal constructions in language *A* and parallel verbal constructions in language *B*, or shifts of order from subject-verb-object in language *A* to verb-subject-object in language *B*. Similar types of rules are constructed for changing rhetorical questions to emphatic statements and for altering certain types of metaphors to related kinds of similes. All such rules may be regarded as formulations of interlingual paraphrase, without attempting, however, to relate such paraphrases to particular types of deep structure.[12]

The important work of Vinay and Darbelnet (1958) on the comparison of English and French served as an important guide to many translators in formulating rules for sets of equivalences, and this same approach is reflected in a number of articles in *Meta*. It is interesting that Wandruska (1969)

reversed the process. Instead of setting up rules for translational correspondence on the basis of comparative linguistic
analyses, he employed translations of texts into various languages as a basis for determining comparative structures. Contrastive linguistics, as represented, for example, in *Papers in
Contrastive Linguistics,* edited by Nickel (1971), likewise has
a number of obviously important implications for any theories
of translation based on surface structures, although contrastive
linguistics is also concerned with deep-structure contrasts.

Before the formulation of generative-transformation grammar by Chomsky (1955a, b) Nida had already adopted an essentially deep-structure approach to certain problems of exegesis. In an article entitled "A New Methodology in Biblical
Exegesis" (1952) he advocated the back-transformation of
complex surface structures onto an underlying level, in which
the fundamental elements are objects, events, abstracts, and
relations. Such an approach was developed essentially for two
purposes: (1) to provide a means of adequate analysis of complicated grammatical structures in Greek and Hebrew, and
(2) to determine the least unambiguous structure that might
then serve as a basis for transfer into other languages. After the development of generative-transformation grammar by
Chomsky and his associates, Nida (1964) and Nida and Taber
(1969) further elaborated their theory of translation in terms
of three stages: analysis, transfer, and restructuring, in which
analysis consists essentially in back-transformation to a near-
kernel level.

A further development in this theory would entail back-
transformation to a completely abstract deep level, with a corresponding restructuring to that level in the receptor language
which would be most appropriate for the audience for which
the translation was being prepared. This is essentially the position advocated by Walmsley (1970). In actual practice, however, the transfer from source to receptor language takes
place at various subsurface levels, depending on the extent
to which the two languages under consideration have corresponding semantic and grammatical structures.

Šaumjan (1973) and Apresjan (1971) strongly advocate a so-
called two-level approach to language structure, which is similar to the distinctions between surface and deep structures,

except for the fact that they would eliminate any ordering in the deep structure. The advantage of such an approach would conceivably be greater formal abstraction and thus a more neutral semantic base, which could then serve as an important theoretical link for both mechanical and nonmechanical translation. Rozencveyg's article on "Models in Soviet Linguistics" (1971) is especially instructive in treating the meaning-text model and the applicative generative model (šaumjan's theory). Both of these models are based on semantic structures, lack linearization of elements, and depend on a calculus of transformations, in which transformations are supposed to proceed by abstract rules one from another without their being listed.

A number of linguists have discussed the relevance of deep structure for translation theory. Vernay (1972) has indicated the significance of a completely abstract semantic deep structure that could theoretically consist of a set of semantic universals and could thus presumably reduce to a minimum the problems of transfer. Walmsley (1970) has advocated the use of transformational theory in the teaching of translation techniques, and Scharlau (1970) has illustrated the ways in which a transformational approach to anaphoric usage can have considerable relevance for translation. Raabe's (1972) treatment of deep structures in terms of contrastive linguistics has likewise emphasized the application of generative-transformational grammar to translation problems.

The concept of underlying structures is especially important for both the theory and the practice of translation. The reasons for this are (1) on the kernel or subkernel levels the syntactic structures of various languages are much more alike (basic underlying sentence structures can probably be reduced to ten or so, whereas the variety of surface structures is relatively numerous); (2) one can more readily identify the semantic structures of subsurface levels and thus be in a position to determine more accurately the extent of equivalence and the need for supplementation or redistribution of semantic components; and (3) on the deeper levels of structure one can more easily determine the symbolic relations and their hermeneutical implications. It is, of course, the surface structures that must point to the deep-structure relations, but it is the analysis of the deep structure that greatly facilitates a comparison of structures and relations.

The practical implications of a deep-structure approach to certain aspects of translation principles and procedures can be clearly seen in the extent to which transformational analyses are employed in the teaching of methods of translating. Even though the approach of Beekman and Callow (1974) is concerned primarily with surface-level structures, they nevertheless include several techniques that rely on the analysis of deep structure. In teaching persons how to translate into a foreign language, one can readily see how a surface-structure approach, based on sets of rules for positional variants, can be helpful, but for teaching persons to translate satisfactorily into their own mother tongue, the use of a deep-structure approach appears to be much more effective than any other system.

There is also evidence that a transformational approach to translating is precisely what most good translators employ anyway, usually without being aware of that fact. The description of translation procedures by Fang (1959) suggests a transformational approach, and it seems clear from comparing texts in simultaneous translating that a high percentage of the syntactic adjustments are made in the direction of kernel structures. Haugen has confirmed that a three-step approach to translation (analysis, transfer, and restructuring) is essentially what he uses in translating from various Scandinavian languages into English.[13]

For the translator, however, there are a number of limitations in the standard theory of generative-transformational grammar. In the early stages of Chomsky's developing concepts, the selection of the sentence as the maximum unit for syntactic analysis proved to be a serious block to important investigations of intersentence structures. Linguistic competence clearly involves paragraph and discourse competence, for both speakers and hearers are able to react consistently to the satisfactory or unsatisfactory character of larger discourse units. Petöfi (1971a, b, and 1972) has been particularly active in elaborating a system for the description of such units and their structural relations. No theory of translation can possibly restrict itself to the treatment of sentences. This becomes conspicuously evident in machine translating, because up to the present time machines have been restricted primarily to intra-sentence analysis and restructuring, and a good deal of postediting is required because of their deficiency.

The standard theory of generative-transformational grammar has likewise failed to recognize the significance of rhetorical features. These must either be buried in the deep structure (only to be resurrected at a very high level in transformation), or they must be set up as a separate late structure. They are obviously significant, for they are important in determining focus and impact. Katz (1972) has suggested a "rhetorical component" in grammar, but he would insist that rhetorical features have no "semantic significance" because they have no "logical significance." Basing semantics on propositional logic is a serious shortcoming in Katz's approach (cf. Moravcsik, 1974), but a rhetorical component in grammar theory can be very useful in the development of translation theory, for it suggests a practical way to deal with various subtle elements of style.

Another liability in the standard theory is the failure to deal with certain lexical structures. The meanings of such English terms as sanctifier and mediator can be best handled in terms of their underlying deep structures, for example, one who makes someone or something holy and one who mediates (or acts as a go-between). Introducing certain types of transforms within the lexical level may not be the simplest way to describe a language, but for the translator it is a highly relevant way to deal with problems of semantic correspondence. Those expressions that are structurally complex in the source language are more likely to be translated in a receptor language not by single lexical units, but by phrases. That is to say, the more structurally complex a lexical unit is in a source language, the more likely it is to correspond to a string of lexical items in a receptor language.

The standard theory of generative-transformational grammar has also tended to neglect the semantics of lexical structures or to apply to lexical structures the same structural methods as were found to be applicable to syntactic units. The binary tree-diagrams of Katz and Fodor (1963) have simply not proven adequate. The most serviceable device for describing the semantic structures of lexical units is a matrix, but, theoretically, one should have a multidimensional matrix in order to describe all the componential features and their inter-relations.

Some of the inadequacies of the standard theory have been supplemented by generative semanticists, but although the emphasis on the primacy of the semantic structure is important, the techniques for dealing with the relating deep and surface structures are rather amorphous. Rather than moving directly from deep structures to surface structures, it seems better to recognize the validity of several subsurface levels, and for the translator the kernel or near-kernel level is a highly useful structural feature.

For the translator both the standard theory (or the extended standard theory) and the generative semanticist theory involve certain important limitations. In the first place, synonymy (and thus meaning) is defined too often only in terms of propositional equivalence. But the fact that two expressions are propositionally equivalent does not mean that they are synonymous in meaning. Propositional logic is simply not adequate to deal with a number of aspects of meaning, especially connotations, focus, emphasis, and foregrounding-backgrounding. Frequently the discussions of synonymy have completely overlooked the essential difference between meaning *(Bedeutung)* and reference *(Bezeichnung)*.

In the second place, the standard theory and generative semantics depend too much on the ideal speaker and hearer. There are no such ideal individuals, and the translator must be concerned with the various types of limitations actual speakers and hearers have.

In the third place, transformationalists tend to deal with linguistic facts apart from actual contexts. Many of the early discussions about grammaticality were in error because phrases were extracted from real contexts. Language cannot be discussed as though verbal communication occurs in a cultural vacuum.

Sociolinguistic Theories of Translation

Dissatisfaction with a strictly linguistic approach to translation is evidenced in Nida's (1964) relating translation to communication theory, rather than to a specific linguistic theory. The use of a communication model resulted from obvious practical anthropological interests and reflected a concern for the role of the receptors in the translation process. Because of the crucial role of the decoders of any discourse, the term target and the phrase target language were dropped in favor of receptor and receptor language.

Catford's theory of translation (1965), although primarily linguistic and related to surface structure equivalences, nevertheless moves in the direction of the context of communication in its emphasis on differences of dialects and registers.

Sociolinguistic theories of translation should not be understood as neglecting linguistic structure. Rather, they lift the linguistic structures to a higher level of relevance, where these can be viewed in terms of their function in communication. The translator can and must be aware of such factors as irony, hyperbole, and litotes, which are frequently not signaled by linguistic signs but by incongruence with the communication context. That is to say, the interpretation of certain expressions depends on the extralinguistic context of the utterance.

The sociolinguistic approach to translation also makes it possible to incorporate the results of philological research. The linguist as such is not concerned with identifying the author, audience, and circumstances of a particular utterance. All that concerns him as a linguist is the fact that a particular utterance is a satisfactory reflection of the speaker's language competence. The sociolinguist is much concerned about the author, the historical backgrounds of the text, the circumstances involved in producing the text, and the history of the interpretation of the text, for all these elements figure in the social setting of the communication. This does not mean that a linguist may not also be a sociolinguist, nor that a linguist cannot also be a philologist, but the methods and framework of analysis differ, and these divergent viewpoints must be kept in mind if one is to undertake a thorough analysis of the various aspects of any communication act.

In terms of a sociolinguistic theory of translation, the translator is compelled to take language performance as serious as language competence. Because an ideal speaker-hearer does not exist among the receptors of any translation, adjustments must be made to the norm of the prospective audience. The responses of receptors must be in terms of actual patterns of response to similar types of texts, and not in terms of what might be regarded as a judicial or legal norm, that is, how people ought to respond. Furthermore, the existing receptor expectancies must be carefully calculated, because such dispositions are important determinatives of reaction. What makes the situation somewhat more complex is that within any group of receptors there are certain decision makers whose influence is much greater than that of others, and their response to a translation cannot be judged even on the basis of how the average person is likely to respond to the text in question. In many instances the more crucial factor is the judgment of those who dictate the canons of acceptability. In a sense, therefore, receptor reaction must be judged on the basis of the social structure of the receptor group—one more crucial reason why only a sociolinguistic approach to translation is ultimately valid.

The fact that patterns of human behavior are constantly subject to change means that literary taste and judgment with respect to types of translating also change. There is, therefore, no permanent set of criteria for judging the acceptability of a translation, but change also implies fluctuation in judgment. Accordingly, one must expect that over a period of time not only will the attitudes of many people change with respect to a translation, but the same individual may react to a particular translation in different ways at different times, depending on his own emotional state or needs.

In sociolinguistic theories of translation the basic model is communication. This was first used by Nida (1964) and then by Nida and Taber (1969), but it has also been extensively employed and developed by Kade (1968) and Neubert (1968), who have found it especially appropriate to their linguistic and sociopolitical views. Thieberger (1972) has also insisted on the relevance of the communication model. The fundamental reason for the use of the communication model is that translation always involves interlingual communication, and this communication is based on the use of a code, namely, language. The basic structure of language as a code and the implication

of this for translating have been clearly summarized by Fourquet (1972).

There are certain aspects of translation that also reflect
closely certain features of information theory. Catford (1965)
has noted how the analysis of equivalences can be treated in
terms of degrees of probability, and Colby's paper (1958) on
the 50 percent redundancy in language helps to explain why
good translations are normally somewhat longer than their
originals.[14]

In actual practice, translators rarely if ever pursue their
work as though they were guided by only one underlying
theory. Most translators are highly eclectic in practice. If they
are confronted with a literary text that has a rather special
history, in the sense that it is derived from various sources and
has been subjected to a variety of interpretations, they tend to
begin with a philological approach to their work. If, however,
a text is nonliterary and the source and receptor languages are
relatively similar and represent basically the same cultural
milieu, the approach is essentially linguistic. If, however, a
translation involves languages that are widely separated in
time and represent quite different cultures, and if the text is
structurally rather complex and the prospective audience possibly varied, the translator is almost compelled to think of his
task in sociolinguistic terms.

What is ultimately needed for translating is a well-for-
mulated, comprehensive theory of translation that can take
into account all the related factors. Because translating always
involves communication within the context of interpersonal
relations, the model for such activity must be a communication
model, and the principles must be primarily sociolinguistic in
the broad sense of the term. As such, translating becomes a
part of the even broader field of anthropological semiotics.
Within the structure of a unified theory of translation it would
be possible to deal with all the factors that are involved in and
influence the nature of translation. These could be assigned
their proper roles and their significance for the process of
translating could be properly weighted on a number of sliding
scales, depending in several cases on the extralinguistic factors
involved.

The fact that translating seems to be a very complex operation should not be surprising. Language itself is complex, but the factors involved in human discourse are even more complex. No simple theory or set of rules can ever suffice to provide meaningful answers to what Richards (1953, p. 250) has described as "probably the most complex type of event yet produced in the evolution of the cosmos."

FOOTNOTES

1. See, for example, Tytler (1790); Cary (1956); Fedorov (1958); Mounin (1963); Revzin and Rozencveyg (1964), Kade (1968), and Nida and Taber (1969).

2. In this paper no attempt is made to deal with the distorted principles and procedures that often characterize translations published purely for commercial profit. In such cases the translator's primary interest is in the number of words he can produce per hour; he exhibits little or no concern for stylistic features or accuracy of content. In the production of translations of this type, the publishers bear a heavy responsibility.

3. See Reiss (1971).

4. Catford's volume (1965) is one of the rare exceptions.

5. See also Dressler, 1970.

6. See Nida (1959), and Nida and Taber (1969).

7. This is one of the features of the translation of *The Living Bible* (Taylor, 1971) which has been most widely cited by its critics.

8. It has been traditional among some Cakchiquel interpreters in Guatemala to reproduce an entire speech of up to an hour in length with amazing accuracy and excellent stylistic adaptations.

9. This is well illustrated in the programs for training translators and interpreters in the institutes associated with the University of Louvain, the University of Saarbrücken, Karl Marx University (Leipzig), and Herriot-Watt University.

10. The one important exception to this is Levý's (1969) treatment of literary texts.

11. See, for example, Dolet (1540), Tytler (1790), Galantière (1951); Savory, (1957), and Lane (1958).

12. See Garvin, Brewer, and Mathiot (1967), and Southworth (1967).

13. From personal communication.

14. See also Nida (1964), Nida and Taber (1969), and Zemb (1972).

REFERENCES

Alverson, H. Determining utterance equivalences in interlingual translation. *Anthropological Linguistics*, 1969, *11*, 247–253.

Andreyev, N. Linguistic aspects of translation. In H. Hunt, Ed., *Proceedings of the Ninth International Congress of Linguists*. The Hague: Mouton, 1964, pp. 625–637.

Apresjan, Ju. D. Ideen und Method der modernen strukturellen Linguistik. Berlin: Akademie-Verlag, 1971.

Arichea, D. Criticism and translation: critical and translational issues in Acts 1.1–11. In R. Bratcher, J. Kijne, and W. Smalley, Eds., *Understanding and translating the Bible, papers in honor of Eugene Nida*. New York: American Bible Society, 1974, pp. 1–14.

Bach, E., and Harms, R. *Universals in linguistic theory*. New York: Holt, Rinehart, and Winston, 1968.

Bailey, C. *Variation and linguistic theory*. Arlington, Va.: Center for Applied Linguistics, 1973.

Balcerzan, E. La traduction, art d'interpreter. In J. Holmes, Ed., *The nature of translation*. The Hague: Mouton, 1970.

Barik, H. A look at simultaneous interpretation. *Language Sciences*, 1973, *26*, 35–36.

Barthes, R. et al. *Analyse structurale et exégèse Biblique*. Neuchâtel, Switzerland: Delachaux et Niestle, 1971.

Bausch, K. Qualité en traduction et linguistique die "differentielle." *Babel*, 1970, *16*, 13–20 (a).

Bausch, K. Übersetzungswissenschaft und angewandte Sprachwissenschaft: Versuch einer Standortbestimmung. *Lebende Sprachen*, 1970, *15*, 161–163. (b).

Bausch, K. Kontrastive Linguistik und Übersetzen. *Linguistica Antverpiensia*, 1972, *6*, 7–15.

Bausch, K. Die Sprachmittlung. In H. Althaus et al., Eds., *Lexicon der germanistischen Linguistik*. Tubingen: Max Niemeyer Verlag, 1973.

Beekman, J., and Callow, J. *Translating the word of God*. Grand Rapids: Zondervan Publishing House, 1974.

Belloc, H. *On translation*. Oxford: Clarendon Press, 1931.

Bierwisch, M. Structuralism: history, problems, and methods. In J. Ihwe, Ed., *Literaturwissenschaft und Linguistik*. Frankfurt-am-Main: Athenäum Verlag, 1971.

Bolinger, D. Transformation: structural translation. *Acta Linguistica Hafniensia*, 1966, *9*, 130–144.

Bremond, C. Le "Modele Constitutionel" de A. J. Greimas. *Semiotica,* 1972, *5,* 362–382.

Brislin, R. Back-translation for cross-cultural research. *Journal of Cross-Cultural Psychology,* 1970, *1,* 185–216.

Brislin, R. Translation issues: multilanguage versions and writing translatable English. *Proceedings of the 80th Annual Convention of the American Psychological Association,* 1972, 299–300.

Brower, R., Ed., *On translation.* Cambridge: Harvard University Press, 1959.

Buber, M., and Rosenzweig, F. *Die Fünf Bücher der Weisung.* Berlin: Lambert Schneider, 1930.

Buzzetti, C. *La parola tradotta.* Brescia: Morcelliana, 1973.

Callow, K. *Discourse considerations in translating the word of God.* Grand Rapids: Zondervan Publishing House, 1974.

Cary, E. *La traduction dans le monde moderne.* Genève: Georg et Cie, 1956.

Cary, E. L'indispensable débat. In E. Cary and R. Jumpelt, Eds., *La qualité en matière de traduction.* New York: Macmillan, 1959, pp. 21–48.

Cary, E. *Les grands traducteurs français.* Geneva: Librairie de l'Université, 1963.

Cary, E., and Jumpelt, R., Eds., *Quality in translation.* New York: The Macmillan Company, 1963.

Catford, J. *Linguistic theory of translation: an essay in applied linguistics.* London: Oxford Press, 1965.

Chafe, W. *Meaning and the structure of Language.* Chicago: University of Chicago Press, 1970.

Chafe, W. Directionality and paraphrase. *Language,* 1971, *47,* 1–28.

Chafe, W. Language and memory. *Language,* 1973, *49,* 261–281.

Chafe, W. Language and consciousness. *Language,* 1974, *50,* 111–133.

Chomsky, N. Logical syntax and semantics: their linguistic relevance. *Language,* 1955(a), *31,* 36–45.

Chomsky, N. *Semantic considerations in grammar.* Monograph series 8, Languages and linguistics. Washington: Georgetown University Press, 1955(b).

Chomsky, N. *Studies on semantics in generative grammar.* The Hague: Mouton, 1972.

Colby, B. Behavioral redundancy. *Behavioral Science,* 1958, *3,* 317–322.

Colby, B. Men, grammar, and machines, a new direction for the study of man. In M. Black and W. Smalley, Eds. *On language, culture and religion: in honor of Eugene A. Nida.* The Hague: Mouton, 1974, pp. 187–197.

Coseriu, E. Semantik, innere Sprachform und Tiefenstruktur. *Folia Linguistica*, 1970, *4*, 53–63 (a).

Coseriu, E. Bedeutung und Bezeichnung im Lichte der strukturellen Semantik. *Commentationes Societatis Linguisticae Europeaeae*, 1970, *3*, 2–18 (b).

Cosmao, V. et al., Eds. *Afrique et Parole*. Paris: Présence Africaine.

Daly, P. Translation as interpretation: some observations on three German translations of a Macbeth speech. In B. Schludermann et al., Eds. *Deutung und Bedeutung. Studies in German and comparative literature presented to Karl-Werner Naurer*. The Hague: Mouton, pp. 336–355.

Darbelnet, J. La traduction raisonnée. *Meta*, 1969, *14*, 135–140.

de Kuiper, A. Aquila redivivus—Idiolectics: a Dutch idiosyncrasy. In R. Bratcher et al., Eds. *Understanding and translating the Bible*. New York: American Bible Society, 1974, pp. 80–85.

Di Pietri, R. *Language structures in contrast*. Rowley, Mass.: Newbury House, 1971.

Dolet, E. La manière de bien traduire d'une langue en autre. *Babel*, 1955, *1*, 17–20, originally published in 1540.

Dressler, W. Textsyntax und Übersetzen, In P. Hartmann and H. Vernay, Eds. *Sprachwissenschaft und Übersetzen*. Munchen: Max Hueber Verlag, 1970, pp. 64–77.

Dressler, W. Textgrammatische Invarianz in Übersetzungen? In E. Gülich and W. Raible, Eds. *Textsorten*. Frankfort: Athenäum Verlag, 1972, pp. 98–112.

Eaton, T. The foundations of literary semantics. *Linguistics*, 1970, *62*, 5–19.

Faiss, K. Ubersetzung und Sprachwissenschaft-eine Orientierung. *Babel*, 1973, *19*, 75–86.

Fang, A. Some reflections of the difficulty of translation. In R. Brower, Ed. *On translation*. Cambridge: Harvard University Press, 1959, pp. 111–133.

Fedorov, A. *Vvedenie v teoriyu perevoda* [Introduction to a theory of translation]. Moscow: Izd. literatury na inostrannyx yazykax, 1958.

Fedorov, A. *Osnovy obŠcey teorii perevoda* [General principles of trranslation theory]. Moscow: Izd. literatury na inostrannyx yazykax, 1968.

Fedry, J., and Saout, Y. Les noms theóphores dans la Bible. *Afrique et Parole*, 1973, *41–42*, 102–113.

Fitts, D. The poetic nuance. In R. Brower, Ed. *On translation*. Cambridge: Harvard University Press, 1959, pp. 32–47.

Fourquet, J. La traduction vue d'une Théorie du language. In J. Ladmiral, Ed. *La traduction* (Languages, series 28). Paris: Didier and Larousse, 1972, pp. 64–69.

Fowler, R. Style and the concept of deep structure. *Journal of Literary Semantics*, 1972, *1*, 5–24.

Galantière, L. On translators and translating. *American Scholar*, 1951, *40*, 435–445.

Garvin, P. Referential adjustments and linguistic structure. *Acta Linguistica*, 1944, *4*, 53–60.

Garvin, P., Brewer, J., and Mathiot, M. Predication-typing: a pilot study in semantic analysis. *Language*, 1967, *43*, part 2, monograph 27.

Gleason, H. *Contrastive analysis in discourse structures*. Monograph series 21; Languages and Linguistics. Washington, Georgetown University Press, 1968, pp. 39–63.

Grandjouan, J. *Les Linguicides*. Paris: Didier, 1971.

Greimas, S. *Sémantique structurale*. Paris: Librairie Larousse, 1966.

Grice, H. Utterer's meaning, sentence-meaning, and word meaning. *Foundations of language*, 1968, *4*, 225–242.

Grice, H. Meaning. In D. Steinberg and L. Jakobovits, Eds. *Semantics*. Cambridge: University Press, 1971.

Grimes, J. *The thread of discourse*. Ithica, New York: Department of Modern Languages and Linguistics, Cornell University, 1972.

Gross, M. Notes sur l'histoire de la traduction automatique. In J. Ladmiral, Ed. *La traduction*. Langages, series 28, Paris: Didier and Larousse, 1972, pp. 40–48.

Guttinger, F. *Zielsprache*. Zürich: Manesse Verlag, 1963.

Halliday, M. Notes on transivity and theme in English, part 3. *Journal of Linguistics*, 1968, *4*, 179–215.

Harris, Z. *Methods in structural linguistics*. Chicago: University of Chicago, 1951.

Harris, Z. *Discourse analysis reprints*. The Hague: Mouton, 1963.

Hartmann, P., and Vernay, H., Eds. *Sprachwissenschaft und Übersetzen*. München: Max Hueber Verlag, 1970.

Harweg, R. Text grammar and literary texts: remarks on a grammatical science of literature. *Poetics*, 1973, *9*, 65–92.

Hatton, H. Translation of pronouns: a Thai example. *The Bible Translator*, 1973, *24*, 222–233.

Haugen, E. On translating from the Scandinavian. In E. Polomé, Ed. *From Old Norse Literature and Mythology: a Symposium*. Austin: University of Texas, Department of Germanic Languages, 1969, pp. 3–18.

Heidolph, K. Kontextbeziehungen zwischen Sätzen in einer generativen Grammatik. *Kybernetika*, 1966, *23*, 274–281.

Hendricks, W. On the notion "beyond the sentence. *Linguistics*, 1967, *37*, 12–51.

Hendricks, W. Methodology of narrative structural analysis. *Semiotica,* 1973, 7, 163–184.

Hetzron, R. The deep structure of the statement. *Linguistics,* 1971, 65, 25–63.

Hjelmslev, L. *Prolegomena to a theory of languages.* Translated by F. L. Whitfield for the original, published in 1943. Bloomington: Indiana University Publication in Anthropology and Linguistics, Memoir 7, 1953.

Hollenbach, B. A method for displaying semantic structure. *Notes on translation,* 1969, *31,* 22–34

Holmes, J. et al., Eds. *The Nature of translation.* The Hague: Mouton, 1970.

House, J. Of the limits of translatability. *Babel,* 1973, *19,* 166–169.

Irmen, F. Bedeutungsumfang und Bedeutung im Übersetzungsprozess. In P. Hartmann and H. Vernay, Eds. *Sprachwissenschaft und Übersetzen.* Munchen: Max Hueber Verlag, 1970, pp. 144–156.

Jakobson, R. *Main trends in the science of language.* New York: Harper and Row, 1970.

Jakobson, R. Verbal communication. *Scientific American,* 1972, *227* (September), 72–81.

Joos, M. *The Five Clocks.* Bloomington: Indiana University Research Center in Anthropology, Folklore and Linguistics, Publication 22. IJAL 1962, 28, no. 2, part V.

Jordan, C. *The Cotton Patch Version of Luke and Acts.* New York: Association Press, 1969.

Jumpelt, R. *Die Übersetzung naturwissenschaftlicher und technischer Literatur.* Berlin-Schöneberg: Langenscheidt, 1961.

Kade, O. Kommunikationswissenschaftliche. Probleme der Übersetzung. In A. Neubert, Ed. *Grundfragen der Übersetzungswissenschaft. Beihefte sur Zeitschrift Fremdsprachen,* 1968, *2,* 3–20.

Kahn, F. Traduction et linguistique. *Cahiers Ferdinand de Saussure,* 1971, *27,* 21–42.

Katz, J. *Semantic theory.* New York: Harper and Row, 1972.

Katz, J., and Fodor, J. The structure of a semantic theory. *Language,* 1963, *39,* 170–210.

Katz, J., and Postal, P. *An integrated theory of linguistic descriptions.* Cambridge: MIT Press, 1964.

Klima, E. Relatedness between grammatical systems. *Language,* 1964, *40,* 1–20.

Koller, W. *Übersetzungswissenschaft, (Bericht über die II Internationale Konferenz "Grundlagen der Übersetzungswissenschaft," Folia Linguistica,* 1969, *5,* 194–221.

Ladmiral, J. *La traduction* (*Langages*, series 28.) Paris: Didier and Larousse, 1972.

Lakoff, R. Language in context. *Language*, 1972, *48*, 907–927.

Lane, A. *Die Fremdsprachenberufe*. Munchen: Isar Verlag, 1958.

Langendoen, D. Presupposition and assertion in the semantic analysis of nouns and verbs in English. In D. Steinberg and L. Jakobovits, Eds. *Semantics*. Cambridge: University Press, 1971, pp. 341–344.

Langendoen, D. Speak and talk: a vindication of syntactic deep structure. In M. Black and W. Smalley, Eds. *On language, culture, and religion*. (*Approaches to Semiotics*, series 56). The Hague: Mouton, pp. 237–240.

Larin, B., Ed., *Teoriya i kritika perevoda*[Theory and criticism of translation]. Leningrad: University of Leningrad, 1962.

Levenston, E. The translation-paradigm: a technique for contrastive syntax. IRAL, 1965, *3*, 221–225.

Levý, J. *Die literarische Übersetzung: Theorie einer Kunstgattung*. Frankfort-am-Maim: Athenäum Verlag, 1969.

Longacre, R. *Discourse, paragraph and sentence structure in selected Philippine languages*. Vols. 1, 2, 3. Washington, D.C.: Institute of International Studies, U.S. Department of Health, Education, and Welfare.

Longacre, R. Sentence structure as a statement calculus. *Language*, 1970, *46*, 783–815.

Lyons, J. *Introduction to theoretical linguistics*. Cambridge: University Press, 1968.

Maillot, J. Andre Gidé, traducteur de Condrad. *Babel*, 1974, *20*, 63–71.

Makkai, A. A pragmo-ecological view of linguistic structure and language universals. *Language Sciences*, 1973, *27*, 9–22.

Maranda, E., and Maranda, P. *Structural models in folklore and transformational essays*. The Hague: Mouton, 1971.

Margolis, J. Quine on observationality and translation. *Foundations of Language*, 1968, *4*, 128–137.

Mathiot, M. Cognitive analysis of a myth. *Semiotica*, 1972, *6*, 101–142.

Mathews, J. Third thoughts on translating poetry. In R. Brower, Ed. *On translation*. Cambridge: Harvard University Press, pp. 67–77.

Mounin, G. *Les problèmes théoriques de la traduction*. Paris: Gallimard, 1963.

Mounin, G. Traduction. In A. Martinet, Ed. *La Linguistique: Guide Alphabetique*. Paris: Éditions Denoël, 1969, pp. 375–379.

Mounin, G. *La Linguistique du XXe Siècle*. Paris: Presses Universitaires de France, 1972.

Neubert, A. Pragmatische Aspekete der Übersetzung. In A. Neubert, Ed. *Grundfragen der Übersetzungswissenschaft.* Beihefte sur Zeitschrift Fremdsprachen, 1968, pp. 21–33.

Neubert, A. Theorie und Praxis für die Übersetzungswissenschaft. *Linguistische Arbeits Berichte*, 1973, *7*, 120–144.

Newmark, P. An approach to translation. *Babel*, 1973, *19*, 3–18.

Nickel, G. (Ed.), *Papers in contrastive Linguistics.* Cambridge: University Press, 1971.

Nickel, G. (Ed.), *Fehlerkunde.* Berlin: Cornelsen-Velhagen und Klasing, Verlag für Lehrmedien, 1972.

Nida, E. *Bible translating: an analysis of principles and procedures.* (rev. ed., 1961), New York: American Bible Society, 1947.

Nida, E. A new methodology in Biblical exegesis. *The Bible Translator*, 1952, *3*, 97–111.

Nida, E. Some problems of semantic structure ans translational equivalence. In B. Elson, Ed. *A William Cameron Townsend en el XXV aninersario del Instituto Lingüistico de Verano.* Mexico: ILV Press, 1961.

Nida, E. Semantic components. *Babel*, 1962, *9*, 99–104.

Nida, E. Bible translating and the science of linguistics. *Babel*, 1963, *9*, 99–104(a).

Nida, E. The translation of religious texts, Babel, 1963, *9*, 3–5(b).

Nida, E. *Toward a science of translating.* Leiden: E.J. Brill, 1964.

Nida, E. Science of translation. *Language*, 1969, *45*, 483–498.

Nida, E. Semantic components in translation theory. *Applications of linguistics.* Cambridge: The University Press, 1971, 341–348.

Nida, E., and Taber, C. *The theory and practice of translation.* Leiden: E.J. Brill, 1969.

Nortman, E., Ed. *Voprosy teorii i praktiki naučotexničeskogo perevoda* [Questions of theory and practice in technological translation]. Leningrad: Znanie, 1968.

O'Brien, J. From French to English. In R. Brower, Ed. *On translation.* Cambridge: Harvard University Press, 1959, pp. 78–92.

Oettinger, A. Automatic (transference, translation, remittance, shunting). In R. Brower, Ed. *On Translation.* Cambridge: Harvard University Press, 1959, pp. 240–267.

Oettinger, A. A new theory of translation and its application. In H. Edmundson, Ed. *Proceedings of the National Symposium on Machine Translation.* Englewood Cliffs, New Jersey: Prentice-Hall, 1961, pp. 363–366.

Oller, J. On the relation between syntax, semantics, and pragmatics. *Linguistics*, 1972, *83*, 43–55.

Oller, J. et al. Close tests in English, Thai, and Vietnamese: Native and nonnative performance. *Language Learning*, 1972, *22*, 1–16.

Oomen, U. Der Übersetzungprozess und seine Automatisierung. *Folia Linguistica*, 1969, *3*, 153–166.

Paepcke, F. Verstehen und Übersetzen. *Linguistica Antverpiensia*, 1968, *3*, 329–351.

Pak, T. Limits of formalism in doscourse analysis. *Linguistics*, 1972, *77*, 26–48.

Payne, R. The possibility of translation. In W. Smith, R. Payne, and F. MacShane Eds. *Translation 73*. New York: Columbia University School of the Arts and the P. E. N. American Center, 1973, pp. 82–88.

Pergnier, M. Traduction et sociolinguistique. In J. Ladmiral, *La Traduction* (*Langages*, series 28), Paris: Didier et Larousse, pp. 70–74.

Petöfi, J. "Generativity" and text-grammar. *Folia Linguistica*, 1971(a), *5*, 277–309.

Petöfi, J. *Transformationsgrammatiken und eine ko-textuelle Texttheorie*. Frankfurt-sm-Main: Athenäum Verlag, 1971(b).

Petöfi, J. Zu einer grammatischen Theorie sprachlicher Texte. *Zeitschrift für Literaturwissenschaft und Linguistik*, 1972, *5*, 31–58.

Phillips, H. Problems of translation and meaning in field work. *Human Organization*, 1960, *18*, 184–192.

Popovič, A. Zum Status der Übersetzungskritik, *Babel*, 1973, *19*, 161–165.

Pottier, B. Linguistique culturelle. In J. Pouillon and P. Maranda, Eds. *Échanges et Communications, Offered to Claude Lévi-Strauss*. The Hague: Mouton, 1970, pp. 609–613.

Praschek, H. Probleme des maschinellen Textvergleichs. *Zeitschrift für Literaturwissenschaft und Linguistik*, 1971, *4*, 51–62.

Rabbe, H. Zum Verhältnis von kontrastiver Grammatik und Übersetzung. In G. Nickel, Ed. *Reader zur kontrastiven Linguistik*. Frankfurt-am-Main: Athenäum Fischer Verlag, 1972, pp. 59–74.

Raffel, B. *The forked tongue: a study of the translation process*. The Hague: Mouton, 1971.

Rayfield, J. What is a story? *American Anthropologist*, 1972, *74*, 1085–1106.

Reiss, K. *Möglichkeiten und Grenzen der Übersetsungskritik*. Munchen: Max Hueber Verlag, 1971.

Reiss, K. Texttyp und Übersetzungsmethode. In G. Nickel and A. Raasch, Eds. *IRAL-Sonderband*, 1972, pp. 98–106.

Revzin, I., and V. Rozencveyg. *Osnovy obščego i mašinnogo perevoda* [Principles of general and mechanical translation]. Moscow: Vysšaya škola, 1964.

Richards, I. Toward a theory of translating. *Studies in Chinese Thought.* American Anthropological Association, Vol. 55, memoir 75, Chicago: University of Chicago Press, 1953, pp. 247–262.

Rieu, R. Translation. *Cassell's Encyclopedia of Literature,* Vol. 1. London, 1954, pp. 554–559.

Robinson, J. *Honest to God.* London: Student Christian Movement Press, 1963.

Romano, A., and Hatton, H. Racine's world and theater: a study of his translation methods and their implication for theory in general. In R. Bratcher et al., Eds. *Understanding and translating the Bible.* New York: American Bible Society, 1974, pp. 152–200.

Rozentsveyg, V. Models in Soviet Linguistics. *Social Sciences,* 1971, *3,* 82–94. Moscow: USSR Academy of Sciences.

Šaumjan, S. Outline of the applicational generative model for the description of language. *Foundations of Language,* 1965, *1,* 189–222.

Šaumjan, S. *Strukturale Linguistik.* (In a series edited by Eugenio Coseriu, International Library of General Linguistics). München. Wilhelm Fink Verlag, 1973.

Šaumjan, S., and Soboleva, P. Syntax and semantics. In J. Rey-Debove, Ed. *Recherches sur les systèmes signifiants.* The Hague: Mouton, 1973.

Savory, T. *The art of translation.* London: Jonathan Cape, 1957.

Schank, R. Conceptual dependency as a framework for linguistic analysis. *Linguistics,* 1969, *49,* 28–50.

Scharlau, B. Die Anaphorik und ihre Relevanz für Übersetzungen. In P. Hartmann and H. Vernay, Eds. *Sprachwissenschaft und Ubersetzen.* München: Max Hueber Verlag, 1970, pp. 48–63.

Schmidt, K. Sprachliche Übersetzung und kategoriales Umdenken. In P. Hartmann and H. Vernay, Eds. *Sprachwissenschaft und Übersetzen.* München: Max Hueber Verlag, 1970, pp. 48–63.

Schmidt, S. Ed. *Text, Bedeutung, Asthetik.* München: Bayerischer Schulbuch-Verlag, 1970.

Smith, W. The hardest work. In W. Smith et al., Eds. *Translation 73.* New York: Columbia University School of the Arts and the P.E.N. American Center, 1973, pp. 33–44.

Smith, W. et al., Eds. *Translation 73.* New York: Columbia University School of the Arts and the P.E.N. American Center.

Southworth, F. A model of semantic structure. *Language,* 1967, *43,* 342–361.

Stanosz, B. Formal theories of extension and intension of expressions. *Semiotica,* 1970, *2,* 102–114.

Taber, C. Traduire le sens, traduire le style. In J. Ladmiral, Ed. *La traduc-*

tion. (Languages, series 28). Paris: Didier and Larousse, 1972, pp. 55–63.

Tanaka, R. Action and meaning in literary theory. In T. Eason, Ed. *The Journal of Literary Semantics,* 1972, *1,* 41–56.

Taylor, K. *The Living Bible.* Wheaton, Ill.: Tyndale House Publishers, 1971.

Teilhard de Chardin, P. *Hymne de l'Univers.* Paris: Éditions du Seuil, 1961.

Thieberger, R. Le langage de la traduction. In J. Ladmiral, Ed. *La Traduction.* Paris: Didier and Larousse, 1972, pp. 75–84.

Tosh, L. Initial results of syntactic translation at the Linguistics Research Center. *Linguistics,* 1968, *42,* 96–116.

Tytler, A. (Lord Woohhouselee). *Essay on the Principles of Translation.* London: Dent, 1790.

Ure, J., Rodger, A., and Ellis, J. Somn: sleep-an exercise in the use of descriptive linguistic techniques in literary translation. *Babel,* 1969, *15,* 4–14, 73–82.

Vannikov, J. *Linguisticeskie osnovy teorii perevoda*[Linguistic principles of translation]. Moscow: Universitet družby naxodov imeni Patrisa Lumumby, 1964.

Vernay, H. Zur semantischen Struktur des Verbalknotens und des Nominalknotens. In P. Hartmann and H. Vernay, Eds. *Sprachwissenschaft und Übersetzen.* Munchen: Max Hueber Verlag, 1970, pp. 93–103.

Vernay, H. Möglichkeiten und Grenzen einer sprachwissenschaftlichen Beschreibung des Übersetzungsvororgangs. In G. Nickel and A. Raasch, Eds. *IRAL-Sonderband,* 1972, pp. 105–116.

Vinay, J., and Darbelnet, J. *Stylistique comparée du français et de l'anglais.* Montreal: Beauchemin; Paris: Didier, 1958.

Walmsley, J. Transformation theory and translation. *IRAL,* 1970, *3,* 185–199.

Wandruszka, M. *Sprachen: vergleichbar und unvergleichlich.* München: R. Piper Verlag, 1969.

Wandruszka, M. *Interlinguistik: Umrisse einer neuen Sprachwissenschaft.* Müchen: R. Piper Verlag, 1971.

Wilss, W. Zur Theorie der maschinellen Sprachübersetzung. In P. Hartmann and H. Vernay, Eds. *Sprachwissenschaft und Übersetzen.* Munchen: Max Hueber Verlag, 1970, pp. 33–47.

Wilss, W. Syntaktischemantische Probleme der automatischen Sprachübersetzung. In G. Nickel and A. Raasch, Eds. *IRAL-Sonderband,* 1972, pp. 117–124.

Winthrop, H. A proposed model and procedure for studying message distortion in translation. *Linguistics,* 1966, *22,* 98–112.

Wolff, H. Translator and publisher. In W. Smith et al., Eds. *Translation 73.* New York: Columbia University School of the Arts and the P.E.N. American Center, 1973, pp. 25–31.

Wonderly, W. *Bible translation for popular use.* London: United Bible Societies, 1968.

Yngve, V. The machine and the man. *Machine Translation,* 1954, *1,* 20–22.

Yngve, V. Framework for syntactic translation. *Mechanical Translation,* 1957, *4,* 59–65.

Yngve, V. A programming language for mechanical translation. *Mechanical Translation,* 1958, *5,* 25–41.

Zemb, J. Le meme et l'autre. In J. Ladmiral, Ed. *La traduction (Langages,* series 28). Paris: Didier and Larousse, 1972, pp. 85–101.

Zvegintsev, V. Structural linguistics and linguistics of universals. *Acta Linguistica Hafniensia,* 1967, *10,* 129–144.

CHAPTER 2

Interpretation, A
Psychological Approach to
Translating

D. SELESKOVITCH*

TRANSLATION IS OFTEN CONSIDERED as a code-switching operation implying that a sequence of symbols from one language is substituted for a sequence of symbols in another language.

In interpretation, on the other hand, ideas are stressed, rather than words or symbols, and this introduces into the code-switching chain an additional segment: language X symbols→interpretation of their intended meaning→conveyance of the intended meaning (as perceived by the interpreter) in language Y symbols. Thus translation is considered as an endeavor to establish linguistic equivalents, whereas interpreting aims at integral communication of meaning, whatever the form of words employed in language X or Y.

Any substitution of one language component for another (be they phonemes or, in their written form, letters, grammatical marks, or lexical items) resulting in a correct linguistic equivalent could be termed *translation*. Thus I would be considered to be translating the pronunciation of my Serbian name by shifting the stress from its original place on the first syllable to the last one in French, to the before last one in Russian, and

*I should like to express my warmest thanks to Barry Jaggers for his cooperation and assistance.

to the third from the end in English! To make my name acceptable to German ears I would have to "translate" the initial unvoiced "S" into a voiced one. This concept of translation would also include transliterations, (sometimes with amazingly clear results as with Serbian *pectopah* = *restoran!*); it would cover grammatical equivalents ('he is reading' = (French) *il est en train de lire,* or (German) *des Vaters* = 'of the father'); however, this mode of translation would be devoted essentially to finding equivalents for lexical items in various languages.

With the code-switching concept of translation, languages as such are compared and assessed; among the most successful results obtained are the bilingual dictionaries, listing possible equivalents between language items. Such an approach, however, has obvious limits: how could a Japanese who does not distinguish between (u) and (oe) be made to understand the phonemic difference between *un enfant de 'deux' ans* and *un enfant de 'douze' ans,* how could past tenses be expressed in Chinese, a language without verbs, and so forth.

Anyone who has studied translation as a code-switching operation will inevitably have been confronted with these and many other similar limitations and will have been impressed by the arduous, not to say impossible, nature of such an undertaking.[1]

Interpretation focuses on the ideas expressed in live utterances rather than on language itself; it strictly ignores all attempts at finding linguistic equivalents (i.e., phrases that could be considered under any circumstances to carry the same meaning) and concentrates on finding the appropriate wording to convey a given meaning at a given point in time and in a given context, whatever that wording (i.e., the formulation used by the interpreter) or the original wording may mean under different circumstances. Interpretation involves the identification of relevant concepts and their rewording in another language in such a way that original and target language wordings may correspond only in their temporary meaning in a given speech performance without necessarily constituting equivalent language units capable of reuse in different circumstances.

Certain language units can be considered as permanent matches with other language units, for instance, figures

(French) *cinq* = five,[2] or names (French) *Londres* = London. Speech equivalents, however, are a different matter. I heard an excellent *sans hesiter* when an interpreter used "gladly," or "to mean business" on hearing a colleague rendering the *"volonté d'aboutir"* of a French statesman.

In both cases the meaning was truly conveyed—although the reader has to take the author's word for it, for as quoted here out of context both "gladly" and *"volonté d'aboutir"* may mean many different things. I have seen many such fleeting equivalents in my investigations of conference interpreting[3]; they crop up daily by the hundreds in the life of conference interpreters. They always stem from meaning, never from language. Language, such as described in grammars and dictionaries, yields many varied meanings to the scrutiny of the scholar; speech performance yields but one meaning to the initiated listener: the thing meant by the speaker.

In theory, code switching and interpretation are poles apart. The former deals with language, the latter with ideas. The former is so unconcerned with ideas that it scorns actual speech as a basis for investigating translatability and is only concerned with the linguistic systems involved. The latter is so unconcerned with language that it denies words or sentences any claim to translatability as long as they fail to merge into a meaningful whole: the discourse.

In real life, translating is a mixture of both code switching and interpretation; this is true of interpreting, too. As soon as a translator works on a text he concentrates on analyzing its meaning and the amount of interpretation involved in his work increases. Thus translation transcends mere code-switching of isolated language units.

That translators refuse to be considered as mere converters of one language into another is brought out clearly by the variety of terms used in French for the result achieved by translation. The brilliant French translator of Forsyth's *The Jackal* entitled his work *"texte français,"* translators of film scripts (for subtitles or dubbing) or of plays tend to use the term "adaptation," others speak of "version," whereas conference interpreters refer to "interpreting." Whatever the term used, however, the process involved and, above all, the ultimate aim of adaptations, versions, and interpretations differ in no way from the translator's daily work. The terminological switch is merely indicative of the desire to break out of the linguistic trammels. All those involved in the process, be they translators, interpreters, adaptors, or what have you, are endeavoring to communicate the *meaning* of the original message, and the difference in method is mainly due to differences in working conditions.

Time, for instance, imposes certain constraints on translating, which does not apply to interpreting: once an idea is set down in black and white, it assumes permanent form, and with the passing of time, form may well predominate over the original meaning so that posterity inherits only the linguistic form containing the message. What other solution does the translator have in such cases than to decipher the language units and to replace them by what he hopes to be equivalent units, in the forlorn hope of expressing the meaning?

A written text is, by definition, a permanent linguistic expression and as such constitutes a permanent temptation to the unwary to invert the logical sequence of translation, that is, to translate first (in the hope of understanding later), rather than to understand before translating. When the translator is not as familiar with the original language, nor as fully cognizant of the subject matter as the native reader, there is an immediate risk that he will resort to linguistic equivalents and that his renderings will no longer stem from the ideas contained in the original text but from the meanings individual words have as such. The association between translation and code switching in many peoples' minds is doubtless because written, that is, permanent, language is an open prey, a free for all, whereas the spoken word leaves no other trace in memory but the meaning it conveyed.

Conference interpreting, which involves only the oral processing of an oral message,[4] is in most cases successful in transcending the linguistic aspects of the message. This is why the theory of interpretation is not concerned with descriptive or comparative linguistics but with speech performance; it studies and compares the original message with that conveyed by the interpreter and endeavors to discern the interplay of thought and language through the evidences supplied by the processes of understanding and expressing.

Professional translators and interpreters are waging the same battle of wits, the communication of human thought. Operational translation, dealing with real-life texts, and conference interpreting are far from being the two extreme processes of code switching and conveyance of ideas. No translation of a human being, however mechanical, is entirely devoid of interpretation, and no interpretation, however freed from the constraints of the original linguistic system, is entirely devoid of code switching. Between the two extremes of purely linguistic translation, on the one hand, and of interpretation entirely based on meaning, on the other hand, there exists a whole concatenation of variables, each containing more-or-less interpretative or translative aspects Thus when we classify an exercise under the term *translation* or *interpretation* we refer more to the predominant aspect thereof than to a clear-cut line of demarcation between them.

Because this chapter intends merely to summarize a theory that purports to throw some light on the performance of speech and of cognitive processes as evidenced in interpreting, it will deal essentially with conference interpreting, but the reader should never loose sight of the fact that much of this theory will equally apply to translation.

The Interpreting Process

Interpreting signifies understanding followed by a rendering of ideas. The interpreter can thus be said to be playing two roles simultaneously in the field of language and communication, two roles that otherwise are always practiced separately: speech, which is the expression of our ideas, and understanding, which occurs when we listen to the speech and comprehend the ideas of the other speaker. The unique feature of interpreting is that these two processes are performed by the same person. Instead of the usual communication between speaker and listener, who invert their respective roles from time to time, there is a communication between three persons, the middleman being at the same time both speaker and listener, although in reverse order: listening and then speaking the same things though not the same words. The duplication of the processes involved in any speech performance makes it easier than is normally the case to observe the interplay of linguistic systems and mental processes in man. Thus, although the number of conference interpreters in the Western world does not exceed a few thousand and interpreting as a profession is of interest to a very few specialists only, the interpreting process per se is of universal interest because it exposes many aspects of the thought/language relationship that remain concealed in ordinary communication.

Interpretation theory studies this dual circuit[5]: speaker's act of speech→interpreter's understanding thereof as listener; ideas of the interpreter/speaker (identical to those of the original speaker)→interpreter's act of speech. It is, in duplicate, the same circuit that constitutes the communication between human beings.

In both the interpreter/listener and the interpreter/speaker (as in the normal listener and normal speaker) roles, the interaction of the manifold influences involved are almost invariably bidirectional. The degree to which interpreter/listener understands the oral message (perception of speech) depends not only on his knowledge of the original language and on the relevant knowledge he possesses of the subject under discussion, but also because he is aware of what has already been said and what a given argument is endeavoring to demonstrate or to refute; this understanding of the situation will, in turn, modify the initial factors. Each new factor the interpreter/listener understands and assimilates increases momentarily his relevant referential knowledge and thereby enhances his capacity to understand the following element of the speech or of other speeches later that day. The same process applies to the language itself, which in the communication process adopts a thousand and one ad hoc meanings in the light of the context that it did not previously contain[6] or to the awareness of shared knowledge inasmuch as the listening public and the interpreter/listener are assimilating meaningful segments of the speech in parallel.

In our examination of the communication process we shall deal cursorily with speaker and listener alike. Speech alone will be of concern to us in the speaker's case; as for the listener, we merely note his existence, thus concentrating on the interpreter/listener and then the interpreter/speaker. The processes of expression and understanding are identical, whether they take place in a speaker/listener relationship of two persons or whether they operate in the same person, but they are more amenable to investigation in the interpreter's case because the same ground is covered twice.

We shall begin with the interpreter/listener, the receiver of speech, and try to determine how his *knowledge* of relevant referents enables him to identify known factors and to construe the unknown.

Knowledge and Understanding

To illustrate the vital role played by extralinguistic knowledge over and above purely linguistic information, let us take the example of an evening spent viewing a friend's safari slides, an experience we have all been forced to undergo at some time or other. For our host, the image shown on the screen conjures up the living reality of the adventure he has just experienced: the crushing heat, the overpowering stench, the people, the shoes that pinched, the back-breaking camel-ride, and the like. For the viewers, the slides will only hold any real interest if, over and above his egocentric fascination with the events he has lived through, the photographer has displayed considerable skill in the art of photography, failing which the viewers will probably be secretly wishing the slides would go by as fast as possible, for they represent no more to the *viewers* than their formal appearance. Thus the differing level of interest shown in the visible forms by projector and viewer is explained by the difference in background knowledge. For the photographer, this instantaneous view of the slide recalls an infinitely vaster experience than the visible symbols; for the viewer, the image evokes no more than previously experienced facts, adequate to enable him to identify trees, flowers, or camels, but totally inadequate to enable him to relive the actual experience of the photographer. The difference in signification in the perception of the same slide by two persons having different experiences of the object represented is thus explained by their difference in knowledge level. In the case of the photographer the memories associated with the fraction of a second represented on the slide constitute the background knowledge used to interpret the image; in the case of the viewer, his only background knowledge is that of various past experiences of a sufficient number of trees of different dimensions and species to enable him to identify *the* tree on the slide as *a* tree. In the case of the photographer, the knowledge based on actual experience may cover a period of several days and his interpretation of the slide will call into play all the diverse relevant factors experienced before, and even after, the photo was taken, whereas the viewer can rely only on the tree pattern resulting from his varied experience of trees which enables him to recognize as belonging to the tree category all individual items that effectively belong thereto.

An interpreter lacking the slightest knowledge of the subject dealt with and developed in a speech is in the same position as a viewer who chances upon an unknown photo. He would identify the language spoken and words, just as the chance viewer would recognize a category of living being or object on a photo, but neither the ignorant interpreter nor the chance viewer would understand the *meaning* of the forms perceived.

An interpreter receiving a speech never receives linguistic units entirely devoid of context (verbal and situational) but rather receives utterances spoken by a person whose position, nationality, and interests are known to him, speaking with a purpose in mind, trying to convince his listeners. Thus an utterance bearing a message differs absolutely from a sequence of words chosen at random, for the former evoke not only their intrinsic linguistic meaning but facts known to all those for whom the message is intended.

As an example, let us take the following situation: I'm standing in the lobby of a Paris hotel, chatting with an English friend. Just behind us is the swinging door leading to the restaurant, with waiters scurrying in and out. One of them shouts as he hurries by: *"Méfiez-vous de la porte!"* (possible translations would be "mind the door," "watch the door," "watch your backs," "watch it"). My English friend grabs me by the arm and leads me a few steps further away from the door, saying, "He wants us to stand clear of the door!" He is reexpressing what was originally said in French, basing himself not on the French linguistic formulation but on his perception of the overall situation, thus establishing the link between what is known implicitly and situationally and what was actually expressed verbally. In other words, my friend was interpreting the waiter's words in the light of his knowledge of the situation. Any meaningful utterance is but the visible part of an iceberg, adequate to enable the intended recipient to work out the appropriate relationship between the visible and the invisible parts and, like the mariner who draws the right conclusions and navigates on that basis, to apprehend the whole on the basis of the part.

Another example will serve to demonstrate the obverse of the same phenomenon. The first paragraph of J. Z. Young's book *The Memory System of the Brain* (University of California Press, Berkeley and Los Angeles, 1966) will be used as "speech": "Probably we should all agree that the question 'How do brains work?' is important and that it would be a good thing to know the answer, but would there be agreement on the form the answer might take? The brain is an exceedingly complicated system and our language and powers of understanding my cat is black are but weak. In what sense therefore can we expect to be able to say: 'I understand the brain'?"

Now in this paragraph, which expresses ideas the author wishes the reader/listener to understand, I have slipped in a phrase ("my cat is black") that in the context selected is entirely devoid of meaning. The *reader* will probably have stopped at this point to reread the passage—the fact that he has a written text before him enables him to do so; but in an oral situation, the *listener* is unable to "play back" the speech. His reaction will be either not to hear the phrase, that is, to ignore it because it failed to trigger any mental process in his mind, or else to draw certain conclusions, not about the phrase but about the speaker himself (is the man suffering from a temporary aberration or is he right out of his mind!).

The important conclusion to be drawn from this example with regard to interpretation is that words or phrases in isolation and entirely out of context cannot be linked to relevant knowledge and, consequently, are not amenable to interpretation. We are left with their lexical and grammatical meaning, identified by our knowledge of the language, but this merely enables us to recognize what is already known to us, it does not unable us to apprehend new information. The situation is the same as the example of slide viewing; words constitute a potential communication, but only become "communication" when the speaker addresses them to a listener for a reason comprehensible to both parties.

The first conclusion to be drawn from the relationship between knowledge of referents and the formulation of the message is that the formulation does not contain the meaning but merely triggers it off; the meaning can only be construed in the listener's mind if he has some knowledge of the subject dealt with. This is what I called *Relevant knowledge of referants*, for, clearly, on each and every occasion the kind of knowledge required for understanding depends on the context. The greatest erudite would be lost if he failed to possess the tiny morsel of ad hoc knowledge *relevant* to the situation. An attempt to define the size of that morsel would be too involved for this chapter. However, by reducing the dimensions of the interpreter's rectangle representing this knowledge on the diagram, I have tried to show that the level of knowledge mastered by the conference interpreter who specializes in interpretation and not in the subject matter under discussion can never equal that of the specialist whose knowledge is *operational* and enables him to *perform* (the surgeon, for example) in his field of endeavor or to *assess* the validity of the arguments put forward by the other speakers. And yet the interpreter must have *some* knowledge in all the multifarious fields with which he deals, and the level of that knowledge must be adequate for understanding.

There are two cases in which a linguistic formulation cannot arouse any meaningful knowledge, so that the listener remains as nearly ignorant as he was before the words were said. The first case arises when no context is provided with the utterance (the words out of context that were just mentioned). This occurs whenever you ask someone who knows another language for the "translation" of a word without giving him the context: "How do you say *this* in French, or *that* in German?" The experienced interpreter will always answer, "What exactly do you mean?" The second case is that of insufficient referential knowledge: the interpreter who is not given any insight of the problems to be discussed does not possess the minimum level of knowledge enabling him *to interpret,* that is, *to understand.* His extralinguistic inadequacy will render obscure, and probably meaningless, most of what he hears, even sentences composed of perfectly ordinary words. In such cases, the interpreter inevitably falls back on linguistic meaning; his translation regresses towards mere language-to-language code switching; he understands the words not in their relevant meaning but in their primary sense, the meaning they most frequently have for him or in which he has heard them used most recently. In such cases, any ambiguity in linguistic meaning will remain ambiguous for the interpreter. Thus an ignorant interpreter hearing *La Mer de Debussy,* Debussy's tone poem *La Mer,* might translate "Debussy's mother" (it is rumored that this bilingual malaproprism was actually perpetrated in all seriousness by a beginner!) The interpreter who translates without understanding is no longer interpreting. His audience will have the impression that he does not know the right words, but in point of fact what he is lacking is the background knowledge to *interpret* the words.

In a normal verbal exchange there are no ambiguities. A word of warning to the student interpreter who may fall into the trap of linguistics, failing to realize that the science of linguistics is essentially devoted to the study of language and not to the application of language to communication. The linguist is perfectly right to state that a language is composed of words that, for the most part, have multiple referential meanings and that grammar fails to render sentences entirely unambiguous. The interpreter would be wrong, however, to conclude that multiple referential meanings or ambiguity can exist in a meaningful message and that they could therefore confront him with a problem. Entirely out of context, without any situational background, a word, a phrase, or even a whole sentence may have several possible meanings. But I will only confuse "kernel" with "colonel" if I hear the word entirely out of context, where no meaning is intended. Similarly, when I hear the sentence "What disturbed John was being disregarded by everyone"[7] I will hesitate between the two possible meanings only if the sentence, instead of bearing a message within a given context, is served up on a syntactical platter entirely out of any context. Now, if "What disturbed John was being disregarded by everyone" constituted a meaningful message for the listener, he would be aware of the circumstances referred to, and this knowledge would rule out the slightest possibility of ambiguity.

Ambiguity only occurs when the extralinguistic information normally attached to any linguistic utterance is lacking in the listener; for this reason the traps and pitfalls are a matter of concern chiefly for machine translation. Although it remains a matter of some concern for the human translator of written texts, it is not difficult for him to find the relevant information outside the text itself, enabling him to settle any problems of linguistic ambiguity. As for the conference interpreter, he is not really concerned at all, for in an oral situation it is only quite exceptionally that he will have any doubts as to the intended meaning of the speaker, only if he were deprived of any prior inside knowledge of the problems under discussion might some doubts occur as to the intended meanings.

The fact that the written word appears more ambiguous than the spoken word requires a short explanation to allay any possible misunderstanding. The written, or rather the printed word is far more accessible to all and sundry, whereas the spoken word is intended for persons physically present (we shall disregard radio and television, where interpretation is only involved on rare occasions) and is therefore nicely adapted to fit the implicit knowledge of the audience. Thus it would appear evident that the greater degree of ambiguity in the written or printed word is not due to the written form of the message but to the fact that, contrary to the spoken word in which speaker and listener know each other and adapt to each other, the written word may be read by many people possessing the linguistic competence but lacking the necessary knowledge to understand the text. The understanding required of a written text in order to translate it does not lie, as is claimed only too often, in choosing for a given word or sentence the right meaning out of several possible meanings, but rather in combining correctly relevant knowledge of the subject matter with the linguistic formulation, so that there remain no alternatives to choose from.

Language and Speech Performance

The listener knows the language in which the speech aimed at him is delivered, but he cannot know in advance the contents of the utterance. His understanding will, therefore, be based on two processes: recognizing the linguistic items perceived and construing the meaning of the message.

It is tempting to consider that the identification of linguistic units is not primarily a matter of understanding but rather of comparison with previous knowledge, that is, that the perception of an individual item will trigger off a mental image of the same item stored in the memory. In reality, however, the process is far more complex. For various reasons the sound reaching the listener's ears is rarely a 100 percent perfect; the speaker's pronunciation is always more or less defective; transmission of sound—either direct, through the air in the case of the consecutive interpreter or indirect, via electronic transmission in the case of the simultaneous interpreter—always involves a fairly considerable loss factor. Thus perception of individual words always involves a certain amount of anticipation based on the interpreter's understanding of the meaning. The interpreter/listener (to be differentiated from the ordinary listener probably only by the fact that he concentrates harder) follows the speaker's train of thought very closely, and he can on the basis of previous meanings predict the probable forthcoming meaning. This predicting process assists him in hearing/understanding the acoustic form of the words by comparing the relatively defective sounds reaching his ear with the predicted meaning. A research project currently under way by M. Lederer at Paris University Sorbonne Nouvelle has demonstrated the occurrence of meaningful segments as understood by the interpreter before the grammatical end of the sentence. They appear at when the listening process changes direction, as it were, and instead of consisting in pure reception becomes largely anticipative.

It is well known that the possibility of fully acquiring a foreign language ceases with adulthood and that most adults living in a foreign country never improve their linguistic abilities beyong the threshold of intelligibility.[8] The all-out effort required when they first learned to speak, the patient practice in listening and pronouncing they indulged in as children, learning gradually to appreciate various shades of meaning, is no longer necessary because they no longer need to acquire the meaningful mental representations they built up when learning their mother tongue. Thus once the main obvious differences between the two phonological systems have been overcome, and once the chief classification of meanings behind the new words is achieved, communication is established in the foreign language by phonological and semantic analogy with the mother tongue. The distorted language, however, is understood by native listeners, for between adults more-or-less incomplete sounds or incorrect use of words in all but exhaustive statements suffice for anyone to identify the meaning. In the speech performance meaning is not built up in the listener's mind in successive stages from sounds to words and sentences, but perceived in the opposite order as soon as the first few words uttered by the speaker are past.

Thus when one *hears* words, one does not really preceive their acoustic form in totality, but rather he identifies a partial sound with representations stored in the memory. The partial sound suffices to trigger off the memory process. As to the sounds themselves reach the listener's ears, they too trigger off a mental image: the phonemes. Human sensory organs do not function like photographic film or magnetic tape; the acoustic magma reaching the ear is broken down into separate items that fit into previously stored sound patterns. The sounds themselves may be extremely defective, but integral perception is unnecessary for hearing, because previous knowledge makes up for the missing sounds.

Such perceptual phenomena tend to remain entirely unheeded by those who communicate in their own language, as linguistic competence masks the amount of either words or sounds that is actually filled in. They are equally irrelevant to written translation in which the printed text is composed of letters in their complete form, and in which the eye is not obliged, like the ear, to perceive sequentially but may now and then linger on a phrase, turn back to a previous passage, or fly over several lines at a time. In interpreting, however, these phenomena play a major part, as may be noted daily by those interpreters who teach or work on recordings made at multilingual meetings. They may become utterly noxious if an interpreter does not know well enough the language he is hearing: in that case he will concentrate all his efforts on perceiving the sounds and words and will pay no more than scant attention to the meaning.

This is indeed the crux of the matter; speech is not merely part of a linguistic system requiring individual segments to be identified; it is first and foremost the message the speaker wants to put across to his audience. This is stating the obvious to any conference interpreter and seems perfectly normal in everyday situations involving conversations in the same language ("What did he say?" wife asks husband, as he puts down the phone. She doesn't expect a verbatim report, word for word, but the essential message contained in the conversation). However, it would not appear to be obvious to those who think of translation in terms of written texts only, and it was certainly entirely misunderstood by the first inventors of machine translation, who apparently felt that it sufficed to replace one word in one language by another word in another language to achieve results.[9]

That being so we should take a closer look at this meaning, the reproduction of which in a linguistic system and a linguistic form different from the original, forms the main substance of what is being taught and researched in the field of interpretation. We shall see that this meaning is both more *and* less than the sum of the meanings of the words used.

As proof of the fact that the meaning of the message is *less* than the sum of the meanings of the words composing it, we should note that the lexical meaning of a word is the result of its use by generations of human beings in many varied circumstances. The lexicographer trying to define it will find thousands of shimmering shades of meaning behind the same words used by different authors (we leave aside etymological considerations here as being outside the scope of this article) and will then classify and describe them with abundant examples. For the child learning his own language, the meaning of a word is built up piece by piece. Every different set of circumstances when he hears it used teaches him to use it himself by successive approximation. Furthermore, the meaning of a word represents no more than an initial approach to the thing or the concept it designates. Familiarity with a vast vocabulary often creates the illusion of having a far-reaching knowledge of the corresponding things or concepts. This tends to confusion between absolute, and therefore nonperfectible, knowledge of the material designation of meaning (i.e., the word) and knowledge of the designated object (the referent), which can never attain completion. The illustration of knowledge created by familiarity with the word is frequently accompanied by a taxonomical error. Merely because the linguistic system uses two separate words, the existence of two distinct concepts is often postulated or, conversely, when the language uses a single word to designate two or more distinct concepts, one will tend to think that there is a single concept.

In the last analysis, words are neither a complete description nor the distinctive appellation of the thing or concept involved, but rather a broad-brimmed hat covering meanings and facets of meaning, classified in an infinite number of ways according to the language under consideration. The variations in taxonomy according to language is ample proof of the fact that language is not a listing of things and concepts according to some natural breakdown but that it involves classification into groups or categories carrying as common denominator the most striking common feature. Where French uses the one word *race*, English has both *breed* and *race*. A *bulb* in English is both something you plant in the hope of growing a tulip and an object that provides electric light; the kinship between the two apparently different concepts is based on shape. French, on the other hand, uses *oignon* for flower bulbs, but the word also means the vegetable onion, whereas an entirely different word *ampoule* (also meaning blister) is used for a light bulb. In German, *Birne* groups together the light bulb and pear concepts (clearly because of similar shapes), whereas *Zwiebel* is used for onion and flower bulb, and so forth.

Now, it may be claimed that this way of designating things on the basis of a characterizing feature, evolved through generations of speakers, is evidence of a general relationship between mental processes and verbal expression that also applies to individual speech performance, that is, to the way mental representations are brought to concrete forms in speech. In a recent article in an American newspaper on the present economic situation I noted the use of three words to express the general fears of recession: *threat, ghost,* and *clouds.* Each of these three words was used with almost exactly the same facet of meaning, each with complete disregard of its other facets. The reader, confronted with three different sensory concretizations on the same meaning had no difficulty whatsoever in receiving the only *relevant* semantic feature involved, whereas the other semantic features of *threat, ghost* and *clouds* remained unnoticed. The interpreter hearing the word *bulb* will never think of glass or electricity or light if the subject of the discourse is tulips. Persons engaged in conversations or, in our case, the interpreter listening to a speech, automatically hear the *relevant* layer of meaning while the many other semantic layers stored with the same word remain dormant. The same applies to whole phrases that express meaning not in a one-to-one relationship between verbal forms and mental representations but through the verbal designation of the dominant feature of the thing meant.

This is why the message conveyed is less than the sum of the meanings of the words it consists of. Words follow neatly upon each other in syntactic arrangements, but never do they in toto line up more than a tiny proportion of their potential meaning, and phrases follow upon each other in the course of the speech without ever bringing out more than salient features of the speaker's non verbal ideas. Arrays of words will never constitute a comprehensive description of the speaker's ideas—any such description would tend towards infinity without ever attaining completeness.

This is an important aspect of interpretation in which the differentiation between the various features of meaning is brought out very clearly in the different clothing put on the message in the other language.

The meaning of a sentence aimed at an audience is also *more* than the sum of relevant meanings carried by individual words, because the listener perceives the nonverbal part of the message at the same time as the words; he grasps the much vaster underlying thought that transpires through the coded message. This is why to interpreters the word *information* does not mean at all the same thing as to communication engineers; the interpreter's task is in no way similar to that of a Morse operator transcribing his message into clear language;

he does not process information in the same way that a signal containing information is processed by identifying the ciphers in the light of preexisting knowledge. The interpreter's job is not done once he has deciphered the signal; he must extract from the fleeting words a lasting nonverbal signification. Interpreting involves construing fresh knowledge by removing it from its verbal, that is, physical, support and integrating it into one's relevant, nonverbal knowledge. Thus for him, *information* means that which in some way modifies his previous knowledge[10] in full concurrence with Piaget's views on assimilation. Thus *information* in the interpreter's sense of the term, stems not so much from the identification of the words themselves as from their interpretation.

Thus interpreting both in the everyday sense of individual understanding and in professional practice means the addition of relevant meaning to previous knowledge to grasp the ideas involved in the message, whereas the reproduction of information in the other language involves retrieving the appropriate thought from this body of knowledge and expressing it in the verbal form best suited to understanding by the audience.

Interpreters invariably use meaning as their basis, for they are aware that their translation would be lacking in effectiveness if they were to take the linguistic code only. The oral nature of speech, which obliges the listener to understand what is being said in a single perceptual pass, the need for the interpreter to put over the original idea in one single transmission, the tense atmosphere often found in meetings involving matters of great import, where the slightest slip, in meaning or expression, is almost unpardonable, have led to consecutive interpretation[11] being used in a manner very much akin to the normal mode of communication. The interpreter has no time to dally over a given word or sentence; because he is forced to operate at the normal tempo of human speech, he must comply with all its characteristics.

The following anecdote is to be found in the *New Yorker*, September 7, 1963: "In the annals of the profession (of conference interpreters), there is even a story of an English consecutive interpreter who sat stonily through an hour-long speech in French, moved only once to make a note on his pad, and then rose and rendered the speech word-perfect in English. A colleague, stirred by professional curiosity, sneaked a look at the pad: on it was written the single word 'however'!" The anecdote may have ventured somewhat further than historical truth would allow, but it does clearly reflect the essential underlying principles of consecutive interpreting: very few notes, serving to jog the memory, but above all, understanding and repeating what one has understood. Thus the speech was certainly not rendered *word-perfect* but *meaning-perfect* or true to meaning.

The fact that consecutive interpreters take so few notes is not only proof that interpreting has hardly anything in common with uncoding and recoding, it also demonstrates the nonverbal nature of thought! One of the most interesting mistakes all consecutive interpreters have made at least once in their careers is rendering the original speech, or at least a few sentences of it, in the original language of the speaker. The widespread nature of that error nullifies any argument that would tend to consider that the interpreter says one word in language Y for a word heard in language X, as if he were functioning like a vending machine that spews forth the right brand of cigarettes if you push the right button. The fact that a speech given in *English* is occasionally rendered in *English*, though in different terms, is compelling proof that in the interpreter's mind the original thought had assumed its nonverbal, shapeless state. Where does the interpreter, in such a case, find his English words to reformulate the original English speech? The only possible answer is in nonverbal thought, for, clearly he has not retrieved them from the *words* of the other language!

Formal Memory—Semantic Memory

In the interpreting process two types of memories can be discerned:[12] the first corresponds to the acquisition, storage, and recall capacity of acoustic shapes and their associated mental patterns, which we might term *acoustic* or *formal* memory; the second, more diffuse and not directly related to sensory perceptions, is the ability to remember meanings, where the current names for acquisition, storage and recall are *understanding, knowing,* and meaningful speech; this is the *semantic memory.*

These two memories, that of language (but also of the familiar noises and shapes that surround us) and that of nonverbal knowledge (resulting also from direct experience where language has not been involved) are the essential mechanisms on which interpretation is based; therefore, they particularly lend themselves to investigation through studies on interpretation.

Let us return to the speech at the point where it has been perceived. It is stored by the interpreter partly in the formal memory, partly in the semantic memory, either in toto (in the case of consecutive) or segment by segment (in simultaneous interpreting) before being rendered. During the memory span within which the speech segments are still materially present in their acoustic shape, the interpreter performs a fantastic sorting process: a tiny portion of the speech segments is processed and stored in the form of language units, whereas the major part of the language segments are processed for content, transformed into mental representations, and stored in the semantic memory. Those speech segments that are returned in their linguistic shapes (either in the original or in the interpreter's language) are what I termed translatable words, [13] that is, figures, proper names, and those words that, in a given field, designate things or concepts which are clearly and identically defined in both languages and which therefore have linguistic equivalents (for example: French: *Parc* de locomotives, English: *Fleet* of engines). In the consecutive mode such words are briefly noted so that the interpreter will unfailingly retrieve them when rendering the speech. In simultaneous, one technique is to reduce the time lag between interpreter and speaker in order to translate the words immediately into the other language, that is, within the memory span of the formal memory, while their acoustic shape is still present. Another technique is to listen to the words intently while retrieving their linguistic equivalent for use at the appropriate time. In both cases the formal memory is used to advantage, but while this uncoding-recoding is going on, the bulk of the speech is transformed in the interpreter's mind into mental representations devoid of any linguistic shape and stored into the semantic memory. These simultaneous operations come into conflict when there is occasional need for concentration on the formal memory. This explains why erroneous figures and names are among the mistakes made most frequently by conference interpreters, a compensating factor being the frequent occurrence of the same translatable words that, as time goes by, makes language switching easier.

As the line of thought of the speaker develops, the speech unfolds and is understood by audience and interpreter. Once heard, any listener could easily render it with a single word (for instance *agrees* or *disagrees*) or summarize it briefly, or even repeat some parts or words that were particularly striking. The interpreter too is able to summarize—and indeed in consecutive interpretation is often requested to do so. In both cases the mental processes involved are the same: both listener and interpreter understand the content of the speech—as opposed to merely recognizing its linguistic components. They both syncretize into nonverbal thought the speaker's arguments that neatly dovetail and support each other. Yet, although the listener would be in no position to repeat the whole speech without omitting the slightest shade of meaning or the tiniest detail, the interpreter can—however long the speech. This is because having to use a different language, he does not repeat the words but rewords the meaning stored in his semantic memory.

The use of another language to reexpress *all* information, however insignificant, reveals far more of the interplay of the two types of memories than the repetition of a statement in the same language—if it could be achieved with proper training. In the latter case it would be well-nigh impossible to determine the mnemonic origin of the utterance, and to decide, for instance, whether the use of identical words was attributable to formal memory or whether a meaningful process had taken place in such a manner that identity of linguistic units was purely fortuitous. Such problems disappear in the case of interpreting. Languages do not tally, and the semantic process stands out clearly in the formulations used by the interpreter to express ideas in the other language; such formulations are entirely different from those words that are merely *translated* and that still bear the mark of the original language.

In simultaneous interpreting it may be asserted as a general rule that the better the interpreter understands the meaning of what the speaker is saying, the less linguistic similarity there is between his discourse and that of the speaker. In consecu-

tive interpreting, the formal memory decays almost completely because of the sheer passage of time, inasmuch as shorthand is never used, because it would interfere with the semantic coding process in the interpreter's mind.

In addition to the dissimilarity in the form of language it is
interesting to note in simultaneous interpreting the time lag
between the interpreter's rendering and the original speaker:
on occasion the interpreter will allow the speaker to run
ahead, whereas at other times he will finish the sentence ahead
of the speaker.[14] This demonstrates that for an oral contribution to be understood, a certain number of words must have
been spoken, but that in most cases the idea is grasped before
the end of the formal linguistic expression. In observing the
interpreter re-expressing the original thought in terms that
are independent from the original wording we can pinpoint
the moment when understanding occurs in the mind of the
interpreter and when meaning breaks away from the shackles
of linguistic symbols. The number of words required before
meaning is established depends on the listener's knowledge of
the subject: the greater the knowledge, the sooner understanding occurs, provided due attention is paid. This ratio of
the total utterance will thus vary constantly. It therefore appears that since on the one hand the speaker arranges the
length and degree of detail of his discourse intuitively according to what he believes to be the average level of knowledge
of his audience, and since on the other hand different listeners
do not require the same amount of words to grasp the speaker's intentions correctly, there is no quantitative relationship
between the informational content and the physical, sensory
support of information. The overriding role of semantic memory would seem thus to be demonstrated, and the evidence
supplied by interpretation may be considered of paramount
importance for the study of cognitive processes involved in
speaking and understanding.

FOOTNOTES

1. Cf. G. Mounin, *Les Problèmes Théoriques De La Traduction*, (Gallimard, Paris 1963)

2. Though, here again, lexical exceptions are far from infrequent: A one-star general (American) = *un général à deux étoiles* (French)

3. D. Seleskovitch, *L'Interprète Dans Les Conférences Internationales* (Minard, Lettres Modernes, Paris, 1968) and D. Seleskovitch, *Language, Langues et Mémoire* Etude de la prise de notes en interprétation consécutive, (Minard Lettres Modernes, Paris, 1975).

4. On occasion, the conference interpreter is obliged to convey a written text; in such cases the process involved is inevitably more akin to translation than to interpretation.

5. "The interpretation circuit" is part of a post-graduate course on the *theory of interpretation* which the author teaches at the Paris University "Sorbonne Nouvelle". For reasons of space, it is possible to give only a brief overview of the subject here.

6. M. Lederer, "La Traduction: Transcoder ou Réexprimer?" *Etudes de Linguistique Appliquée, Exégèse et Traduction* 12, (Didier, Paris, 1973)

7. Chomsky, *Language and Mind* p. 124. Consider, for example, the following sentence: "What disturbed John was being disregarded by everyone." It is clear, first of all, that this expression has two distinct interpretations. Under one interpretation, it means that John was disturbed by the fact that everyone disregarded him; under the second, it means that everyone was disregarding the things that disturbed John.

8. On the 'threshold' of linguistic learning see Déjean and Pergnier, ESIT.

9. See M. Lederer " 'Equivalences' ou Intelligence," *Bulletin L'Interprète* XXIX/ *2*, 1974 (Case Post. Stand 388, Genève).

10. I well recall the evening in April 1945 in Belgrade, liberated six months previously, where I was monitoring the German radio and the last verbal convulsions of the enemy. That evening, after the traditional symphonic extract, the announcer proclaimed *"Der Führer ist gefallen"* (Hitler is dead). These four words conjured up in my mind the end of a nightmare far more intensively than the news of the preceding allied victories had ever done. This short sentence changed the world, not by its intrinsic value but by virtue of the information it conveyed, the irreversible transformation of reality . . . a new historical era was born.

11. In the consecutive mode of interpretation, the interpreter awaits the end of the speech before taking over. He does not learn the speech

by heart any more than he notes it down in shorthand; thus he will only memorize or jot down a few words. Rooted as it is in understanding and in making one's audience understand, consecutive interpreting is real "interpretation." Although still used not infrequently today in bilingual meetings, its main use is to train students to handle information intelligently. Thus, once they begin their professional life, working preponderantly in the simultaneous mode, they will avoid falling into the trap of code switching. This pitfall is all too seldom avoided by untrained interpreters or by those whose training has been limited to vocabulary drills; in such cases, their performance at best will leave the audience guessing at what the speaker might have meant or, at worst, cursing the speaker as a mental defective. In her report to the *Royal Commission on Bilingualism and Biculturalism*, R. Nilski stresses the same point: "In interpreters schools, the emphasis should be on developing mental grasp and agility, on creating an awareness of the thought processes involved in both direct oral communication and communication across a language barrier, rather than on mechanistic transposition and automatic vocabulary drills, which produce an unintelligent and often unintelligible reproduction of the original message."

12.   See also Jean Delay, *Les Maladies de la Mémoire* (Presses Universitaires de France, Paris, 1970).

13.   D. Seleskovitch, *Language, Langues et Mémoire, etude de la prise de notes en interprétation consécutive*, (Minard Paris, 1975).

14.   Some noninterpreters, attempting to teach interpreting, have noted the existence of a time lag between speaker and interpreter and, taking it to be the key to the mysterious working of simultaneous interpreting, have endeavored to increase the distance between utterance and repetition in a word-for-word drill, failing to realize that the distance at which the interpreter operates is not a deliberate artifice, but a variable factor based on *semantic* and *not* on formal memory!

REFERENCES

Barbizet, J. *Etudes sur la Mémoire*. Paris: L'Expansion Scientifique Française, 1964 and 1966.

Chomsky, N. *Language and mind*. New York: Harcourt, Brace, Jovanovich, 1972.

Delay, J. *Les Maladies de la Mémoire*. Paris: Presses Universitaire de France, 1970.

Ecole Superieure d'Interprètes et de Traducteurs de l'Université de Paris (ESIT), Monographies: Perfectionnement linguistique (Déjean and Pergnier), 1975.

Lederer, M. Transcoder ou Réexprimer. *Etudes de Linguistique Appliquée*, No. 12. Paris: Didier, 1973.

Lederer, M. Equivalences ou Intelligence? *Bulletin L'Interprète*, 1974, *29* (2), Geneva: Case Post. Stand 388.

Mounin, G. *Les Problèmes théoriques de la traduction*. Paris: Gallimard, 1963.

Nilski, R. *Conference interpreting in Canada*. Royal Commission on Bilingualism and Biculturalism. Ottawa: The Queen's Printer, 1969.

Seleskovitch, D. *L'Interprète dans les conférences internationales, Problèmes de langage et de communication*. Paris: Minard, Lettres Modernes, 1968.

Seleskovitch, D. Vision du Monde et Traduction. *Etudes de Linguistique Appliquée*, No. 12, Paris: Didier, 1973.

Seleskovitch, D. *Langage, Langues et Mémoire—Etude de la prise de notes en interprétation consécutive*. Paris: Minard, Lettres Modernes, 1975.

CHAPTER 3

Perspectives and Limitations of a Didactic Framework for the Teaching of Translation*

WOLFRAM WILSS

ANYONE WHO TRIES to answer the question of the extent to which translation can be taught and learned systematically must first make sure that his explorations are not interpreted as only another contribution toward clarifying an issue that has played an important part in foreign-language pedagogy in recent years. It is a well-known fact that under the influence of behavioristic learning theory as developed by Skinner, the role of translation in foreign-language teaching has been critically assessed. The issue is still controversial; whereas at first the grammar-translation method, under the impact of the direct method, was widely regarded as irrelevant for language teaching, there are now indications on an increasing scale that, owing to the progress of cognitive-code learning theory, translation is re-establishing itself as a useful and legitimate tool of foreign language teaching with a markedly higher degree of didactic and methodical sophistication than previously.[1]

Independent of the discussion on foreign language pedagogy regarding the full, partial, or zero relevance of translation in language teaching and within quite a different conceptual framework, problems of the preconditions, perspec-

*This chapter was originally written in German. It was translated by the author with the help of Richard Brislin, who acted as translation editor.

tives, and limitations of a didactically and methodically sound approach to the teaching of translation (TT) have emerged in one other area, namely in the field of teaching translation to would-be professional translators (and interpreters). There are at the moment three universities in Germany, in Germercheim/Mainz, Heidelberg, and Saarbrücken, that offer specific, interdisciplinary programs for future translators with two obligatory foreign languages and one obligatory nonlanguage complementary subject (in Saarbrücken technology, economics and law, in that order). In comparison with modern language departments, such as English, French, or Russian, the problems of the didactic and methodical structuring of TT within a program for future professional translators possesses much more weight and curricular topicality, because here TT is not just one problem within the many still-to-be-solved problems of foreign language teaching, but an issue of primary importance. This is evident from the fact that the development of the translational (translatory) competence, that is, the ability to reproduce technical, common language and literary texts adequately in the target language, constitutes the overriding (pivotal) learning target on which all curricular components—native-tongue training, controlled second-language acquisition, common language, technical and literary translation classes, (comparative) area studies and, last but not least, courses (lectures and seminars) in the science of translation (ST)—are focused.[2]

If one realizes the outstanding importance of TT in all curricula for future professional translators, it is at first sight surprising that the problems of TT efficiency have thus far played only a secondary role in the framework of empirical pedagogical research. It is, therefore, no wonder that the development of learner group-specific, text-typologically differentiated methods of TT is still in its infancy. This is probably true not only for the three West German university institutes for translating and interpreting, but also for comparable university schools abroad. It is symptomatic of the present unsatisfactory state of affairs that the term *Ubersetzungsdidaktik* (translation pedagogy) is a fairly new coinage and that the manifold problems associated with this term have only recently provoked noticeable interest among linguists engaged in ST.[3]

The relatively slow crystallization of TT into a self-contained subfield of ST is, above all, because ST in its various ramifications is a late starter in modern linguistics and has therefore had some difficulties in asserting (and defending) its theoretical and methodological dignity. This has entailed a time lag in the emergence of the applied science of translation (AST) under which TT can be subsumed together with other applied branches, such as the development of a hierarchy of translation difficulties, error analysis (foreign language/native tongue), and translation criticism. The explanation of this time lag is that a subject matter which has become the object of scientific research can be made amenable to applied aspects only after it has been deeply explored in its own theoretical and methodological dimensions. The rather late appearance of ST as a new, autonomous subdiscipline of descriptive-synchronic comparative linguistics is the result of the predominantly monosystematic orientation of present-day linguistics and of the speeding-up in recent years of the construction of formal syntactical models aimed at the filling up of the acutely-felt "theory gap" of modern linguistics. The investigation of translation problems could not be accommodated in the system-dominated research paradigm of modern linguistics, because it operates along other lines of thought than ST, which is mainly occupied with interlingual text-pragmatic and text-idiomatic issues. There is no doubt that the development of syntactical models is extremely important for basic (theoretical) linguistic research. On the other hand, their explanatory power is limited in cases in which the explanation of the functioning of human language in concrete communicative situations is at stake.[4] Here is a legitimate opening for the ST: its starting point is that translation is an interlingual transfer process that can be broken down into a finite number of basic components. It leads from a written source language (SL) text to an optimally equivalent target language (TL) text and presupposes the syntactic, semantic and text-pragmatic understanding of the original text. The primary task of the ST is to analyze, under functional aspects, those linguistic and psycholinguistic factors that are constitutive in any translation process. Hence ST is a branch of linguistics that is characterized by the perpetual interplay of descriptive, explanatory, and normative perspectives.

The number of translation problems included is impressive

enough, but the problem situation is acutely sharpened by the fact that AST is, at least at present, unable to provide a satisfactory answer to the question of the measurability of translational competence. It is, therefore, extremely difficult for AST to describe learning targets in detail and to develop an adequate TT framework. AST cannot provide a satisfactory answer to the question of the professional minimum qualifications of a translator, above all, because *the* translational competence as a uniform qualification for professional translation work is, to all intents and purposes, nonexistent and probably also nondefinable. Two implications from this are evident:

1. The need to differentiate between a number of discourse-type-specific competence areas such as technical translation, common-language translation, literary translation, and Bible translation (see the introductory chapter by Brislin).

2. The need to differentiate between two competence directions for translation from foreign language to native tongue, and vice versa.

Even if we ignore the need for subcategorization, for example, in the area of technical translation, we must distinguish eight translational competence ranges, each of which covers a specific field of professional translation activities. Each of the eight competence ranges is in its turn composed of two subcompetences, a SL receptive and a TL reproductive competence. Both subcompetences are in complementary relation and together constitute the basis of translational competence. Such competence is an imperative prerequisite for a translator to be able to translate semantically, syntactically, and/or stylistically complex texts from various discourse areas with the necessary minimal degree of communicative equivalence.

Because translational competence is an interlingual competence, it is clearly marked off from the four traditional monolingual skills: listening, speaking, reading, and writing. It is, as it were, a supercompetence requiring as a precondition a comprehensive syntactic, lexical, morphological, and stylistic knowledge of the respective SL and TL and the ability to synchronize these two monolingual knowledge areas and thus to bring about a communicatively effective interlingual transfer.

In order to put AST on a solid pedagogical footing, it is

necessary to look at translation process in such a way as to make clear that it is not a linguistic operation but a psycholinguistic activity that brings two language levels, lexis and syntax, functionally together. In its attempts to pin down the process, ST can fall back on various trends in contemporary linguistics. Relatively meager stimuli seem to have been suggested for AST from transformational grammar (TG), and this is primarily due to two reasons.

First, TG has thus far failed to develop a bilingual or even multilingual performance model as required by ST. Rather, TG still seems to be focused on the clarification of the concept of linguistic competence against the background of idealized monolingual sender/receptor relations. This restriction makes itself felt in the absence of a consolidated effort to develop procedures for the discovery of the complicated interplay between linguistic rule systems on the one side and concrete, situationally determined linguistic performance on the other, as well as for the exploration of the communicative side of linguistic usage. It follows from this that it is the function of language, so fundamental for ST, that has remained outside its theoretical research paradigm. Els Oksaar is therefore right in stating, "Linguistic form is to some extent a function of social context . . . and the ability to communicate effectively involves more than what is implied in Chomsky's rather narrowly defined view of linguistic competence."[5]

Second, TG has developed stringent descriptive procedures that, particularly in the description of syntactically and semantically complex sentences, will entail such complex derivational structures that the much propagated elegance, simplicity, and transparence of generative tree structures might in many cases turn into the opposite.

Nevertheless, there have been attempts to utilize TG for ST and thus to develop TT-operational strategies. This was, however, only possible at the cost of a good deal of its conceptual stringency and the coherence of its descriptive procedures. This becomes apparent if one examines critically the rather vague use of the two terms basic sentence and transformational component[6] by Walmsley, or Nida's and Taber's concept of the near-kernel[7] which has so far defied a precise definition, presumably because it is a heuristic device requiring redefinition for each individual textual segment (unless a text is largely composed of standardized or phraseologically petrified linguistic units).

Such conceptual adaptations and extensions may be pedagogically permissible or even necessary; however, their descriptive and explanatory power for TT is somewhat doubtful, because they concern translation process questions that AST should be able to solve adequately without explicit reference to TG.

As a result, AST would be well advised to make use of linguistic models that are aimed at the rule-oriented description and explanation of the communicative competence of the language user and at the same time guarantee or facilitate an optimal degree of explication of psycholinguistic TT problems. Hence what AST requires in the way of a basic frame of reference will probably have to be adapted from functionally and socially oriented language description models that, according to Ferdinand de Saussure, belong to the realm of "external linguistics." This term was critically examined by Jutta Quasthoff, who has suggested a distinction between linguistic usage theory and performance theory on the pattern of the differentiation between universal pragmatics and empirical pragmatics.[8]

As a complement to its linguistic frame of reference, AST, and for that matter TT, need a pedagogical working hypothesis tailored to the specific teaching and learning features of TT, of which the following three seem to be of topmost importance:

1. TT, as a rule, is practiced collectively rather than individually; the learner group consists of students who are instrumentally motivated. All members of a group possess a relatively homogeneous SL and TL command which they have acquired in an early phase of controlled secondary-language acquisition and of native-language training. Thus they fulfill the linguistic and pedagogical preconditions for active participation in an hierarchical, problem-oriented TT system.

2. TT is both prospective (SL/TL directed) and retrospective (TL/SL directed). On the one side, it is designed to preclude translation errors by developing and internalizing adequate transfer strategies; on the other side, it has a remedial function, that is, it has to take care of translational errors which have actually occurred in going from SL to TL.

3. Each text contains a specific range of linguistic and extralinguistic translation difficulties. In addition, the difficulties may either be on the receptive side (i.e., they have their root in the phase of SL text understanding) or in the reproductive side (i.e., they occur in the phase of the TL reproduction of the SL text). Difficulties are possible in all cases in which a one-to-one correspondence between SL and TL textual segment cannot be effected without a deviation from the TL system or usage norms, thus forcing the translator to work out compensatory transfer strategies on the syntactical or lexical level.

Translation difficulties can, at least to a large degree, be isolated in their respective context; if one wants to eliminate them it is necessary to build up a teaching and learning situation that must take account of all the contextual factors relevant for TL text reproduction. The pedagogically easiest-to-handle translation unit is the sentence, because it reveals a self-contained network of the often complicated interplay of lexis and syntax. The sentence, as it is understood here, is a syntactically structured, communicatively controlled, context-sensitive combination of linguistic signs that are formally marked off from other sentences of the same text by means of punctuation marks. Within the framework of a sentence-based TT, all teaching methods are permissible that take into account the three factors which constitute the translation result, namely, the communicative intention of the text to be translated, the stylistic competence of the SL text author, and the translational competence of the translator. According to my own experience, the following five-step TT operation is particularly useful, because it drives home the interplay between SL analyzing techniques, prospective (SL/TL) transfer strategies, and retrospective (TL/SL) testing procedures:[9]

1. Syntactic, semantic, and stylistic analysis of the SL sentence against the background of its textual concatenation with preceding and subsequent sentences of the same text.

2. Description, classification, evaluation, and weighing of the lexical, syntagmatic, syntactic, and stylistic translation difficulties.

3. Optimal elimination of ascertained difficulties with the help of compensatory transfer procedures, if necessary, via one or several translation interim stages.

4. Critical assessment of the semantic and stylistic equiva-

lence of the translation with the help of text-immanent yard-sticks, with possibly revision of decisions and qualitative scaling of translation alternatives.

5. Back-translation of the translated sentence into the SL for operational comparison of the stylistic arsenal of the SL and the TL and the bidirectional description of interlingual equivalence relations.

The TT power of this framework will now be examined with the help of a German original sentence and its English equivalent. It figures as the introductory sentence of a functionally two-pronged text providing information on industrial and economic aspects of the Saarland and is at the same time intended to draw new industry into the Saarland: "Das Saarland Standort Ihres neuen Betriebes—Produzieren und Verkaufen inmitten der EWG."[10] It is a text that Katharina Reiss, in her text typology based on Karl Bühler's "Organonmodell", would clas-

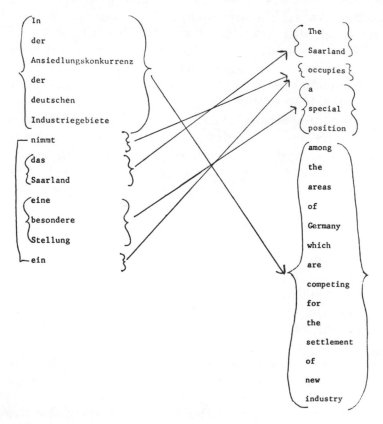

sify as a semantically marked text.[11] According to Albrecht
Neubert, who has taken the existence of different degrees of
translatability of texts as the starting-point for an attempt at
systematic text classification, the text in question is of denota-
tive nature, and as such both SL and TL-oriented. Independent of the competence of the translator, it is fully translatable,
because what the translator has to have in mind as his primary
objective is the semantic equivalence between the SL and the
TL text.[12]

1. a) *SL syntax*
The German sentence contains four constituents that function at the same time as translation units:
a complex prepositional phrase (PP) with a post-modifying
genitive attribute at the front-end of the sentence; first
element of a two-element verbal phrase (VP) with predicate function;
simple nominal phrase (NP) with subject function; simple
NP with object (complement) function; second element of
the two-element VP.
A syntactic alternative of this sentence, without modification
of the functional sentence perspective would be possible if
we were to shift the subject phrase to the front-end of the
sentence:
"Das Saarland nimmt in der Ansiedlungskonkurrenz der
deutschen Industriegebiete eine besondere Stellung ein."
The syntactic structure of this sentence can be described as
follows:
simple NP with subject function;
first element of a two-element VP with predicate function;
complex PP with post-modifying genitive attribute;
simple NP with object function;
second element of a two-element VP with predicate function.[13]

1. b) *SL semantic analysis*
Semantically, the sentence is clearly marked. It contains
two semantic foci, one at the front end of the sentence (Ansiedlungskonkurrenz) and another at the rear end of the
sentence (besondere Stellung). The compound "Ansiedlungskonkurrenz" is nonlexicalized (and, being an ad-hoc coinage, nonlexicalizable) and only contextually fully under-

standable. As far as the syntactico-semantic transparency is concerned, the order of syntactic units as chosen by the SL author—with the front-end position of the complex PP—is a better solution than my own alternative, because the two elements of the VP stand nearer to each other and therefore make it easier for the receptor to arrive at the sentence meaning. In organizing his sentence syntactically, the SL author has obviously obeyed the principle Otto Behaghel in 1932 formulated as follows: "Das oberste Gesetz ist dieses, dass das geistig eng Zusammengehörige auch eng zusammengestellt wird."[14]

1. c) SL stylistic analysis

Stylistically, the sentence is characterized by the usage of an extremely complex semantic unit (PP). It leads to a surface structure that deliberately suppresses the explicit formulation of the semantic dependency relations between the two constituents of the compound so important for grasping the sentence meaning. Thus it fully exploits the means of expression offered by the German language for cutting down explicitness to a bare minimum and for the economic organization of sentence structure.

2. Translation difficulties and

3. their elimination.

Translation difficulties occur in connection with the German PP whose nucleus is formed by the compound Ansiedlungskonkurrenz. According to information obtained from native English speakers, a rank-bound translation on the basis of a one-to-one correspondence (*settlement competition) would not be in harmony with English usage norms and must therefore be discarded (it is only feasible as the first stage of a pedagogically conceived "multiple-stage translation").[15] In order to arrive at an adequate translation result, it is necessary to embark on a complex syntactic paraphrasing operation which results, as the illustration shows, in a rank-free translation and ends up in a complete rearrangement of the original sentence. The right-left organization of the German sentence gives way to a left-right organization in English. In addition, the German clause is inflated in English to a sentence (clause and sentence here used here as technical terms). Doubtless the English sentence, with its formally and functionally coextensive structure, is more easily comprehensible than the German clause, with its high degree of syntactic compactness and syntactico-semantic context-sensitivity. Instead of a heavily condensed PP which is a typically nominal-style means of expression, the English translator has preferred a more voluminous verb-centered way of expression entailing a syntatic upshift from word-group rank to clause rank which is, psychologically speaking, much less demanding than the structurally more involved German clause.

4. Translation equivalence

Translation equivalence has, as Wolfgang Dressler was able to show,[16] a syntactic, a semantic and a stylistic dimension, in ascending order. The English relative clause is in nonisomorphic syntactic correspondence to the German PP; it explicatoo, as said before, the implicitly expressed semantic dependency relations of the German compound. Nevertheless, one cannot really say that the English sentence is more informative than its German counterpart, because it does not contain any noticeable additional information that could be isolated contextually.

Stylistically, SL and TL sentence are incompatible as a result of the rank-free translation of the German PP. The degree of stylistic equivalence between the SL and TL sentence can therefore be determined only indirectly. If it is true that in a denotationally marked text, nominal style and verbal style can coexist side by side, because, as Roman Jakobson has stated, "in its cognitive function, language is minimally dependent on the grammatical pattern,"[17] then the two sentences can be regarded as equivalent also in respect to style.

5. Back-translation

If one tries to retranslate the English sentence into German, it becomes obvious that the relative clause can be taken over into German on the basis of a one to one correspondence.

This permits the following four conclusions:

1. Within the realm of straightforward syntactic structures, German and English are much more similar than in the field of transformationally derived surface structures.

2. Within straightforward syntactic structures, literal translation[18] is a legitimate procedure, because here explicit syntactic relations are also explicit semantic relations. This is, by the way, a transfer factor that has hitherto not received systematic treatment in TT.

3. In the case of literal translation, the often-proclaimed principle of irreversibility[19] or unidirectiionality[20] of the translation process must be relativized.

4. In the surface realizations of textual segments, such as the one discussed here, German seems to be more flexible and more capable of stylistic modulations than English. In German it would be just as well to say: "Unter den Gebieten, die im Wettbewerb um die Ansiedlung neuer Industrien stehen (liegen), nimmt das Saarland eine besondere Stellung ein" (probably not yet possible, at least not in written German, would be: "Das Saarland nimmt eine besondere Stellung ein unter den Gebieten, die im Wettbewerb um die Ansiedlung neuer Industrien stehen").

The example presented here offers sufficient evidence of what a TT approach combining descriptive, explanatory, and evaluative components is able to perform for the cognitive analysis of the TP and the underlying contextual factors:

1. It shows how syntactic, lexical, and psychological features mutually influence each other and how the translator must study the text to achieve a translation product which is in line with TL usage norms.

2. It supplies important cues as to which interlingual structural divergencies need intensive TT treatment (in their respective contextual embedding).

3. It facilitates a distinction between language-specific and universal properties of a textual segment and is therefore, in connection with other TT methods,[21] able to make a valuable contribution to the envisaged expansion of translational intuition into a cognitively based translational competence. Such a competence is necessary for mastering complex translation problems as the ones posed by the German PP, which is a good example of "die gegenläufige Tendenz von ökonomischer, d.h. kurzer und in diesem Sinne einfacher Oberflächenform und perzeptueller Komplexität andererseits."[22] PPs of this type are particularly interesting, because

the underlying nominalizing transformation cannot be imitated in English. In going from SL to TL, it must, therefore, be back-transformed into a verbal-style way of expression, with all SL logical-semantic dependency relations being held constant in the TL:

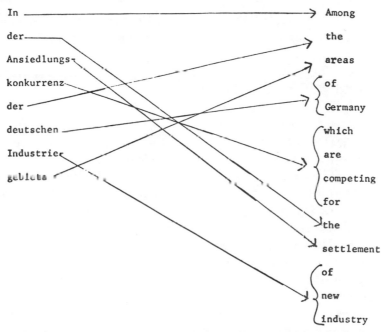

Such back-transformations which affect cognitive disambiguation are a frequent phenomenon in German-English translation because of the uneven arsenal of nominal-style means of expression in these two languages.

AST can neutralize resulting translation difficulties by building up TT procedures that do not emphasize the uniqueness of the individual problem but which are focused on recurrent features of interlingual transfer. The answer to the question of the extent to which transfer procedures are generalizable is important, because it might help the translator to develop an empirically testable translational "minimax-strategy"[23] which guarantees both a reasonable input-/output relation in professional translation work and a fairly high degree of textual equivalence of SL/TL means of expression. In adopting this line of approach, AST would probably be able to bring scientific exactness and creative thinking in TT together—of course, within the limitations determined by the complexity of the subject matter to be investigated.

The development of multistage TT operations seems advisable for several reasons:

1. They enable the translator to give a critical account of the transfer procedures leading from the SL text to the TL text.

2. They are apt to demonstrate undogmatically the complexity of the translation-learning process.

3. They can help minimizing inadequate assessment of translation performance.

4. They can be practiced by the student without the translation teacher being present all the time.

5. They can make a substantial contribution to the development of a TT meta-language which facilitates the verification (or falsification, for that matter) of translation decisions and translation evaluation statements.

6. They can promote the urgently needed consolidation and unification of ST terminology.

It should be added, however, that the applicability of TT operations checklists is limited. Anyone who is experienced in the concrete problems of translation work is aware of the fact that the translator may at any moment be confronted with textual segments in which the overcoming of syntactic, semantic, and text-pragmatic problems is so complex and multifaceted that even the most sophisticated TT operation is only of partial help. This would compel the translator to take refuge in nongeneralizable creative thinking and rather unique transfer procedures. AST, therefore, is in the same boat as the translation theory which Flora Amos (as early as 1920 and until today unrefuted) has characterized as follows: "The theory of translation cannot be reduced to a rule of thumb. It must again and again be modified to include new facts . . . In translation there is involved enough of creation to supply the incalculable element which cheats the theorist . . . it is this incalculable quality in creative work that has made theorizing on the methods of translation more than a mere academic exercise."[24]

AST must, as a result, put up with the undoubtedly discomforting fact that it has to investigate a subject matter that permits only limited theoretical insights, and can therefore only partially—certainly less than the theory of translation—be systematized and formalized.[25] This is because a pedagogical approach is always less systematic than a theoretical approach and, by definition, cannot possibly reach the same level of abstractness as the general, universally applicable theory of translation, with its primarily deductive-axiomatic frame of reference. Hence AST-obtained results can only be of a statistical nature. However, this is an advantage rather than a disadvantage, because exhaustive regularization of translation problems would require an a-priori exhaustive regularization of all human communication (linguistic performance). This is something nobody can seriously hope or wish for, because it would mean the end of all creative linguistic performance. If one accepts the inherent limitations of the standardization of linguistic behavior, there is no reason for 1 1 resignation or defeatism. One can venture the hypothesis that TT can be planned and organized, at least in some parts, to a considerable extent in such a way as to allow factorization of problems into their linguistic, cognitive, and pedagogical components, and the condensation of empirical translational insights into translational statistical rules. Such a TT concept would definitely be preferable to TT methods that are limited to the intuitive ad hoc solution of isolated translation difficulties, thereby sweeping basic TT problems—intentionally or unintentionally—under the carpet.

To start the working out of linguistically and pedagogically systematic TT operations, AST should in the initial stage limit itself to the investigation of relatively standardized linguistic utterances, with relatively rigid syntactic, contextually comparable configurations occurring rather frequently in human communication. This would probably permit the derivation and collection of translation data that could facilitate a translational transfer of training. Data of this nature could then be tested for their TT multiplication (snowball) effect,[26] allowing conditioned predictions on translational behavior in going from SL to TL.[27] This does, however, not mean that such transfer regularities would ever obtain the status of transfer algorithms, that is, unexceptionally applicable and exhaustively determined translational rules. This is impossible because the relation between form and function in linguistic communication is heteromorphous,[28] which means that syntactic, semantic, and stylistic features can interlingually be expressed in different ways. It is, therefore, my opinion that the term "teaching algorithm",[29] which is fairly frequent in the discussion of pedagogical issues, is inappropriate for TT. The algorithmic streamlining of transfer regularities is irrelevant, too, because, as Hans Lenk has convincingly shown[30] (and has become apparent from the stagnation of machine translation), the realization of a cybernetic theory of cognition is rather utopian.

On the other hand, the discovery of recurrent TT types is a necessity, because such translational "standard events" can take over an important relief function in the calculus of translational activity and increase the volume of positive transfer results per text. Any translator is aware of the fact that a translation is always a mixture of creative transfer operations and predetermined transfer automatisms—often with uneven proportions of cognitive and routine performance relative to the degree of difficulty of the SL text and the interlingual synchronizing competence of the translator.

Thus if AST wants to present concrete results that can be applied in practical translation work, it must try to define significant TT teaching and learning fields and to initiate translational learning processes that permit, according to the principle of contextual generalization,[31] the progressive transition from cognitively controlled translation processes to associatively controlled transfer mechanisms. It goes without saying that the operational conditioning of the future translator does not amount to a behavioristic or unitary TT model. Such a model is out of the question for three reasons:

1. Interlingual transfer automatisms exist only in certain discourse areas with relatively standardized meanings (contents) and with an appreciable proportion of phraseologically solidified, semisolidified, or communicatively prepatterned utterances with relatively rigid interlingual equivalence relations.

2. A unified TT methodology would not be recommendable at a time when pedagogically and linguistically sound TT operations are just reaching the point of asserting themselves

within AST; as long as AST is in an experimental stage, it would be ill-advised to throw the principle of plurality of TT methods overboard.

3. Systematic TT operations as suggested in this chapter are not merely meant to equip the future translator with translational skills in an accumulative, theory-precluding sense of the word; they are also conceived as a means to help him develop rational problem-solving strategies with testable optimality criteria, and to make him conscious of the fact that translational behavior always rests on cognitively analyzed translation procedures and the ability for contextual discrimination.

This, incidentally, is a fact that provokes the question whether the distinction between rule-governed and habit-oriented learning theories is really as important as it is maintained in some circles,[32] or whether it would not be more possible in the interest of the many still-to-be-clarified pedagogical issues to adopt a critical approach and to combine behavioristic and cognitive aspects of teaching and learning into a comprehensive down-to-earth learning theory.

It is obvious that the recognition, internalization, and application of transfer regularities represents a program that requires long-term planning. But the investment, although of considerable size, may well be worthwhile. If translation is to be regarded as a process of the communicatively controlled substitution, combination, and compensation of interlingually identical, partly identical, and nonidentical textual elements that are definable and isolatable to some extent, two conclusions can be drawn:

1. It should be possible to develop learner-group-specific and discourse-type-specific translational factor-analysis procedures and thus to explain many syntactic, lexical, and text-pragmatic translation difficulties.

2. It should also be possible to develop transfer strategies and transfer techniques with a noticeable transfer-of-training effect.

If AST sees its main task in the amalgamation of theoretical, descriptive and applied aspects of interlingual transfer, it should be fairly immune to the notorious charges of being insufficiently geared to practical needs or of being a cause of widening the gulf between theory and practical translational work. Moreover, if AST conceives its target as a dynamic process of continued synchronization of the theoretical and methodological issues on the one side and concrete linguistic utterances on the other, it would reach the dimension of a branch of comparative-descriptive linguistics, which might legitimately be called Übersetzuungslinguistik (translation linguistics). It would have to cope with a subject-matter in which four interdependent factors, description, explanation, evaluation, and extrapolation of translation difficulties and their elimination by pertinent transfer strategies, constitute the complex area of TT research.

FOOTNOTES

1. Jäger, Übersetzen und Übersetzung im Fremdsprachenunterricht, *Deutsch als Fremdsprache,* 1972, 9(5), 257–264; E. Muskat-Tabakowska, The function of translation in foreign language teaching. in J. Fisiak (Ed.), *Papers and studies in contrastive linguistics,* vol. 1. Poznan, 1973, pp. 131–139; B. Sepp, Überlegungen zur Funktionsbestimmung der Übersetzung im Fremdsprachenunterricht, in G. Nickel (Ed.), *PAKS-Arbeitsbericht No. 7.* Stuttgart, 1973; W. Wilss, Die Funktion der Übersetzung im Fremdsprachenunterricht, *Neusprachliche Mitteilungen,* 1973, 26(1), 16–24.

2. W. Wilss, Das Studium des Übersetzens und Dolmetschens. *Deutsche Universitätszeitung,* 1973, 18, 162–165.

3. V. Kapp (Ed.), *Übersetzer und Dolmetscher.* Heidelberg, 1974.

4. E. Oksaar, Sprache und Denken. *Zeitschrift für Germanistische Linguistik,* 1973, 1(3), p. 328.

5. E. Oksaar, Sprachliche Interferenzen und die kommunikative Kompetenz. in H. Pilch and J. Thurow (Eds.), *Indo-Celtica, Gedächtnisschrift für Alf Sommerfelt.* München, 1972, p. 133.

6. J. Walmsley, Transformation theory and translation. *International Review of Applied Linguistics in Language Teaching,* 1970, 8(3), 185–189.

7. E. Nida and C. Taber, *The theory and practice of translation.* Leiden, 1969; M. Masterman, Bible translation by "kernel." *The Times Literary Supplement,* March, 1970, pp. 299–301.

8. J. Quasthoff, *Soziales Vorurteil und Kommunikation—Eine sprachwissenschaftliche Analyse der Stereotyps.* Frankfurt, 1973.

9. H. Blankertz, *Theorien und Modelle der Didaktik.* München, 1970.

10. I am grateful to Gisela Thiel, one of my colleagues in Saarbrücken, for drawing my attention to this text.

11. K. Reiss, *Möglichkeiten und Grenzen der Übersetzungskritik Kategorien und Kriterien für eine sachgerechte Beurteilung von Übersetzungen.* München, 1971.

12. A. Neubert, Pragmatische Aspekte der Übersetzung. *Grundfragen der Übersetzungswissenschaft, Beihefte zur Zeitschrift Fremdsprachen II,* Leipzig, 1968, pp. 21–33.

13. Another syntactical alternative—with modification for the functional sentence perspective—would be: "Eine besondere Stellung in der Ansiedlungskonkurrenz der deutschen Industriegebiete nimmt das Saarland ain."

14. O. Behaghel, *Deutsche Syntax,* Bd. 4, Heidelberg, 1932.

15.   C. Voegelin and F. Voegelin. Anthropological linguistics and translation. *To Honor Roman Jakobson.* The Hague, 1967, pp. 2159–2190.

16.   W. Dressler, Textgrammatische Invarianz in Übersetzungen? in E. Gülich and W. Raible (Eds.), *Textsorten. Differenzierungskriterien aus linguistischer Sicht.* Frankfurt, 1972, pp. 98–106.

17.   R. Jakobson. On linguistic aspects of translation. in R. Brower (Ed.), *On Translation.* New York, 1966, p. 236.

18.   Contrary to a widespread assumption, "literal translation" and "word-for-word translation" are not synonymous. "Word-for-word translation" is oriented toward the syntactic rule systems of the source language, "literal translation" toward the syntactical rule systems of the target language.

19.   K. Bausch, Übersetzungswissenschaft und angewandte Sprächwissenschaft. Versuch einer Standortbestimmung. *Lebende Sprachen,* 1970, 25, p. 161.

20.   L. Spalatin, Contrastive methods. *Studia Romanica et Anglica Zagarabiensia.* 1967, 23, p. 29.

21.   K. Reiss. Ist Übersetzen lehrbar? in G. Nickel and A. Raasch (Eds.), *IRAL-Sonderband: Kongressbericht der 4. Jahrestagung der Gesellschaft für Angewandte Linguistik.* Heidelberg, 1972, pp. 69–82.

22.   R. Bartsch. Gibt es einen sinnvollen Begriff von linguistischer Komplexität? *Zeitschrift für Germanistische Linguistik,* 1973, 1(1), p. 17.

23.   J. Levy. Translation as a decision process. *To Honor Roman Jakobson: Essays on the Occasion of His Seventieth Birthday,* vol. 2. Den Haag, 1967, p. 1179.

24.   F. Amos. *Early theories of translation.* New York, 1920.

25.   J. Juhasz. Probleme der deskriptiven Linguistik im Universitätsunterricht. *Annales Universitatis Scientiarum Budapestinensis de Rolando Eötvös Nominatae.* Budapest, 1973; G. Wienold *Die Erlernbarkeit der Sprachen.* München, 1973.

26.   C. van Parreren. *Lernprozess und Lernerfolg.* Braunschweig, 1972.

27.   To test this hypothesis, I have started a research project in Saarbrücken on the syntactical, semantic, and TT problems of the reproduction of English participial constructions in German. The first interim results permit the assumption that in going from English into German, there are transfer trends involved which can be regarded as dynamic transfer patterns helping the translator to streamline his translation performance.

28.   E. Koschmieder. Heteromorphe Zuordnung von Zeichen und Punkten in der Sprache. *Beiträge zur allgemeinen Syntax,* Heidelberg, 1965, pp. 189–198.

29.   U. Bonnekamp, Sprachlehrforschung. in W. Koch (Ed.), *Perspektiven der Linguistik I.* Stuttgart, 1973.

30.   H. Lenk. *Philosophie im technologischen Zeitalter.* Stuttgart, 1971.

31.   G. List. *Psycholinguistik. Eine Einführung.* Stuttgart, 1972, p. 56.

32.   John B. Caroll argues similarly in his paper, "Contrastive analysis and interference theory," in J. Alatis (Ed.), *Report of the Nineteenth Annual Round Table Meeting on Linguistics and Language Studies,* Georgetown University, 1968, p. 114. "I am not convinced, that is, that there is any real difference between a "habit" and a "rule," or between a "response" and a "rule-governed performance" . . . I deny the allegiation that the use of the term *habit* necessarily implies some sort of simple-minded association theory."

CHAPTER 4

Translation and Sign Languages

RYAN D. TWENEY AND HARRY W. HOEMANN

A SIGNIFICANT FRACTION of the world's population does not possess a vocally encoded linguistic system as a first language. For most congenitally deaf individuals, and for those who become profoundly deaf prior to the acquisition of spoken language, some form of sign language will constitute the earliest linguistic system, and it will be the one most likely to be utilized in ordinary social interaction. It thus becomes of great practical interest to consider the unique problems of translation when a sign language is the source language, the target language, or both.

Furthermore, much recent attention has been directed toward sign languages because of their intrinsic interest as semiotic systems (Stokoe, 1974). As a natural extension of that interest, "intersemiotic translation" (Jakobson, 1959), involving sign language to spoken language conversion and vice versa, is deserving of study, both for its intrinsic value and for the light it can shed on intersemiotic relations in general.

The process of translation is one in which meaningful utterances in one linguistic system are converted into related meaningful utterances in another system. Most research on translation has involved conversion among spoken linguistic systems, in spite of the fact that definitions of translation generally fail to restrict the domain to that of speech. Intersemiotic translation, however, has not generally been considered by researchers in translation or in linguistics. The restriction of translation interest to spoken languages is doubly unfortunate because it has eliminated certain theoretical and empirical issues from consideration.

In the case of spoken languages, a number of empirical studies of simultaneous translation have shown that interpreters lag behind speakers, and tend to fill in pauses in the speaker's utterances with "bursts" of translated material (Oléron and Nanpon, 1965; Barik, 1973). It is not known, however, whether the phenomena observed result from the necessity of an ordered, linear sequence in the transmission of speech or whether they result from constraints on the ability of the translator to simultaneously encode utterances in one speech code while decoding utterances in another. This issue could be approached by careful consideration of the behavior of simultaneous translators encoding sign into speech, speech into sign, and sign into sign, and comparing the results with the more commonly studied speech-into-speech encoding. Further, only in sign language can true simultaneous production of two languages occur. Because sign languages are generated manually, they are unique in permitting simultaneous generation of a spoken and a signed message. A clergyman addressing a mixed group of deaf and hearing individuals might simultaneously *say* "The congregation will please rise" and *sign* "church group please stand" (where each word is a gloss for a single sign). Similar phenomena can be observed in deaf educational institutions, where lecturing activity may present a simultaneous sign translation. Study of this activity should be rewarding for the light it can shed on the cognitive processes related to encoding in language.

The neglect of consideration of sign languages by translation research can be seen as part of a much wider general neglect of sign systems by language scientists and educators. Because the approach to deaf education in the Anglo-Saxon countries has, until very recently, emphasized the acquisition of oral language skills, research on deafness has also ignored the properties of sign languages. The same orientation has assumed that prior acquisition of a sign system can interfere with the acquisition of oral skills. The first point is dealt with later. The second point has never been put to adequate empirical test. It is worth nothing, however, that Charrow and Fletcher (1974) found that deaf adolescents whose first language was sign performed better on the Test of English as a Foreign Language than comparable deaf adolescents who lacked sign as a first language. If anything, then, prior sign useage may facilitate rather than hinder acquisition of an oral code.

A number of misconceptions about the nature of sign are current. Two deserve special mention: (1) the belief that sign languages are pantomimic and therefore understandable by anyone regardless of their native tongue, and (2) the related belief that sign languages are not really languages at all but simply an extension of such nonlinguistic gesture systems as the use of finger-pointing to represent objects. Of course, the acceptance of either point of view would radically alter the conceptualization of translation issues involving manual language. The first myth, in fact, suggests that there are *no* issues for translation theory, because any human being ought to be able to "translate" a manual representation into its meaning. The second myth, that sign systems are trivially deictic, need not lead to the same radical conclusion, but it does suggest that some aspects of manually encoded communications may be difficult or impossible to translate, because they derive from nonlinguistic expressive gestures.

Recent research in the linguistic and psycholinguistic properties of sign languages makes it possible to present evidence suggesting that sign languages are functional linguistic systems. The first part of this chapter summarizes some of the relevant evidence, and serves as the basis for the second part, which examines the application of the findings to existing sign language translation issues.

The Nature of Sign Languages

A sign language is any linguistically structured communication system in which meanings are mapped primarily onto gestures made by the arms, hands, torso, and face of the communicator. Such systems need to be carefully distinguished from gestural encodings of vocal languages (Stokoe, 1974). Thus finger spelling, the representation of an alphabet by hand gestures, is not a manual language, but a manual encoding of a vocal language. For people with knowledge of English, finger spelling is exactly analogous to the transmission of English texts by writing. In both finger spelling and reading, the receiver's ability to decode the sender's message is wholly dependent on his knowledge of another language system, together with a set of arbitrary correspondence rules. True sign languages, on the other hand, can be correctly decoded only if knowledge of the internal structure of the manual language is possessed by the receiver; knowledge of English is irrelevant. Clearly, the use of finger spelling involves no important issues of translation. Manual languages are generally used, however, in conjunction with finger-spelled terms from the dominant spoken language. Such variation means that "pure" sign language is not often observed, and that the relationship between sign language and the dominant system needs to be taken into account. Sign languages must also be distinguished from pantomimic communication systems, in which a gesture is a kind of acting out of the meaning. Very few signs possess pantomimic quality to a sufficient degree to allow meaning to be apprehended directly. Rather, nearly all signs represent meanings conventionally, like spoken words (Hoemann, in press; Stokoe, 1972).

A variety of manual language systems exist and are in contemporary use. As with vocal languages, geographical differences are found, and historical change is known to occur. Thus, although French sign language and American sign language (ASL) are related historically, they differ greatly today. British sign language also differs substantially from ASL. Manual languages show considerable variation within national borders. The relative social isolation of deaf children in residential schools in the United States has lead to a proliferation of local dialects. In fact, dialect variants peculiar to a single residential school for the deaf are not unusual and may persist within the surrounding adult deaf linguistic community.

The use of manual languages is affected by constraints of social acceptability. Stokoe (1972) has applied Ferguson's (1959) notion of diglossia to the description of manual language useage. Two variants, H (high, or formal) and L (low, or conversational), are easily identified. In America, the H sign order corresponds closely to English word order, and extensive finger spelling may be utilized to encode English articles and prepositions. Such devices are not generally found in L variants, although finger spelling may be utilized for particular words without conventionalized manual equivalents. Differentiating only two categories is, in a sense, artificial, because a continuum of useage exists. Further, the use of H and L depends not only on the particular social demands of the situation, but also on the background of the signer—for example, whether he or she has attained command over English syntax. Similar differences as a function of sociolinguistic variables have been described (for spoken languages) by Labov (1972b) and Bailey (1973). The differentiation of H and L sign useage in America is similar to the differentiation of vernacular Black English from Standard English among Black Americans (see, e.g., Houston, 1969; Labov, 1972a). It is now quite clear from the evidence that variation in the useage of particular phonological rules is a characteristic feature of speech systems. Thus the use of "are-less" constructions (e.g., "They going to the store") among Black American speakers is related in a lawful fashion to situational constraints and to the perceived formality of the situation (Labov, 1972a). That a similar situation exists within ASL has been argued by Woodward (1973, 1974) who has shown that systematic variation exists among deaf adult signers in Washington, D. C., and Montana.

Manual languages have been subjected to repeated attempts to modify, or to create anew, lexicons and syntactic mechanisms. Deaf educators have generally made such attempts with an educational purpose in mind. Because the social communities of deaf individuals are relatively isolated and more-or-less segregated from speaking communities and because of the prevalence of residential schools for the deaf, these attempts have been surprisingly successful. The earliest (and the most successful) was that of the Abbe Charles Michel de l'Épée, who in 1776 published an extensively elaborated systematic sign language he had developed while working in the Institution des Sourds et Muets in Paris, France (Bender, 1970). This system was later modified by his successor, Roch Ambroise Sicard, who decided that the original system was overly methodical and overly burdened with irrelevant syntactic devices derived from French. Sicard thus eliminated certain regular structures in de l'Épée's version and incorporated many naturally occurring sign structures found among deaf individuals. The result was an easily learned and transmitted language that eventually evolved into the contemporary

American and French sign languages. Sicard's system was brought to the United States by Thomas Hoplins Gallaudet in 1816.

In recent years several attempts have been made to modify ASL for educational purposes (Bornstein, 1973). All share a common goal, that of making the learning of English easier. As just one example, Anthony's "Seeing Essential English" (SEE) provides a system that closely parallels English structure. Analogs of English articles, function words, prepositions, and conjunctions are included. The utility of such systems is still an open question. To the extent they become utilized in future educational settings, however, it is probably safe to predict that they will influence the structure of vernacular ASL in the direction of greater similarity to English. This, in turn, would have clear implications for the translatability of signed utterances and for the assumptions that a translator can safely bring to the translation process.

Brief mention is necessary for certain special-purpose manual languages. The best known, American Indian sign language, is now extinct but once served widely as a form of intertribal communication. Extensive descriptions of its lexicon were made by Mallery (1881) and Clark (1885). The origin of the system is unknown. Kluge (1885) described a monasterial sign language used by monks who observe silence for religious reasons. Cistercian sign language is now undergoing rapid change and may soon become extinct (Barakat, 1969). Formal descriptions do not yet exist for any of these systems. Although translation involving such languages was at one time of great practical importance, the need for translation has disappeared almost completely.

The Linguistic Structure of Sign

Surprisingly little attention has been paid by linguists to the formal description of the linguistic properties of sign. Until Stokoe's work appeared in the early 1960s, the Indian sign language descriptions of Mallery and Clark provided the only discussion of sign linguistic structure (their work was at the level of an informal "school grammar," rather than in terms of a formalized descriptive approach).

The seminal application of modern linguistic analysis was due to Stokoe (1960), who first described ASL in terms of the contrastive categories of structural linguistics. In looking for minimally contrastive formatives in sign, Stokoe isolated combinatorial units, called *cheremes* (after the Greek *chéir, cheirós* —hand), which are analogous to phonemes in vocalic languages. Three types of cheremes can be described, a place marker, or *tab*, a hand configuration marker, or *dez,* and a movement marker, or *sig.* The sign for girl, for example, consists of moving (sig) the ball of the thumb (dez) along the signer's cheek (tab). If a different dez were used, say, the outstretched palm instead of the ball of the thumb, then the meaning of the sign would differ (in this case, the result would be the sign for brown).

Complete description of the cheremics of ASL would consist of a list of all cheremes, together with an indication of the range of allocheric variation and the distributional constraints imposed on cheremes. Sign cheremes represent conventionalized structural patternings of the total set of produceable gestures (Stokoe, 1974). Although no complete description has been attempted for any sign language, Stokoe has supplied a fairly complete list of cheremes for ASL, together with at least some information on allocheric variation and on distributional constraints. Morphocheremic description, that is, description of the interaction of cheremic units within signs, has, however, barely been started.

Stokoe's classification does present certain problems. In the first place, the elaboration of three types of cheremes appears a priori, and has less linguistic motivation than one would like. To be sure, phonemes can be divided into two classes, vowels and consonants, in much the way cheremes have been divided into three (cheremes, however, represent simultaneously cooccurring features). The analysis of a particular phoneme as a vowel can be done on the basis of several criteria, all of which are known to be relevant to the production of speech (e.g., presence of vocal tract resonance). For cheremes, however, no such rationale can yet be provided. One can imagine a classification of speech sounds based on tab, dez, and sig components involving the tongue, lips, and vocal cords. All speech could be described in this fashion, but the description would not be directly related to the linguistically relevant parameters. The necessity of relating *acoustic* distinctive features to *articulatory* distinctive features has been much discussed in the speech perception literature (e.g., Stevens, 1971). Some support for the adequacy of Stokoe's system can be derived from the results of short-term memory studies. Bellugi, Klima, and Siple (1975) found that errors in memory for signs occurred along dimensions predicted by a cheremic analysis. Thus the sign for noon was mistakenly recalled as tree, a sign that differs only in the type of movement (i.e., along the sig dimension). Other errors occurred along dez or tab dimensions, or along some combination of more than one dimension.

The lack of linguistic motivation is especially evident for the distinction between dez and tab. Whereas some tabs (the forehand, say) are never used as dez, others (the hand turned palm up, with the fingers held together) can be used as tab or as dez. Stokoe has attributed this problem to the inadequacy of morphocheremic description, a full account of which would, presumably, deal with such difficulties. The problem may, however, be more basic. If the analysis of signs into three dimensions is insufficient (i.e., if a different categorization is required), then no amount of morphocheremic description is likely to clarify the difficulty. It is apparent, for example, that a fourth dimension will be needed to represent the relative orientation of the dez hand in a given sign. The possible inadequacy of the cheremic description system goes beyond the need for such straightforward supplementation, however. Clearly, future research needs to be directed to this issue.

ASL syntax still awaits its Stokoe. Few serious attempts using the techniques of modern linguistic analysis have been made to describe fully the syntactic mechanisms found in ASL. McCall (1965) provided a "grammar" of ASL based on the generative-transformational principles of Chomsky's (1957) model. McCall's corpus consisted, however, of English glosses of all of the filmed utterances of a number of signers at a social gathering. No use was made of signer's intuitions about grammaticality, nor, in fact, was any attempt made to separate well-formed from ill-formed utterances. Further, McCall's grammatical rules derived sentences from other, kernel sentences, rather than from deep structures. As a result, McCall's grammar provided only the most superficial description of ASL syntax. Woodward (1972) has provided a very small fragment of a transformational grammar of ASL which avoided the difficulties associated with McCall's work. Only 11 rules were formally described, however, making Woodward's grammar little more than a demonstration of what might be possible.

Stokoe (1972) has described a number of possible approaches to the linguistic description of sign syntax, of which two deserve comment here. He is, first of all, very negative about the possibility of applying generative transformational principles to the description of manual systems. According to Stokoe, the fundamental assumption that a grammar relates *sounds* and meaning makes generative theory useless, unless one is willing to say that sign languages are derivative from spoken languages. It does not seem to us, however, that this is a necessary assumption within generative theory. Were a generativist interested in describing sign using transformational principles, there is no reason why the fundamental principle could not be modified to involve relations between *gestures* and meaning. The point seems to have little force. Stokoe is also critical of the need for sequential ordering of phonological elements which he claims are necessary for the operation of transformational rules on the phonological level. The simultaneous production of sign elements, however, renders such a scheme unworkable, according to Stokoe. Again, however, we do not feel that this is a necessary characteristic of a generative account, since only terminal-level rules need be involved in the ordering of elements in an utterance. Of course, Stokoe is correct in asserting that generative accounts have not been developed. We can look forward to the day when they do become available.

Stokoe is more favorable about the possibilities of applying Ceccato's (1961) operational model of syntax to the analysis of sign. This approach, developed for use in computer applications, utilizes a lattice or network of relationships between the fundamental content-elements of a sentence. The model operates by elaborating links between elements, links between sets of linked elements, and so on. Unlike generative systems, there is no need for the principal relationships to be hierarchically related. Generative grammars handle sentence embedding processes by first deriving hierarchial trees with incorporated

S nodes, followed by the application of transformational processes to provide ordering, inflections, and specific lexical interpretations. Operational grammars, however, provide for ordering of only major segments, whereas elements within segments can remain unordered. This feature, according to Stokoe, permits the lack of syntactic ordering constraints in sign language to be easily represented. Of particular interest in Stokoe's discussion is his claim that operational analysis of sentences in both ASL and English reveals, greater intertranslatability than would be expected from a generative analysis. The underlying lattice for an utterance may be the same in both languages, even though the realization of each lattice element in the ASL utterance may be very different from its realization in English. As interesting as the suggestion appears, however, it is speculative until such time as formalized operational grammars of a sign language become available.[1]

Can anything definite be said about the nature of syntax in sign languages? In fact, the emergence of sign language research is so recent that very little has been done. The relative lack of order constraints has been referred to. Although this characteristic is shared by some spoken languages, ASL lacks, to a very great degree, not only order constraints but sign-level inflection markers to indicate grammatical role. The absence of both ordering and morpological inflection has been used to argue that sign languages lack linguistic structure (Tervoort, 1968). Yet, in ASL, grammatical role is indicated using a number of inflectionlike devices. Thus deictic reference to agents and patients in ongoing discourse is provided by the manual indication of a kind of stage in front of the signer. Particular individuals are located on the "stage" initially by pointing, and can later be referred to by reference to the particular location. This device reduces need for personal pronouns in ASL (though finger-spelled pronouns sometimes occur in ASL as importations from English).

Psycholinguistic Properties of Sign Languages Several lines of research have been initiated by psycholinguists interested in the functional properties of sign language. The work is indirectly relevant to issues of translation insofar as any finding which indicated a functional deficiency relative to spoken languages would need to be considered in translation programs.

To date, however, evidence for deficiencies, except in very specific circumstances, has not been found. The account given here must be brief—a fuller review is given by Bonvillian, Charrow, and Nelson (1973).

The most basic psycholinguistic question involves communicability. Can sign languages serve as an effective channel for the transmission of messages from a sender to a receiver? Hoemann (1972) taught young deaf children a simple competitive game, and then required that the children in turn teach the game to another child. Deaf children communicating in ASL and finger-spelled English were not as effective as comparable hearing children using English. Specific problems included a tendency of deaf children to explain in detail some single feature of the game, such as rolling the die or moving a counter, without indicating the way in which the game was to be won. The finding thus may be due to deficiencies in social or in cognitive development rather than to a characteristic of the language medium. Using deaf adolescents, Jordan (1974) found that ASL was *more* effective than English used by hearing adolescents. Jordan used a picture-description task in which the sender was required to describe one picture out of a multiple array and the receiver was required to choose the correct target picture from an identical array. Together with the Hoemann study, the results suggest that relative communicative effectiveness may be content-specific. It is possible that highly visualizable arrays are more readily encoded in a sign language than in a spoken language, whereas abstract material (like game rules) are more readily encoded by a spoken language. The hypothesis has never been directly tested.

Schlesinger (1971) required deaf adult users of Israeli Sign Language (ISL) to describe simple actor–action–object–indirect-object pictures to another deaf adult. Performance was surprisingly poor, even when multiple sentences in ISL were used to describe each picture. Schlesinger suggested that the grammatical encoding of object–indirect-object relationships may not be a linguistic universal, since it appears not to be found in ISL. The conclusion is, however, premature since ISL may rely heavily upon deictic mechanisms which were not available in the experimental situation used. Thus, if ISL distinguishes object from indirect object by relative location on an

imaginery stage, rather than by order relationships or inflections, then Schlesinger's task may have worked against his
subjects. This conjecture is supported by the results of a study
by Bode (1974) in which deaf ASL users performed at a very
high level on a task similar to Schlesinger's. Bode's subjects
were matched for their knowledge of ASL, thus ensuring use
of a mutually understood code by her subjects—a precaution
not utilized by Schlesinger.

Few studies have been conducted of the perception of sign
languages. Tweney, Heiman, and Hoemann (in preparation)
studied the effect of temporal interruption of a signed message
on intelligibility of the message. The rate of interruption and
the degree of linguistic structure in the message were varied.
A high degree of resistance to such disruption was found. Further, well-formed strings of signs were more resistant than
syntactically well-formed but meaningless strings or random
strings, suggesting that syntactic and semantic structure play
a functional fole in sign as in speech (Heiman and Tweney,
1975). Sign language, like spoken language (Miller, 1951), appears to utilize linguistic structure to add redundancy, thereby
increasing the ease of transmission of messages (Fodor, Bever,
and Garrett, 1974). Future research is needed to determine
the exact mechanisms used by sign language to achieve this
result.

Translation of Sign Languages

From what has been said about the nature of sign languages,
there is no reason to expect translation involving sign languages to be radically different from translation involving
spoken languages. This conclusion follows because there is no
linguistic or psychological evidence that sign languages are
functionally inferior to spoken languages or that they rely on
different principles of linguistic organization. Research on this
issue is still very limited, to be sure, but it seems unlikely to us
that major surprises are to be expected. The specific linguistic
characteristics of sign language still need to be detailed, along
with specific psycholinguistic properties. But the evidence to
date suggests that all language rests on the same set of universal cognitive capabilities whether it is based on manual encod-

ings or on acoustic encodings.[2] Research on translation of sign languages should, therefore, be able to build on prior findings in translation theory and research.

The general conclusion receives pragmatic support from the fact that sign language interpreting is widespread. Large numbers of adult deaf persons rely on manual systems of communication and need interpreters to render the spoken language into signs and vice versa. Such services have traditionally been rendered on a volunteer basis by persons whose parents were deaf or who learned sign language from professional contact with deaf persons. In the past decade there has been a concerted effort to professionalize interpreter services for the deaf. In 1964 a registry of interpreters for the deaf was organized (Quigley, 1965). Its constitution calls for publication of a registry of persons qualified to serve as interpreters and the development of standards of certification. Examination and certification procedures were implemented at a national evaluation workshop held in Memphis, Tennessee in 1972. Persons seeking certification are now required to take an examination in expressive translating (verbatim signing of an English presentation), or in expressive interpreting (freely rendering an English presentation in colloquial sign language with freedom to paraphrase), or in reverse interpreting (rendering a colloquial sign language presentation into spoken English). An examination in comprehensive interpreting skills (translating, interpreting, and reverse interpreting) is also available. Professional training for interpreters is available at several educational institutions in the United States. It is interesting to note that professional training for interpreters has been available in the USSR for many years (Godin, 1967).

Interpreting from one sign language to another is infrequent but is manifested at international conferences, such as the annual meetings of the World Federation of the Deaf. In international dealings some unusual circumstances can occur. A perhaps apocryphal story concerns a noted American educator of the deaf who wished to converse with a French colleague. A deaf person served as the educator's interpreter by speech-reading French and translating into sign, and by translating the educator's signs into spoken French!

Translations intended to be relatively permanent (as distinguished from the immediate and ephemeral interpretation of conversation) are beginning to emerge for sign languages. Literary works, particularly drama and poetry, are being translated into sign language in several centers. Particularly notable are the efforts of the National Theater of the Deaf in New York City and the efforts of the Drama Department of Gallaudet College, which has been in existence since 1892 (Newman, 1971). Although most of the translation has been from spoken language to sign, original dramatic works scripted in sign language have appeared. Most notable is Gilbert Eastman's *Sign me Alice* (1974), which has been translated into an annotated, glossed version of written English.

Translation of dramatic works has revealed the same difficulties that are well known in spoken translation. As Jakobson (1959) has indicated, the lack of grammatical correspondence between one language and another does not prevent translation (although unit-by-unit equivalence may not be possible). But if particular grammatical categories (genders, say) carry semantic impact in one language, then translation may not be possible: "Only creative transposition is possible" (Jakobson, 1959, p. 238). This difficulty may be especially characteristic of sign-to-spoken translation. George Detmold, in the introduction to the English translation of Eastman's play, indicated that "the play makes clear sense as an English script; but the thousand little jokes, puns, and word-plays are missing, as well as the lyric beauty of some passages, if the play is read simply as English" (Eastman, 1974, p. vii).

Sign languages possess limitless possibilities for the expression of emphasis and emotion, perhaps to a greater degree than for spoken languages. Thus body movements, elements of dance, and facial expressions can be combined with a signed message in a way not possible in most spoken languages. Further, the articulation of particular signs can be extended over longer or shorter distances, stretched out or shortened temporally, or delivered simultaneously with other messages. The use of such mechanisms in sign can be seen not only in drama but in the modern dance performances of Gallaudet College students and in signed hymns in religious services for the deaf. Formal, group signing of a hymn lacks acoustic melody, but substitutes expressiveness and beauty of an entirely different sort.

All interpretation and translation activity involving sign language suffers from a fundamental practical problem: no true dictionaries or grammars exist for any sign language. The importance of this factor is suggested in the following comment by Bates:

Translators may be divided into four kinds: those who neither use nor need dictionaries; those who need them and use them; those who need them but don't use them; those who would like them but have to do the best they can without. (1936, p. 99).

All sign language translators are, of necessity, in the fourth category. The importance of the problem is suggested by the late historical appearance of adequate translations of Greek and Latin works into English (Amos, 1920). Until appropriate dictionary materials were available, nearly all translations left a good deal to be desired (see Tytler, 1791, for an early consideration of some of the problems). Dictionaries do not, of course, provide more than word-level translation, and so capture only one level of meaning (Nida, 1964). Nevertheless, they can provide a translator with helpful guides to the rendering of passages at all stages of translation, and are especially helpful when the translator is himself not a native user of both of the languages. The relation of dictionaries to translation activity is reciprocal—just as dictionaries assist in translation, the knowledge gained by translators is important and useful in the preparation of dictionaries. In fact, the basis of modern dictionaries can be found in Renaissance times when interlinear glosses of classical texts were common (Amos, 1920). It was then a short step to the preparation of lists of frequently used terms from the gloss (Starnes and Noyes, 1946).

A number of bilingual sign language–English dictionaries have been produced in recent years (as well as dictionaries in other languages—see Bornstein and Hamilton, 1972), and are, of course, helpful in translating. They are not true dictionaries, because all relate a sign to its closest English equivalent. Multiplicity of meaning is rarely indicated, and the total number of signs indexed is still very small. Stokoe, Casterline, and Croneberg (1965) have provided the most extensive and the most widely used such dictionary, a work which is currently under revision. Signs are described using a cheremic notational system, supplemented with articulation notes and photographs. Some hints on usage are provided. Signs are grouped on the basis of the locus of execution. The listing within each tab group is alphabetical in the sense that entries for particular signs are arranged in an order based in part on the closest finger-spelled letter that is equivalent to some part of the sign. Thus if a sign is formed with an extended index finger, it is listed under G, because the finger-spelled letter G is similarly formed. This method of organization is external to sign language as such, although it makes the dictionary more useable for beginning signers who already know a spoken language.

Can true sign language dictionaries be created? In theory, there is nothing to prevent this, but substantial practical difficulties exist. Film or video tape is the obvious medium, but would clearly be an awkward way to record entries. Imagine the difficulty of using a tape recorded dictionary of a spoken language! What is called for, obviously, is a notational system that permits the rapid and clear recording of sign language utterances. No such conventionalized and accepted notational system is in existence, although attempts to create one have been made (with only limited success).

Bébian (1825) developed a system of conventionalized symbols to represent hand shapes, body parts, movements, and "Points physionomiques" to indicate different methods or styles of articulation. The system was able to represent most sign language gestures in written form, but it suffered from the intrinsic limitation that the dimensions chosen for written representation were not motivated by linguistic considerations. The approach of Stokoe, Casterline, and Croneberg (1965) is far superior in this regard because it used dimensions that do have linguistic importance. This does not, of course, completely describe any one sign, but it does allow all of the critical aspects to be captured—the rest is allocheric variation and need not be represented. (Of course, this assumes the descriptive adequacy of the system—a point which has been challenged earlier.)

All notational systems suffer from a lack of clear representation of the dynamic characteristics of signs. This is true even for those systems that have relied on pictorial representation of signs. Thus Fant's (1972) introductory text used photographs of signs. Hoemann and Hoemann (1973) used line drawings in a set of flash cards for student use. Klima and Bellugi (1972) attempted to capture some of the dynamic aspects of signing by using multiple-exposure photographs. None of the systems of representing signs is completely adequate, however. All require extensive verbal descriptions of each sign to supplement the visual, pictorial representations. Although one picture may be worth a thousand *words,* one *sign* may need a thousand pictures!

An interesting notational problem emerges when English glosses of signed messages are prepared. There is, of course, the expected difficulty arising from the lack of single word equivalents for particular signs—a difficulty found in preparing glosses for any language. In addition, most ASL useage in the United States involves varying amounts of interpenetration from English. Thus, as a result of classroom instruction, deaf individuals are able to rely on finger-spelled English words to supplement lexical deficiencies in ASL. This is especially necessary when technical matters are being discussed; ASL lacks technical vocabulary, and makes up for it by finger-spelling (or in some cases, by pantomime). Such variation needs to be clearly represented in the preparation of textual glosses.

A particular research tool that relies heavily on translation has been utilized to shed light on the nature of sign language. The method, known as back translation (Brislin, 1970; Werner and Campbell, 1970), uses two bilingual translators and a text in a source language (SL) which is to be translated into a target language (TL). One translator prepares an initial TL version of the SL text. The other translator then retranslates the TL version into the SL. The two SL versions can be compared, and the differences taken into account in the preparation of a new TL version. The cycle (SL to TL to SL) can be repeated until both SL versions are equivalent. The procedure provides evidence for the adequacy of translations of the TL version and an operational method for achieving an adequate translation of any text. Furthermore, inspection of the kinds of SL constructions that are difficult to translate can be used to formulate recommendations for the preparation of easily translated text (Sinaiko and Brislin, 1973).

Back-translation procedures can also be useful for investigating the properties of particular languages, because they provide a means of evaluating the extent to which meaning is preserved in translation and the strategies by which meaning is encoded. Two studies have been reported in which back translation procedures were applied to the investigation of the properties of ASL. In the first (Tweney and Hoemann, 1973), lists of complex English sentences were presented to adult deaf subjects who were required to generate an ASL version for each sentence. The videotaped ASL statements were presented to another set of subjects who were required to prepare English-language versions. The meaning of the original sentences was preserved in 63 percent of the observations. The original grammatical structure remained unchanged in only 27 percent of the back translations, however. The results tentatively suggest that ASL may serve as an adequate system for encoding the meaning of a variety of English sentence types even when complex grammatical constructions with no ASL counterparts are involved.

The second study introduced modifications in the back-translation procedure (Hoemann and Tweney, 1973). The target-language version was prepared by a hearing informant who had learned ASL as a first language from deaf parents. The informant was instructed to use colloquial ASL and to avoid literal translations of the English original. Finger spelling was prohibited. Relatively long English texts of 150 to 200 words were used to ensure presence of a meaningful context. Videotaped ASL translations were shown to adult bilingual subjects, who were instructed to write down in English the gist of the text. Because memory for details was not of primary interest, subjects were allowed to view the tape as many times as they desired and to make changes in their translations after each viewing. The results of the second study clearly showed that ASL was an adequate linguistic medium for transmitting many kinds of complex information. The meaning losses that did occur were in all cases either trivial details or obvious from the context.

Whether ASL is equally able to encode technical prose for which specialized vocabulary may be lacking remains a question for further research. A ban on finger spelling for such material may prove to be inappropriate. Thus translators in a back-translation experiment involving English and Vietnamese often left a technical English word intact or transliterated the word using Vietnamese characters (Sinaiko and Brislin, 1973). Finger spelling is the only comparable strategy available to translators working in a sign language.

At the present time the body of data from back translation of sign language is relatively small; however, additional applications of back-translation procedures to the study of sign languages offer numerous possibilities for further research. It is interesting that translation may help elucidate the nature of sign language. It is hoped that the results will, in turn, aid translation efforts.

Conclusion Sign languages have only recently become the object of scientific research. This chapter has, as a result, ranged fairly widely to represent the work that has been done. For the same reason, we have attempted to point out some areas in which more research appears to be needed. At present, very little can be said with certainty about the specific translation problems encountered in dealing with sign languages. Much of what we have presented amounts to common wisdom rather than demonstrated fact. Nevertheless, two conclusions are, we feel, particularly clear: (1) sign languages, insofar as they possess the functional properties of language in general, present no inherently unsolvable problems for translation theory, and (2) sign languages do have unique properties that must be taken into account in translation activity. Future work must delineate the phenomena that fall under each heading. Translation of sign languages, like translation in general, can be completely effective only when it is based on linguistic and psycholinguistic knowledge concerning each language involved.

FOOTNOTES

1. Advances in the computer processing of language have, however, gone in a somewhat different direction. Instead of focusing on syntactic relationships, the most successful (e.g., Winograd, 1972) rely on semantic and logical interpretation of syntactic structure.

2. This issue is treated at more length in Bellugi (1974); Tweney, Hoemann, and Andrews (1975); and Tweney, Heiman, and Hoemann (in preparation).

REFERENCES

Amos, Flora Ross. *Early theories of translation.* New York: Columbia University Press, 1920.

Bailey, Charles-James N. The patterning of language variation. In Richard W. Bailey and Jay L. Robinson, Eds. *Varieties of present-day English.* New York: Macmillan, 1973, pp. 156–186.

Barakat, Robert A. Gesture systems. *Keystone Folklore Quarterly,* 1969, *14,* 105–121.

Barik, Henri C. Simultaneous interpretation: temporal and quantitative data. *Language and Speech,* 1973, *16,* 237–270.

Bates, E. Stuart. *Modern translation.* London: Oxford University Press, 1936.

Bébian, R. A. *Mimographie, ou essai d'ecriture mimique, propre a regulariser le language des sourds-muets.* Paris: Louis Colas, 1825.

Bellugi, Ursula. Some aspects of language acquisition. In Thomas A. Sebeok, Ed. *Current trends in linguistics: Volume 12, Linguistics and adjacent arts and science.* The Hague: Mouton, 1974, pp. 1135–1158.

Bellugi, Ursula; Klima, Edward S. and Siple, Patricia. Remembering in Signs. *Cognition: International Journal of Cognitive Psychology,* 1975 (In press).

Bender, Ruth E. *The conquest of deafness: A history of the long struggle to make possible normal living to those handicapped by lack of normal hearing.* Revised Edition. Cleveland: Case Western Reserve University Press, 1970.

Bode, Loreli. Communication of agent, object, and indirect object in signed and spoken languages. *Perceptual and Motor Skills,* 1974, *39,* 1151–1158.

Bonvillian, John D., Charrow, Veda, R., and Nelson, Keith E. Psycholinguistic and educational implications of deafness. *Human Development,* 1973, *16,* 321–345.

Bornstein, Harry. A description of some current sign system designed to represent English. *American Annals of the Deaf,* 1973, *118,* 454–463.

Bornstein, Harry, and Hamilton, Lillian B. Recent national dictionaries of signs. *Sign Language Studies,* 1972, *1,* 42–63.

Brislin, Richard W. Back-translation for cross-cultural research. *Journal of Cross-Cultural Psychology,* 1970, *1,* 185–216.

Ceccato, Silvio. *Linguistic analysis and programming for mechanical translation.* Milan: Giangiacomo Feltrinelli, Editore, Undated (1961) (Technical Report No. RADC-TR-60-18, United States Air Force).

Charrow, V. R., & Fletcher, J. D. English as the second language of deaf children. *Developmental Psychology,* 1974, *10,* 463–470.

Chomsky, Noam. *Syntactic structures.* The Hague: Mouton and Co., 1957. "Janua Linguarum, Series Minor, No. 4"

Clark, W. P. *The Indian Sign Language, with brief explanatory notes of the gestures taught deaf mutes in our institutions for their instruction . . .* Philadelphia: L. R. Hamersly & Co., 1885.

Eastman, Gilbert C. *Sign me Alice: A play in sign language.* Washington, D.C.: Gallaudet College Bookstore, 1974.

Fant, Louis J. *Ameslan: An introduction to American Sign Language.* Silver Springs, Md.: National Association of the Deaf, 1972.

Ferguson, Charles A. Diglossia. *Word,* 1959, *15,* 325–340.

Fodor, J. A., Bever, T. C., and Garrett, M. F. *The psychology of language: An introduction to psycholinguistics and generative grammar.* New York: McGraw-Hill, 1974.

Godin, Lev. Interpreters for the deaf in Russia. *American Annals of the Deaf,* 1967, *112,* 595–597.

Heiman, Gary W., and Tweney, Ryan D. The intelligibility of temporally interrupted American Sign Language as a function of linguistic organization. Paper presented at the 55th Annual Meeting of the Western Psychological Association, Sacramento, California, April 26, 1975.

Hoemann, Harry W. The development of communication skills in deaf and hearing children. *Child Development,* 1972, *43,* 990–1003.

Hoemann, H. W. The transparency of meaning of sign language gestures. *Sign Language Studies,* 1975, In press.

Hoemann, Harry W., and Hoemann, Shirley A. *Sign Language Flash Cards.* Silver Spring, Md.: National Association of the Deaf, 1973.

Hoemann, Harry W., and Tweney, Ryan D. Is the Sign Language of the deaf an adequate communicative channel? *Proceedings of the American Psychological Association,* 1973, 801–802.

Houston, Susan H. A sociolinguistic consideration of the Black English of children in northern Florida. *Language,* 1969, *45,* 599–607.

Jakobson, Roman. On linguistic aspects of translation. In Reuben A. Brower, Ed. *On translation.* Cambridge: Harvard University Press, 1959. Harvard Studies in Comparative Literature, pp. 232–239.

Jordan, I. King, Jr. A referential communication study of linguistically adult, deaf signers. Paper presented at the First Annual Sign Language Conference, Gallaudet College, Washington, D.C., April 27, 1974.

Klima, E. S., and Bellugi, U. The signs of language in child and chimpanzee. In T. Alloway, L. Krames, and P. Pliner, Eds. *Communication and affect: A comparative approach.* New York: Academic Press, 1972.

Kluge, F. Zur Geschichte der Zeichensprache. Angelsächsische indicia Monasterialia. *Internationale Zeitschrift für Allgemeine Sprachwissenschaft,* 1885, *2,* 116–137.

Labov, William. *Language in the inner city: Studies in the Black English vernacular.* Philadelphia: University of Pennsylvania Press, 1972 (a).

Labov, William. *Sociolinguistic patterns*. Philadelphia: University of Pennsylvania Press 1972 (b).

Mallery, Garrick. Sign language among North American Indians, compared with that among other peoples and deaf-mutes. In J. W. Powell, Ed. First Annual Report of the Bureau of American Ethnology, 1881, pp. 263–552. (Reprinted 1972, The Hague: Mouton & Co.).

McCall, Elizabeth A. A generative grammar of Sign. Unpublished Master's Thesis, Department of Speech Pathology and Audiology. University of Iowa, 1965.

Miller, George A. *Language and communication*. New York: McGraw-Hill, 1951.

Newman, Pat. Gallaudet on stage. *Hearing and Speech News*, 1971, *39*(1), 12–15.

Nida, Eugene A. *Toward a science of translating*. Leiden: E. J. Brill, 1964.

Oléron, P. & Nanpon, H. Recherches sur la traduction simultanée. *Journal de Psychologie Normale et Pathologique*, 1965, *62*, 73–94.

Quigley, Stephen P., Ed. *Interpreting for deaf people: A report of a workshop on interpreting*. Washington: U.S. Department of Health, Education, and Welfare, 1965.

Schlesinger, I. M. The grammar of Sign Language and the problems of language universals. In J. Morton, Ed. *Biological and social factors in psycholinguistics*. London: Logos Press, 1971.

Sinaiko, H. Wallace, and Brislin, Richard W. Evaluating language translations: Experiments on three assessment methods. *Journal of Applied Psychology*, 1973, *57*, 328–334.

Starnes, DeWitt T., and Noyes, Gertrude E. *The English dictionary from Cawdrey to Johnson 1604–1755*. Chapel Hill, N.C.: The University of North Carolina Press, 1946.

Stevens, Kenneth N. Perception of phonetic segments: Evidence from phonology, acoustics, and psychoacoustics. In D. L. Horton and J. J. Jenkins, Eds. *Perception of Language*. Columbus, Ohio: Merrill Publishing Co., 1971.

Stokoe, William C., Jr. Sign Language structure, an outline of the visual communications systems of the American deaf. *Studies in Linguistics*, Occasional Paper #8, Buffalo, N.Y., 1960.

Stokoe, W. C., Jr. *Semiotics and human sign languages*. The Hague: Mouton, 1972.

Stokoe, William C., Jr. Classification and description of sign languages. In Thomas A. Sebeok, Ed. *Current trends in linguistics, Vol. 12: Linguistics and adjacent arts and sciences*. The Hague: Mouton, 1974, pp. 345–372.

Stokoe, William C., Jr., Casterline, Dorothy, and Croneberg, Carl. *A diction-

ary of American Sign Language. Washington: Gallaudet College Press, 1965.

Tervoort, B. T. You me downtown movie fun? *Lingua,* 1968, *21,* 455–465.

Tweney, Ryan D., Heiman, Gary W., and Hoemann, Harry W. Psychological processing of sign language: The functional role of syntactic and cheremic structure. In preparation.

Tweney, Ryan D. & Hoemann, Harry W. Back translation: A method for the analysis of manual languages. *Sign Language Studies,* 1973, *2,* 51–80.

Tweney, Ryan D., Hoemann, Harry W., and Andrews, Carol E. Semantic organization in deaf and hearing subjects. *Journal of Psycholinguistic Research,* 1975, *4,* 61–73.

Tytler, Alexander Fraser (Lord Woodhouselee). *Essay on the principles of translation.* London: J. M. Dent & Co., no date (First published 1791).

Werner, Oswald, and Campbell, Donald T. Translating, working through interpreters, and the problem of decentering. In R. Naroll and R. Cohen, Eds. *A handbook of method in cultural anthropology.* Garden City, N.Y.: Natural History Press, 1970.

Winograd, Terry. Understanding natural language. *Cognitive Psychology,* 1972, *3,* 1–191.

Woodward, James Clyde, Jr. A transformational approach to the syntax of American Sign Language. In William C. Stokoe, Jr. *Semiotics and human sign languages.* The Hague: Mouton, 1972.

Woodward, James C., Jr. Inter-rule implication in American Sign Language. *Sign Language Studies,* 1973, *3,* 47–56.

Woodward, James C., Jr. A report on Montana-Washington implicational research. *Sign Language Studies,* 1974, *4,* 77–101.

PART 2

Social and Behavioral Sciences

CHAPTER 5

Empirical Studies of Simultaneous Interpretation: A Review and a Model.

DAVID GERVER

FORTUNATELY, OR UNFORTUNATELY, unlike many reviews of research in a particular field, the present discussion of empirical studies of simultaneous interpretation cannot start with the admission that the reviewer was almost defeated by the vast literature on the topic. Although a few books and a number of papers on practical and theoretical aspects of simultaneous interpretation have appeared over the years in such journals of interpretation as *Babel, Meta, Fremdsprachen* (Leipzig), or the Russian periodical for translators *Tetradi Perevodchika*, there has in fact been disappointingly little actual research carried out on the subject by either psychologists, linguists, or teachers of simultaneous interpretation. Library searches and requests for information to all the major schools of simultaneous interpretation revealed only a dozen or so authors whose work was available for review. Regretably, a number of papers by Russian authors mentioned by Chernov (1973) have had to be omitted from the discussion because their work was not obtainable in the West. The reviewer's task, then, has been more one of sifting through the mass of data presented by some of the authors rather than through some of the data presented by a mass of authors!

Apart from the very few psychologists whose work is to be reviewed, almost no authors of books or papers on human skills, cognitive psychology, or psycholinguistics even mention the complex skills involved in simultaneous interpretation. The principal exceptions are Welford (1968) and Neisser (1967). Welford discusses simultaneous interpreters' ability to listen and speak simultaneously within the context of a discussion of single-channel theories of human information processing, that is, theories based on the supposition that attention can be paid to only one activity at a time. Welford suggests that simultaneous interpreters acquire the ability to listen and speak simultaneously because, after much practice, they learn to ignore the sound of their own voices. As will be seen later in the discussion, the picture is rather more complicated than Welford suggests. Neisser, in *Cognitive Psychology*, a book which has had a significant effect on contemporary approaches to cognitive psychology and human information processing, limits his mention of simultaneous interpretation to a discussion of simultaneous interpretation as evidence against a motor theory of speech perception: "In a sense simultaneous translation is a form of 'shadowing'.[1] However, it is not words or articulatory movements that are shadowed. The translator, who is obviously attending to, and understanding the incoming stream of speech, cannot possibly be imitating the speaker's vocalizations. His own vocal tract is occupied with an entirely different output."

In an extensive survey of problems involved in foreign-language teaching (with particular emphasis on the teaching of Russian) Leont'ev (1973) deplores the lack of knowledge about simultaneous interpretation and calls for research on the mechanisms involved.

However regrettable it may be, the reasons for this neglect are perhaps not too difficult to find. First, the phenomenon is a comparatively recent one, and although conference interpretation had been practiced for some time, simultaneous interpretation only really came into its own after its use at the Nuremberg trials, with the increase in organizations of international cooperation, and with the ever increasing number of international conferences on cultural, social, political, and scientific themes. Second, the task is extremely complex: though simultaneous listening and speaking rarely occurs in everyday verbal behavior, simultaneous interpreters manage not only to listen and speak simultaneously for reasonable lengths of time, but also to carry out complex transformations on the source-language message while uttering their translation in the target language. From the point of view of cognitive psychologists the task is a complex form of human information processing involving the perception, storage, retrieval, transformation, and transmission of verbal information. Furthermore, linguistic, motivational, situational, and a host of other factors cannot be ignored.

This very complexity has no doubt daunted many who might otherwise have been interested in the subject, the problem being one of defining and isolating both the independent and dependent variables, as well as being able to find experimental designs capable of handling the multiplicity of factors involved and the relatively small numbers of sufficiently skilled interpreters available at any one time in any one place with a particular combination of languages. It would be premature to say that research on simultaneous interpretation is at anything but a preliminary stage; much of the research to be discussed being primarily concerned with description rather than experimental manipulation or theoretical elaboration. Even so, it is not too early to attempt a step-by-step description, or model, of the process, and this will be presented at the end of this chapter, bearing in mind that most of the studies to date have been concerned with interpretation to and from English and French, English and German, and English and Russian, and that there has been no replication of any of the studies in other language combinations. This point is quite important, for as Průcha points out in a recent review of Soviet psycholinguistics (Průcha, 1972), the findings of Anglo-Saxon psycholinguists working in English have not always been replicated by Russian investigators working in their own language. The same may, of course, be true for other languages.

Because the skills developed by simultaneous interpreters are not characteristic of bilinguals in general,[2] certain problems in the study of bilingualism will be either ignored, or barely touched on in the following discussion, such as the effect of the context within which a bilingual learns his languages (Ervin and Osgood, 1954) or the nature of the mechanisms of storage and retrieval of linguistic information in bilingualism (Kolers, 1968; Macnamara, 1967). The general framework of the discussion is, therefore, that of recent research and theory in the psychology of memory, attention, and language.

As Barik has pointed out (Barik, 1973), a number of questions spring immediately to mind in relation to the simultaneous interpreter's task. How does the interpreter carry out all the activities involved in simultaneous interpretation? What strategies must the interpreter employ in order to distribute his attention most effectively between input, translation, and output? What aspects of the source language message affect his performance, and how does he segment almost continuous input? What difficulties arise in the course of the task, and to what extent does personality affect performance? To what extent can the study of the interpreter's speech pattern, and the content of his translation provide clues to the processes involved? Before proceeding to the attempts at answering these and similar questions, it is instructive to bear in mind an interpreter's own view of the task. Glemet (1958) has been discussing consecutive interpretation:

With simultaneous interpretation the basic problems are the same: the "phenomenal" problems are more acute. Your "intellection" of the speech need not be so thorough, but your response to words must be quicker than before. The speaker speaks, and you are speaking too. If memory plays little part, neither does the personal element in the reconstruction of speech. Your sentence must, of necessity, follow the pattern of those which the speaker has pronounced. Circumlocutions are impossible. You cannot hear ahead. Your rendering will naturally tend to be verbatim, but, of course, what you say must make sense, and word for word translation may not. As you are following the speaker you start a sentence. But as you start a sentence you are taking a leap in the dark, you are mortgaging your grammatical future; the original sentence may suddenly be turned in such a way that your translation of its end cannot easily be reconciled with your translation of its start. Great nimbleness is called for to guide the mind through this syntactical maze, whilst at the same time it is engaged upon the work of word-translation. Listening intently, translating half-unconsciously, consciously intervening to redress the formas and balances of syntax, touching up, putting in fillers—these are some of the demands of simultaneous interpretation.

"Early" Research

The first lengthy discussion and analysis of simultaneous interpretation appeared in a master's thesis by Paneth (Paneth, 1957), herself a former conference interpreter. Although concerned primarily with the training of simultaneous interpreters, Paneth also discussed some of the problems involved in simultaneous listening and speaking for the interpreter, and from observations of interpreters at actual conferences she noted that interpreters would often lag from 2 to 4 seconds behind the source-language speaker. She also discussed the problems of how the interpreter segments the input, and what use he might make of the pauses in the source language speaker's delivery in order to speed up his own output. These problems and a number of others discussed by Paneth have since been taken up by other investigators, and are discussed below.

The first experimental studies in this area both appeared in 1965 (Oléron and Nanpon, 1965; Treisman, 1965). Treisman was concerned with the effects of the sequential constraints of messages on two speech transmission tasks, rather than with the study of simultaneous interpretation per se. The tasks were shadowing and simultaneously interpreting. Although some of her subjects were bilingual, none had any previous experience in simultaneous interpretation. Treisman compared the effect of the redundancy of the source language message on ear-voice span (the number of words or seconds the interpreter or shadower lagged behind the speaker) and accuracy of performance. Redundancy was found to have an effect on the number of words correctly shadowed or interpreted, and grammatical constraints were found to be more important than semantic constraints in shadowing than in interpretation. Not unreasonably, Treisman attributed the greater ear-voice span for interpreting than for shadowing to "the increased decision load imposed by the more complex transformations between input and output." Ear-voice span was also studied by Oléron and Nanpon (1965), who calculated ear-voice spans from recordings of a number of simultaneous interpreters translating different lengths of passage from and to a number of different languages. They found that delays could range from 2 to 10 seconds, and they suggested that the extent of the delay in interpretation is determined by the relative difficulty of organizing the incoming material. The interpreter must grasp a certain amount of material before he begins to translate, the amount varying with the position in the sentence of certain key words such as the verb. On the other hand, as Oleron and Nanpon pointed out, because of limitations in short-term memory capacity, the interpreter cannot afford to lag too far behind. The problem of the amount of information the interpreter requires before starting to translate was also discussed by Goldman-Eisler (1972) and is discussed later in this chapter. Oléron and Nanpon also examined the accuracy of the translations they had obtained, both in actual conference, and in laboratory, conditions, and noted numbers of errors of omission and addition, and that oral translations tended to be longer (in terms of words) than formal written translations of the same passages.

Two further papers involving simultaneous interpretation appeared in 1967, but it was not the main focus of the study in either case. In the first of these, Lawson (1967) was principally concerned with selective attention for speech, that is, the ability to attend selectively to some aspects of verbal input while rejecting others. Lawson asked bilingual English-Dutch subjects to simultaneously interpret different types of text both from and to English and Dutch. Her subjects were not professional interpreters. Although her subjects interpreted the texts they heard in one ear, in the other ear they received passages of English or Dutch text or statistical approximations to text in each language. Subjects were instructed to translate the text on the left or right ear, and the number of omissions in their translations were counted under the different input conditions for the nonattended ear. The degree of interference from the nonattended channel varied according to the language and the text on that channel, more omissions occurring with input in the same language as in the attended ear and from a different passage of prose. Lawson discussed her results in terms of stimulus factors facilitating interference between the channels. Paneth (1957) and others had mentioned the ability of some experienced interpreters to carry out other tasks, such as writing letters, while interpreting in the booth. Lawson's experiment, while not directly relevant to the questions as to what type of task might be carried out concurrently with simultaneous interpretation or to what extent this is possible, does have some bearing on the type of auditory interference likely to affect interpreters' performance.

In the second paper Goldman-Eisler (1967) discussed the role of patterns of speaking and pausing in reading, spontaneous speech, and simultaneous interpretation. In previous papers with Henderson and Skarbek (Henderson et al., 1966a, 1966b) Goldman-Eisler had suggested that cumulative graphs of successive time periods of speech and silence, plotted for individual speakers, show that periods of long pauses and short speech bursts alternate with periods of short pauses and long speech periods, and that this repeated pattern reflects cycles of acts of planning and production in speech. It was suggested that hesitant steep slopes are related to planning and fluent shallow slopes to the outcome of the planning. Goldman-Eisler (1967) examined the temporal patterns of speech and pausing in samples of spontaneous speech, reading of prepared texts, and simultaneous interpretations of texts from and to English, French and German, and found that the above-mentioned rhythmic property could be detected in all three conditions when pausing constituted at least 30 percent of the total time spent in speaking and pausing. Both this finding and Goldman-Eisler's further discussion in the same paper of the relationship between rhythmic structure and interpreters' redistribution of speech time/pause time ratios in the input text are open to criticism. The problem is not only whether the patterns of speaking and pausing described by Goldman-Eisler are indicative of the cognitive activity, but also whether the patterns themselves are true patterns or artifacts of the method used to detect them. Schwartz and Jaffe (1968), and Jaffe et al. (1970) demonstrated that computer-generated random sequences and random graphs also show the same stepwise patterns that Goldman-Eisler and Henderson et al. claim provide evidence for cognitive rhythm. According to Jaffe and his colleagues, therefore, the evidence for cognitive rhythm may be more an artifact of the experimenter's judgment when searching for patterns in the data than the result of a cognitive process.

In the paper mentioned above Goldman-Eisler also discusses the effect of source-language speech rate on the temporal rhythm of the interpreters' output. A more relevant question

from the practising interpreters' point of view is the effect of
input rate on the interpreter's ability to interpret effectively.

Source Language Input Rate

Most interpreters agree that a slow, monotonous delivery
can be as stressful as a very fast staccato one. Seleskovitch
(1965), for example, suggests that an input rate of between 100
and 120 words a minute is a comfortable one for simultaneous
interpretation, and that rates between 150 and 200 words per
minute provide an upper limit for effective interpretation.
The effect of source language presentation rate on interpreters' performance was studied by Gerver (1969). Ten simultaneous interpreters were asked to either simultaneously interpret or to shadow a prerecorded passage of French prose
presented at increasing rates of 95, 112, 120, 142, and 164
words per minute. Simultaneous interpretation and shadowing were compared on a number of parameters in order to
ensure that any changes in performance in simultaneous interpretation at the faster input rates could be attributed to the
processes involved in simultaneous interpretation rather than
to difficulties in perception or simultaneous listening and
speaking per se. The proportion of the text correctly shadowed
only decreased significantly at input rates of 142 and 164
words per minute, but the amount correctly interpreted decreased with each increase in input rate. Shadowers maintained a constant ear-voice span of between 2 and 3 words at
all input rates, but interpreters' ear-voice spans increased from
5 words at 95 words per minute to an average of 8½ words at
164 w.p.m. It was also found that while shadowers were able
to increase their own articulation rates, pause less, and speak
for longer periods as input rates increased, interpreters maintained a fairly steady output rate, paused more, and spoke less.
Transcripts of shadowing and interpreting responses were also
examined for errors of commission, omissions, and self-corrections. The optimal input rate for simultaneous interpretation
was between 95 and 120 words per minute, confirming Seleskovitch's suggestion. Normally simultaneous interpreters
might try to optimize their work load by working at a steady
rate and maintaining a balance between the rate at which they

interpret, and the rate at which new material arrives, under conditions of speed, noise, or other stress; however, they may adopt certain strategies for coping with information overload. For example, Chernov's suggestions regarding strategies used by interpreters to compress the source language text (Chernov, 1969), mentioned below, or some of the "adjustment procedures" which Miller (1964) found his subjects employed when attempting to cope with information overload during a task involving continuous responding to various visual and auditory signals: (1) Omission, or not processing the information when there is overload; (2) escape, or cutting off the input; (3) error, or incorrect processing and failure to correct; (4) Queueing, or delaying responses during heavy load periods, and catching up during any lulls that occur; (5) filtering, or systematic omission of certain types of information; (6) approximation, or loss precise response when there is not time for details. Examples of the first four of these strategies were found in interpreters' performance at faster input rates, but the transcripts of the translations were not examined for evidence of the last two strategies.

A different approach to the possible effect of source language input rate was taken by Chernov (1969). Chernov counted the number of syllables in each of three English passages, and then obtained simultaneous interpretations into Russian of the same passages by four student interpreters. Both the target language versions and written translations were found to contain many more syllables than the English originals. The interpretations were, however, shorter than the written translations. Chernov then compared interpretations of the same passages by experienced interpreters with the English original, and found they contained fewer syllables. Chernov suggests that when the source language is presented at a faster rate than the interpreter's own speech rate, or the target language translation is longer than the source language text, the experienced simultaneous interpreter must employ strategies involving either lexical or syntactical compression if he is not to lag too far behind, and omit part of the source language message. The lengths of simultaneous interpretations were also compared with the lengths of source language texts by Krušina (1971), who compared the number of words needed in English, French, and German to translate 100 word passages in Czech. The passages in all three languages were 30 to 40 words longer than the Czech originals. A syllable count revealed, however, that all three translations contained fewer syllables than the Czech, with the English texts being the shortest. Krušina argued that it is, therefore, misleading to describe rate in terms of words per minute when in fact more syllables will be uttered per unit time in some languages than others, even though the number of words may be the same. Although Krušina presents data comparing actual utterance rates in syllables per minute for actual interpretations in French, German, and English, as well as the Czech source text, and argues that the English syllable rate is the slowest, a statistical reanalysis of the date he presents revealed no significant differences between either the source language or the target language utterance rates.

It is interesting to apply Krušina's method to Chernov's examples, for though Chernov reported expansion in the number of syllables when comparing English passages with Russian simultaneous interpretations of the passages, the number of words concerned did not differ very much. In any case, there is a problem in employing the syllable as a measure either of length of passage or of articulation rate. Although it is reasonable to assume that in describing the length of a passage, or the rate at which it is spoken, one is attempting to convey some measure of the rate at which information is produced or transmitted, it is not clear that the syllable is a suitable unit for this purpose. Syllables as phonological units do not necessarily correspond with morphemic or semantic units, and it is surely meaning rather than sound that we are concerned with in discussing translation.

The Effects of Poor Listening Conditions on Interpreters' Performance

Continuous skilled tasks involving the sharing of attention and data transformation are particularly susceptible to the detrimental effects of environmental noise, as has been demonstrated by Broadbent (1958) and Woodhead (1958). It is not surprising, therefore, to find that simultaneous interpreters are particularly sensitive to poor listening conditions, whether because of inadequate sound insulation in the interpreter's booth or inadequacies in the conference amplification system.

A study on the effects of noise on simultaneous interpreters' performance was carried out by Gerver (1972a, 1974). Twelve professional conference interpreters shadowed or simultaneously interpreted into English six prerecorded excerpts from articles in the French edition of the UNESCO Courier. The passages were heard without noise, with a moderately noisy background, and against a very noisy background. The principal findings were that, although more was omitted both in shadowing and interpreting as noise increased, significantly more errors were made in interpreting than shadowing under both moderately and very noisy backgrounds. Furthermore, in spite of the increase in errors, the ratio of simultaneous interpreters' corrections to errors of commission remained almost the same in all three listening conditions. It was also found that, though there were greater ear-voice spans for interpreting (about 5.7 words) than for shadowing (about 2 words), the ear-voice spans remained fairly constant in good and bad listening conditions. These results suggested that in order to maintain a constant ear-voice span in difficult listening conditions, the simultaneous interpreters in this particular study were prepared to sacrifice accuracy by lowering their response criteria, that is, by accepting more errors without attempting to correct them.

Further analyses of the temporal characteristics of subjects' performance demonstrated a retarding effect of noise on simultaneous interpretation as compared with shadowing. This was shown in decreased articulation rates and increased unfilled pause times.

Pinhas (1972) discusses some of the factors that might affect a simultaneous interpreter's performance when coping with exceptionally difficult and noisy listening conditions, such as those encountered when trying to interpret communications from spacecraft or from the moon. Pinhas raises the question, often discussed among teachers of interpretation, of whether it is better to interpret *into* or *from* one's mother tongue. Although, as Pinhas points out, there is no empirical data on which to base their judgments, various branches of the United

Nations have maintained over the years that it is better to interpret into the mother tongue, whereas teachers of interpreting at Lomonosov University in Moscow have maintained that it is better to interpret from the mother tongue. The arguments rested basically on a disagreement as to whether decoding or encoding were the most important aspects of interpretation. The United Nations case was based on the supposition that more stylish, fluent, and accurate interpretations will be made into a language spoken without accent, and of which one has the better grasp of vocabulary and grammar. The Lomonosov viewpoint is based on the argument that such may be the case for many of the types of political material interpreted at United Nations meetings which are highly redundant both in form and content and only have to be attended to every so many words. It would not be the case with scientific and technical texts, however, where more often than not every word has to be accurately perceived. Under these conditions it is necessary to have a perfect grasp of the source language, and this must, therefore, be the mother tongue. As a result of difficulties encountered in attempting to interpret Apollo 14 transmissions, Pinhas suggests that interpretation should be *into* the mother tongue under good listening conditions, and with general texts, but *from* the mother tongue when interpreting technical texts and/or under difficult listening conditions. An empirical test of Pinhas' suggestions should not be difficult to devise.

A further aspect of the effects of noise on interpretation is the effect of noisy listening conditions on the conference audience. An experiment on the effect of noisy listening conditions on an audience's ability to comprehend and recall simultaneously interpreted text was carried out within the context of a comparison of simultaneous and consecutive interpretation and their relative effectiveness in conveying information (Gerver, 1972a). Whereas simultaneous interpreters may occasionally encounter noisy listening conditions, the conference listener will nearly always have to listen to the interpretation against a highly variable level of background noise from inside or outside the conference hall, from the relatively poor quality of sound transmitted by most headsets, or (in the case of simultaneous interpretation) from interference from the voice of the speaker whose speech is being interpreted. Under these circumstances it would appear that, given an equivalent translation (in terms of the information conveyed), consecutive interpretation, which is carried out when the floor speaker has finished, should be more effective in conveying information to the listener than simultaneous interpretation. Two experiments were carried out comparing simultaneous and consecutive interpretation in this context. In the first experiment, 15 subjects with minimal or no knowledge of French listened under simulated conference conditions to three French prose passages, together with the simultaneous interpretations of the passages into English, and 15 similar subjects listened to the same three passages followed by consecutive interpretations from the same professional interpreter. The interpreter was allowed to familiarize himself with the passages beforehand, and the consecutive and simultaneous interpretations for each passage were checked to ensure that the same information was available in each version. After listening to each passage and its interpretation the subjects were asked 10 questions relating to the passage. No differences were found in retention and comprehension scores for the simultaneous and consecutive conditions.

In order to examine the effect of adverse listening conditions on an audience's ability to retain information presented in either simultaneous or consecutive interpretation, the above experiment was repeated with four groups of subjects and two types of interference. In one condition both the source language speech and its interpretations were heard against a background of white noise in the lecture theatre. In the second condition subjects heard source-language speeches and interpretations against a background of noise in their headsets. No significant differences were found in subjects' comprehension and recall test scores for the two noisy listening conditions, but higher mean scores were obtained for responses to consecutive than to simultaneous interpretations, and noise in the headphones caused a slightly greater decrease in comprehension scores for simultaneous than for consecutive interpretations.

Although a choice between simultaneous and consecutive interpretation is rarely an issue in present-day conference planning, from the point of view of the different skills involved it would be interesting to compare the abilities of skilled interpreters to transmit information correctly with the two techniques. There are two forms of consecutive interpretation: (1) Continuous, in which the interpreter waits until the source language speaker has finished his entire speech before delivering his version, and (2) discontinuous, in which the interpreter delivers his version at breaks in the source language speaker's output. Van Hoof (1962) points out that in recent times consecutive interpretation has gradually given way to simultaneous interpretation at most international conferences, but that it may be the preferred type of interpretation at small meetings, such as committees and roundtables, where two languages suffice. Although consecutive interpretation is often thought to be superior to simultaneous in terms of accuracy and style, its use will inevitably lengthen conference proceedings. It should be remembered, however, that the process itself may be less stressful for the interpreter than simultaneous interpretation, insofar as he does not have to listen and speak simultaneously while translating. The basic skill developed in consecutive interpretation is that of taking rapid notes in various "shorthand" forms (shorthand from the point of view of mnemonic codes rather than a system of shorthand as such), and reconstructing the original message on the basis of the notes (see Seleskovitch, 1973, for an analysis of this process). Although this may often enable the interpreter to deliver a more accurate and stylistically acceptable translation than would be the case with simultaneous interpretation delivered under time pressure (though even this remains to be empirically demonstrated), the results of the two experiments described above suggest that given equally accurate translations, there may be no reason to prefer one form of interpretation over the other solely on the basis of the listener's ability to gain information from either form of interpretation.

Segmentation of the Source-Language Message

Barik (1969) has suggested that source-language pauses might delineate units of meaning for the interpreter, and thus assist with the segmentation of the almost continuous stream of source-language input. There have been two attempts to study this question. In the first, Goldman-Eisler (1972) suggested that simultaneous interpreters have their own ways of segmenting the input. She suggests three ways in which the source language message can be segmented: encoding the "chunks" of speech between pauses as they occur in the source language (identity); starting to encode before the source language "chunk" has ended (fission); stringing two or more input "chunks" and then encoding (fusion). Of a large number of responses from six professional interpreters working from and to English, French and German, Goldman-Eisler found 11 percent identity, 48 percent fission, and 41 percent fusion responses. Further analysis of the identity responses showed that significantly more occurred at faster than at slower input rates and when translating from German than from French or English. Analysis of responses to read, rather than spontaneously spoken, texts in German and French revealed that significantly more fission responses occurred to French than German texts, but that there were significantly more German than French fusion responses. Goldman-Eisler concluded that whether simultaneous interpreters used input "chunks" or imposed their own, segmentation appeared to be a function of the language being translated, and that larger "chunks" were stored after translating German than French or English.

The use made by interpreters of source-language pauses to segment the message was also studied by Gerver (1971), basing his experiment partly on Suci's (1967) demonstration of the validity of pauses as indices of perceptual or processing units of language. Suci's subjects were asked to repeat, with normal intonation, passages recorded in a monotone at a regular rate of two words per second. The location of subjects' pauses relative to phrase structure was assessed, as well as their ability to recall material. Suci found that subjects' pauses tended to segment passages into phrases, and that phrases were more readily learned than nonphrase segments. Johnson (1970) also demonstrated that phrases bounded by pausal locations are learned and recalled as units. With these findings in mind, Gerver (1971) asked his subjects (students completing a course in simultaneous interpretation) to simultaneously interpret two types of prerecorded passage of French prose: passages spoken with normal stress, intonation and pausing and passages with minimal stress and intonation, with all pauses of more than 0.25 second eliminated from the recording. All texts werre spoken at the same rate. An immediate constituent analysis of all the French texts was carried out, as well as analyses of the locations of pauses of more than 0.25 second or more in both the input passages with pauses, and subjects target language translations. Of 105 source language pauses, 84 occurred at major constituent boundaries, 21 at minor constituent boundaries, and none within minor constituents. When the locations of pauses in the target language were compared with source language pause locations it was found that 55 percent occurred after words at major constituent boundaries in the source language (89 percent of these occurring at the same position as source language pauses), 30 percent between minor constituents, and 15 percent within constituents. When the source language pauses were eliminated 32 percent of target language pauses occurred at source language major constituent boundaries, 42 percent between minor constituents, and 26 percent within minor constituents. It was also found that significantly more was correctly interpreted in the pause than the no-pause condition. It was concluded that source-language pauses do assist simultaneous interpreters in segmenting, decoding, and encoding of source-language messages.

A different approach to segmentation was taken by Goldman-Eisler (1972) in an analysis of the linguistic structure of the words comprising interpreters' ear-voice spans when simultaneously interpreting from and to English and French and from German to English. The majority of EVS's were found to consist of at least a complete predicate expression (defined as NP + VP). Goldman-Eisler also defined 7 types of ear-voice span unit: adverbial expressions; NP + VP without object; NP + VP complete with object, adverb, and so on; NP + VP complete with some components of the next clause; end of clause; end of clause continuing into next clause. The average EVS appeared to be between four and five words, and the majority were found in the last three categories. Data are also provided regarding the frequencies of occurrence of these different categories of EVS in interpreting from each of the three languages.

Simultaneous Listening and Speaking

Some writers have suggested that in order to avoid the strain of continuous simultaneous listening and speaking, simultaneous interpreters try to make use of the brief silences (unfilled pauses) in the source-language speaker's speech. Goldman-Eisler (1968), for instance, suggests that ". . . . the intermittent silence between chunks of speech in the speaker's utterance is a very valuable commodity for the simultaneous interpreter; for the more of his own output he can crowd into his source's pauses, the more time he has to listen without interference from his own output." Goldman-Eisler does not, however, present any evidence in support of this hypothesis. Barik (1973) investigated the hypothesis by means of a computer analysis of temporal characteristics of recordings of source language speakers' and interpreters' speech. Employing a pause criterion of 0.60 second, Barik first of all obtained the total times spent by the two speakers in each of four possible states: both speakers pausing, both speakers speaking, source speaking-interpreter pausing, source pausing-interpreter speaking. Barik calculated the proportion of source speakers pause time that the interpreter would be expected to speak were his speaking independent of source language pauses, compared these figures with those actually obtained, and concluded that simultaneous interpreters do make greater use of source-language pauses than would be expeected on the assumption that the interpreter's delivery is independent of intervals of speaking and pausing in the source language speakers delivery.

The suggestion is, then, that simultaneous interpreters would endeavour to optimize their use of source-language pauses to reduce the amount of time spent in simultaneous listening and speaking. Barik also goes on to suggest, however, that a contributory factor in interpreters' use of source language pauses might be due to source language pauses having a greater likelihood of occurring in between units of meaning, and that since interpreters are concerned with translating meaning rather than with word-for-word translation they would consider such units before starting to translate, and would therefore be more likely to start speaking during source-language pauses than during source-language speech.

The questions of the position of source-language pauses in relation to the linguistic structure of the utterance, and of what units might be involved in the process of simultaneously interpreting a source language have been discussed above, but it is worth bearing in mind some shortcomings in the notion that simultaneous interpreters will try to reduce simultaneous listening and speaking time by filling source language pauses in the way suggested by Barik and Goldman-Eisler.

Although, intuitively, the hypothesis appears a reasonable one, it is doubtful whether such a strategy could be actively used most of the time because the length of the majority of unfilled pauses in speech would in itself render the strategy useless. Goldman-Eisler (1968), for instance, found that the majority of pauses were of 1 second or less in a variety of speaking situations in English. Barik (1969) examined pause durations in various types of material used as source-language text in his study (different languages, read texts, spontaneous speech, etc.), and found average unfilled pause durations of 0.92 to 1.98 seconds. The differences between Goldman-Eisler's and Barik's mean pause time values can perhaps be accounted for on the bases of the difference in criteria for a pause, and in method of presentation of the data; Goldman-Eisler employed an interval of 250 milliseconds as criterion and presented the distribution of pause lengths, whereas Barik presented only the average values with a criterion of 0.60 second. In a computerized analysis (Gerver, 1972b) of 3- to 5-minute segments of recordings of 10 English speakers made at conferences, and employing a pause criterion of 250 millisecond, the writer found that out of a total of 804 source language pauses, 48 percent were between ¼ and ½ second, 23 percent between ½ and ¾ second, 12 percent between ¾ and 1 second, 13 percent between 1 and 2 seconds, and only 4 percent over 2 seconds. The distribution was similar for a more limited sample of four 5-minute recordings from French speakers at the same conferences. Obviously such figures will vary depending on the language, the speaker, the topic, and a variety of other factors, but equally obviously, there is very little a simultaneous interpreter can do to avoid filling the majority of pauses if he is already speaking.

Gerver (1971, 1972a) calculated the articulation rates in

words per minute in English for a number of simultaneous interpreters working from French to English with a number of different texts spoken at different rates, and in good and poor listening conditions, and found articulation rates ranging from 96 to 120 words per minute. When speaking at these rates very little can be crammed into pauses of even from 1 to 2 seconds, although it is possible that within longer source language pauses the interpreter might try to speed up his articulation rate in order to be clear of as yet untranslated material when the speaker starts speaking again. Whether and how frequently this does happen remains to be demonstrated, however. In any case, analysis of a number of 3-minute samples of different interpreting situations (Gerver, 1972a) demonstrated that even when a fair proportion of the total time is spent in simultaneous listening and speaking the interpreters performance does not necessarily suffer: over 85 percent of the source-language text was correctly interpreted when an average of 75 percent of the total time was spent in simultaneous listening and speaking. Further analyses of 14 recordings of from 5 to 20 minutes, made of six simultaneous interpreters working from French to English at two international conferences showed that on average they spoke for 64 percent of the source-language speech time.

To what extent is having to listen and speak simultaneously likely to affect the performance of the concurrent tasks involved in simultaneous interpretation?

Pintner (1969) examined the effects of simultaneity of listening and speaking, and subjects' practice at the task on ability to repeat sentences, and answer yes/no or why questions under three experimental conditions: in between auditorily presented sentences, overlapping with the presentation of these stimuli, and simultaneously with their presentation. Four groups of subjects took part in the experiment: experienced simultaneous interpreters, student interpreters in their sixth semester of training, student interpreters in their first semester, and first-semester students of other subjects with no experience of simultaneous listening and speaking.

In terms of numbers of words correctly repeated, or questions correctly answered, the simultaneous interpreters' performance was not significantly affected either by the task or the condition, but both simultaneous interpreters and the sixth-semester students performed better than the other two groups on the overlapping and simultaneous tasks. The results of this experiment, therefore, demonstrate that simultaneous interpreters can carry out a complex cognitive task while simultaneously listening and speaking, whereas less experienced and untrained subjects have some difficulty with such tasks.

Although Pintner did employ simultaneous interpreters in her study, they were not interpreting. The question as to whether simultaneous listening and speaking in itself impairs performance on a cognitive task was also to some extent answered by Gerver's (1974b) experiment. Trainee simultaneous interpreters, approaching the end of an intensive course in interpreting, listened to, simultaneously interpreted into English, or shadowed (repeated as they heard) recordings of passages of French prose from the UNESCO Courier. After each passage subjects were given a test of comprehension and recall. If simultaneous listening and speaking in itself impairs ability to comprehend, store, and recall, then test scores for both of the simultaneous tasks should be lower than for merely listening. The additional task of translating could still further impair either interpreters' ability to understand and retain what they hear, or the more complex analysis of the incoming message which is necessary in order to translate, rather than merely repeat it, would assist in comprehension and recall.

In fact, since test scores were higher after listening than after simultaneous interpretation or shadowing, comprehension was impaired by simultaneous listening and speaking. Significantly higher scores after interpretation than after shadowing indicated, however, that simultaneity of listening and speaking affected comprehension more when simple repetition of the message was involved than when the task involved the more complex decoding and encoding of simultaneous interpretation. Both Pintner's and Gerver's studies demonstrate that where a person has the experience that even experienced students of simultaneous interpretation have of simultaneous listening and speaking, the simultaneity of function does not in itself hinder the performance of concurrent cognitive tasks, although it may place some limits on efficiency of performance.

Analysis of Interpreters' Output

Apart from the more generalized temporal measures of input and output rates, speech and pause times, ear-voice spans, and words correctly interpreted under different listening conditions discussed so far, there have also been more detailed analyses of what the interpreter says in his translation. It is to be hoped that these, too, will provide cues to the processes involved in simultaneous interpretation.

In an analysis of the translations of six subjects simultaneously interpreting to and from French and English, Barik (1971) provides a fairly detailed description of various types of omission, addition, substitution, and other errors of translation that overlap with and extend the error categories described by Gerver (1969, 1974a). Barik describes four types of omission: (1) skipping, or the omission of single words, such as qualifiers; (2) comprehension omissions, or omissions of larger units due to a failure of comprehension on the interpreter's part; (3) delay omission, in which the interpreter appears to have got too far behind; (4) compounding omission, due to regrouping of elements from different clause units of the original text. Barik also found that interpreters made certain additions to the original text, such as qualifiers or connectives not found in the source language passage. Barik's subjects also made more elaborate and extraneous additions to the source text than those already mentioned, as in the following:

Source language. . . . Je dois rester conscient de ce qui est juste . . .
Target language. . . . I must be aware and conscious of what is just and fair . . .

Barik also found that substitutions and errors could be grouped into two categories of semantic error, one involving mild errors or substitutions, more or less retaining the meaning of the original, the other, more serious errors involving a substantial change of meaning. There were also a number of reversals in translation of the order in which items had been presented in the source language, for instance:

Source language. . . . to contrast the French and English language . . .

Target language. . . . établir le contraste entre les langues anglaise et
francaise . . .
Source language. . . . the drill of these materials in the classroom and
the laboratory . . .
Target language. . . . la presentation de ces materiaux en laboratoire
et salle de classe . . .

Barik suggests that such reversals are interesting because of
the light they might shed on the mechanisms involved in the
storage and retrieval of information in simultaneous interpretation. Similarly, further study of the type of interference from
the source language found in translations by Barik might aid
the understanding of linguistic independence. Barik found occasional source-language pronunciations or words occurring in
interpreters' translations, but perhaps the most interesting aspect of such intrusions is how seldom they occur in relation to
a simultaneous interpreters' total output over a given period
of time. This finding lends force to Macnamara's observation:
"One of the most remarkable aspects of bilingual performance
—so obvious in fact that it has scarcely been mentioned in the
literature—is the bilingual's ability to keep his languages from
getting mixed up." (Macnamara, 1967).

Both Barik's and Gerver's methods of classifying errors and
omissions are open to the objection that the criteria used are
purely subjective. This objection can to a certain extent be met
when independent judges are employed, but an alternative
approach to the evaluation of translations, and one which
necessitates the use of independent judges, was employed in
Gerver's (1974a) study on the effects of noise. Two independent judges evaluated transcripts of each translation on two
scales developed by Carroll (1965) in order to compare human
with machine translation. Both scales were nine-point scales.
The first, the intelligibility scale, was employed to assess the
degree to which the interpreter's translation of a passage
sounded like normal well-thought-out prose, and would be
understandable in the same way as if it had been originally
spoken in the target language.

Although the translated version of a passage may sound or
read well, it may bear little relationship to the original in terms
of the meaning conveyed. Carroll approached the question of

the fidelity of a translation by converting it into the complimentary question as to whether the original contained any information that would supplement, or contravert, that conveyed in the translation. The scale of Informativeness, then, pertains to how informative the original passage is perceived to be *after* the translation has been seen and studied. If the translation already conveys a great deal of information, the original may be said to be low in informativeness, relative to the translation being evaluated. If, however, the original conveys more information than the translation it will be rated high in informativeness. Two judges were employed in Gerver's study. Both had experience of marking translations from the French up to a first-year-University standard. They were not informed that they were participating in an experiment, and were simply asked to evaluate transcripts of translations by assigning them to points on the separate nine-point scales of intelligibility and informativeness. There was a high degree of agreement between judges' ratings' which showed a significant decrease in the rated intelligibility together with a significant increase in the informativeness of the original passage in relation to the translations, as noise increased.

A further aspect of translations produced by simultaneous interpreters that provides clues to the processes involved in the task is the fact that occasionally simultaneous interpreters will correct themselves in the course of interpreting. Paneth (1957) pointed out that even though interpreters often state that they have no idea of what has been said, they sometimes demonstrate that they are aware of what has been said, they sometimes demonstrate that they are aware of what they are saying by revising as they translate. Welford (1968) in a discussion of sequential processes in the performance of skilled tasks states that simultaneous interpreters acquire the ability to listen and speak simultaneously after long practice because they learn to ignore the feedback from their own voices. Welford goes on to state that simultaneous interpreters often have little idea of what they are saying, or confidence that it is correct, and that their voices often seem strange to them while interpreting. Inspection of translations made by simultaneous interpreters both in the laboratory and at conferences, demonstrates, however, that some attention to some form of feedback must occur, because interpreters do correct both the sound and the meaning of what they are saying as they say it. The first three of the following examples occurred during an experiment reported in Gerver (1974), the last three were obtained from recordings made at a conference:

Table 1: Examples of self-corrections made during simultaneous interpretation

Source	*Interpreter*
(1) . . . est imprimé . . .	. . . is imprinted—is printed . . .
(2) Sur tous les continents . . .	Especially on the continents—on all the continents
(3) Aussi bornée que cette activité . . .	Just as limited as this—however limited this activity
(4) . . . for psychologists . . .	. . . pour des psocho-psychologues . . .
(5) . . . in physical education . . .	. . . dans l'édifis-l'éducation physique . . .
(6) . . . which will be published this month	. . . qui doit sortir d'ici-au cours de ce mois-ci

Gerver (1974a) suggests that in these and other examples of self-correction the simultaneous interpreters appear to have been carrying out a monitoring procedure similar to Miller, Gallanter, and Pribram's (1960) TOTE or test-operate-test-exit. The interpreter generates a target-language response, which may pass a first test, and is uttered, but is then tested again. If the second test is passed, the interpreter may proceed to the next item; if not, he "operates" again by generating a further response to the same stimulus, and so on. The significance of self-corrections for an understanding of the processes involved in simultaneous interpretation, as well as suggestions regarding the type of mechanism that could incorporate such behavior are discussed in the final section of this chapter.

Stress and Personality

Although the question of individual differences in personality, and the ability to withstand the stresses involved in the career of a simultaneous interpreter (e.g. the constant information load during interpretation, the confined environment of the interpreting booth, fatigue, and the effects of environmental noise) is often discussed by professional interpreters, virtually no research has been carried out in this area. This is particularly regrettable in view of the importance of adequate selection procedures both for training and subsequent career placement. A number of suggestions for research in this area were discussed in reports of the Association Internationale des Interpretes de Conference Health Committee (1969), and of the Alpbach Conference (1968), in particular the need for objective selection tests and the design of the working environment. Discussions of the design of interpreters' booths are available in two reports from Belgium and Holland (Bergman, 1973; Joosting, 1970), both of which contain detailed discussions of the optimal working conditions for simultaneous interpreters.

Two studies can perhaps be regarded as attempts to initiate research on personality and performance. Howells, in an unpublished report on the personality characteristics of simultaneous interpreters presented the results of a pilot study in which he interviewed 11 experienced professional interpreters, obtained assessments of their job performance, and asked them to complete the Cattell 16 PF Personality Questionnaire. Although it is not possible to draw any general conclusions on the basis of so tentative a study on so small a sample, Howell's results may provide ideas for further research. Ten of the interpreters were rated as good and dependable, and five of these were judged to be more imaginative. An interesting outcome of the interviews was that the interpreters felt that although there is a creative element in good interpreting, the fact that the content of the interpretation was always initiated by others was a source of frustration. In other words, although the job appears to demand creative effort, it may often deny full creative satisfaction. From the responses to the personality questionnaire, it would be fair to characterize the group as a whole as intelligent, assertive, independent, self-sufficient, resourceful, imaginative, and creative. Because the sample was so small and no control group of subjects who were not interpreters was included in the study, it is not possible to say whether these characteristics are typical of successful interpreters, or of any group of successful professionals of similar age and background.

The second of these studies was carried out by Gerver as part of the investigation on the effects of noise on the performance of simultaneous interpreters. It has been suggested that highly anxious individuals have a low tolerance for noise (Broadbent, 1957), and it might therefore be expected that interpreters with a relatively high general level of anxiety would perform less well under noisy listening conditions than less anxious subjects. Anxiety is often discussed in terms of arousal level, or the general level of arousal of the central nervous system. The relationship between arousal level and performance is usually assumed to take the form of an inverted U, in that performance improves to an asymptote as arousal level increases, after which any further increase in arousal coincides with a decline in performance. In order to assess the relationship between anxiety and interpreters' performance under noise stress, the 12 interpreters in Gerver's study were asked to reply to the questions on the neuroticism scale of the Eysenck Personality Inventory, a short scale which correlates highly with other measures of anxiety. The importance of individual differences in response to stressful working conditions was demonstrated by the relationship between EPI neuroticism scale scores and the proportions of the input texts correctly shadowed or interpreted. With a simple task such as shadowing there was only a small nonsignificant correlation between N scale scores and performance at different noise levels. With the more complex task of simultaneous interpreting, however, although there was no correlation between N scale scores and performance in good listening conditions, there was a positive (but not quite significant) correlation between the two measures under slight noise stress, indicating that subjects with higher N scores tended to perform better than those with lower N scores. Furthermore, there was a significant negative correlation between neuroticism scores and performance at the highest level of background noise, which demonstrated that subjects with higher scores tended to perform worse than those with lower scores. It would appear, then, that a tendency to higher anxiety under stress may be an advantage for simultaneous interpreters when working under moderately stressful listening conditions, but a liability when a greater degree of stress is involved.

An Information Processing Approach to Simultaneous Interpretation

Finally, it does not appear premature to discuss what can be guessed about the processes involved in simultaneous interpretation within the context of current theory and research in human information processing, with particular attention to the roles of memory and attention in the task.

The role of memory in simultaneous interpretation has been discussed by various writers. Van Hoof (1962), referring to the number of tasks simultaneous interpreters must carry out at the same time, talks of split memory or attention. Hromosová (1972) refers to simultaneity and the interaction between short- and long-term memory as three-track memory: as the source language starts, the interpreter begins to store, as he stores he also brings into short-term memory his knowledge of the vocabulary and grammar of both source and target languages, then while pronouncing his translation, the cycle continues.

A review of the experiments discussed so far, however, reveals a rather more complex picture: ear-voice span data suggest that some form of short-term buffer memory is involved; in order to account for the ability of interpreters to translate while further information is received, a relatively short-term working memory is required; the ability of interpreters to monitor and correct their own output suggests a short-term output buffer memory; finally, there must be long-term storage of lexicons and grammars of both source and target languages, interacting with the other processes involved with the reception, transformation and production of language. These suggestions are incorporated in the flow chart model, or rather approximation of simultaneous interpretation shown in Figure 1. There are two main aspects of the process as described in Figure 1:

(1) Permanent structural features such as the various types of memory systems described above.

(2) Control processes which can be selected at the option of

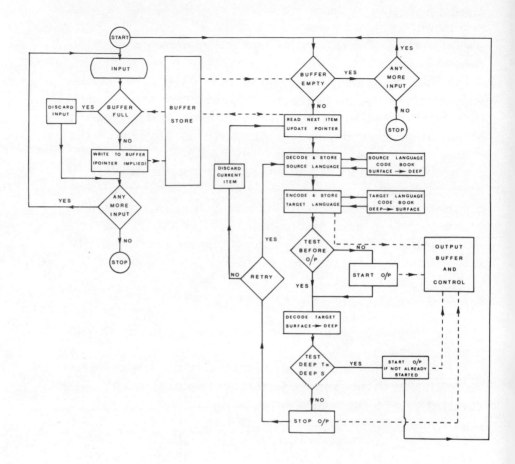

Figure 1: A model of the simultaneous interpretation process.

the interpreter, and which may also determine the distribution of attention to the different components of the task.

It can be argued that, although the main focus of the interpreter's activity is on the actual translation of a message, information may be acquired simultaneously in a buffer storage, while a running comparison can be carried out between output and previous input. The model is consistent with recent discussions of research in both memory (Norman, 1968), and attention (Kahneman, 1973). Norman, for instance, has also suggested that a number of storages may be involved in human information processing: "Any analysis of complex data processing devices indicates the need for numerous storage devices. Temporary storage mechanisms are needed to maintain the results of intermediate steps of analysis. Small buffer memories are needed at each interface of peripheral equipment to the central system to improve the efficiency of operations." Kahneman (1973), reviewing recent research on the problem of attention concludes that, though attention is limited, the limit varies from moment to moment, and the amount exerted at any one time depending primarily on the demands of concurrent activities. Recent research reviewed by Kahneman also demonstrates that, contrary to previous beliefs (Broadbent, 1958; Welford, 1968), attention can be shared between various tasks, allocation being a matter of degree, and under the control of a person's temporary intentions as well as permanent dispositions. At high levels of task load, however, attention becomes almost unitary. Thus in simultaneous interpretation an interpreter can, under normal circumstances (i.e., good listening conditions, moderate input rate, and easily grasped source language material) easily divide his attention between the various functions described in the flow chart, but when, for instance, coping with difficult listening conditions, and/or difficult subject matter, attention might be focused on decoding or encoding and monitoring of both input and output might suffer.

Input procedures Source-language input is received in short-term buffer storage, which is monitored and is under the control of what might be called an input routine that is sensitive to the state of the environment (e.g., whether source language input is available), to the state of the buffer store (e.g., whether further input can be accepted, or whether recent input is fading), and also implement whatever strategy the interpreter employs for segmentation of the input message.

Short-term operational memory. The term operational memory was suggested by Posner (1967) for memory involved in the active reinstatement of permanently stored information, which seems a particularly appropriate description of the type of process involved when an interpreter accesses information regarding source and target language, and carries out the operations involved between perception of the source language message and vocalization of the translation. In the flow chart these would involve all the operations after retrieval of information from short-term buffer storage.

Decoding and Encoding

In an interesting paper on methodological aspects of simultaneous interpretation Kade and Cartellieri (1971) called for research in the subject in order to provide an understanding of the complex skills involved and a scientific base for the training of interpreters. They discuss the problem of what they term the phase shift: the delay between receiving part of the source-language message and uttering the target-language translation, discussed elsewhere in this chapter as ear-voice span. They suggest that interruptions and short breaks in the source-language speaker's speech, together with redundant parts of his speech, assist the interpreter in catching up with the speaker so that every so often he will be able to start afresh. In effect, Kade and Cartellieri propose that simultaneous interpretation involves a stochastic model of listening and speaking in which ". . . . the interpreter builds up within himself an expectation pattern which gets more and more unambiguous with every entity of the source language text he has received." In other words, the interpreter as listener makes probabilistic inferences about the future development of a sentence on the basis of what he has just heard; his own utterances are then based on these predictions, becoming more determined as the source language sentence proceeds.

This view is similar to Hockett's Markovian model of language perception and production (Hockett, 1961), and appears to be the same as that put forward by Chernov (1973) as a psycholinguistic model of simultaneous interpretation. Chernov suggests a probabilistic model of recoding in simultaneous interpretation based partly on a theory of what is termed probabilistic prognosis proposed by Feigenberg (1967). Probabilistic prognosis is defined as the ability to utilize past experience to organize future activity. This is not simply another way of describing learning, but implies an active Markov process. Chernov reports an experiment in which interpreters were asked to simultaneously interpret from Russian to English a number of texts which included passages designed to instigate a misleading set in the interpreter. Chernov reports that 75 percent of subjects' responses to such passages appeared to be according to their expectations rather than what they actually heard, but does not state how many interpreters or how many passages were involved. He suggests that in listening to the source-language message, the simultaneous interpreter generates and attempts to verify hypotheses about the input, using both linguistic and nonlinguistic cues. Factors such as the interpreter's experience with the subject being discussed, his assumptions about the speaker's intentions (e.g., whether wit or sarcasm are intended), as well as the overall context, also affect the interpreter's predictions.

Although there can be little doubt, as Chernov's results and remarks made by interpreters themselves demonstrate, that simultaneous interpreters will sometimes predict what the speaker is about to say, a Markovian model cannot in itself provide an adequate basis for the understanding of translation during simultaneous interpretation. In the first place, there are the general objections to Markov processes as models of either the perception or production of language (Miller, Galanter, and Pribram, 1961; Miller and Chomsky, 1963; Rommetveit, 1968). As far as this discussion is concerned, the principle objections are twofold: a listener could only recognize sequences of words on the basis of his past experience with similar sequences, but there are too many grammatical sequences of even 20 words (in English at least, and the same observation is no doubt true of other languages) for a person to hear and learn in a normal lifetime. There will, therefore, be vast num-

bers of grammatical sequences of any length which the interpreter would never have heard before, and would not be able
to decode or use as the basis for generating successful hypotheses about source-language texts. A Markovian model would
also generate many word sequences that would not be grammatical sentences, and would not be able to generate some
which were, as in the case of embedded sentences. Secondly,
if simultaneous interpreters were relying on prediction based
on probabilistic inferences from semantic, syntactic, and situational cues, it would be interesting to speculate what would
have been stored in recent memory where they correct themselves. When the sequence predicted and subsequently translated and uttered is altered, and corrected, it is obvious that
what has just been uttered has been compared with some
representation of what was actually heard, as well as with its
context. If the predicted sequence were stored, (and perhaps
heard as well) then there might not be a mismatch when utterance and message were compared, but if the message stored
were the one that was heard, but not predicted, then a mismatch might well occur where the two do not coincide. The
very fact that interpreters do appear to store information that
is at odds with what they utter (as shown by their corrections),
demonstrates that anticipation and prediction are not the sole
processes involved.

Clearly then, whether simultaneous interpreters do, on occasion, take advantage of the redundancy of the source language message in order to predict parts of the message, an
alternative model is required. The flow chart refers only
briefly to the processes involved in decoding the source language message and its subsequent encoding in the target language. Obviously, it is this aspect of the process that is of the
greatest interest for a linguistic analysis of the translation process in simultaneous interpretation, but only a brief outline can
be attempted within the framework of what is essentially a
psychological rather than a linguistic description of simultaneous interpretation.

In the flow chart the first instruction, decode and store,
accesses a code book enabling the interpreter to decode the
phonetic representation of each segment of the source language message, and understand it in terms of its underlying

structure and meaning in relation to the context. The decoded message remains available both for encoding in the target language and for comparison with the resulting utterance. The terms surface and deep refer to the sounds, words, and sentences heard and uttered by the interpreter, and to his understanding of their meaning. These terms do not necessarily imply any particular generative transformational theory of language. The distinction between the surface and deep structures of sentences is by no means a recent one, and can lead to some interesting speculations regarding what an interpreter must "know" about his different languages. Wundt (1890) was among the first to suggest that sentences have two simultaneous levels of organization: the associative phrase relations at the surface level indicated by the order of words in a sentence, and the logical relational concepts at the deeper level (i.e., subject, predicate, and object) expressing the internal relations among the words and phrases of a sentence. One example used by Wundt was "Caesar crossed the Rubicon" and "The Rubicon was crossed by Caesar" in which the underlying relations, or deep structure, are the same, even though word order (surface structure) differs. Another, often quoted example of a sentence in which the actual order of words does not coincide with, or directly reveal, underlying relationships is "Flying planes can be dangerous." The surface structure is the same for both interpretations of the sentence, that is,

(1) To fly planes can be dangerous.

(2) Planes that are flying can be dangerous.

It is only a knowledge of the deep structures that would enable an interpreter to translate this sentence, and indeed translation from (for instance) English into French would immediately disambiguate the sentence, the context assisting the interpreter in choosing the correct deep structure. On the other hand there are sentences such as "J'ai lu la critique de Chomsky," or "J'ai trouvé ce fruit délicieux" that the interpreter might find it difficult to disambiguate unless very specific contextual cues are also provided.

The two last examples were taken from Ruwet (1968), who also provides an example of identical deep structures, which by virtue of the different transformations available in each language, lead to different surface structures in English and

French. The English sentence "John has been given a book by Paul" is perfectly grammatical, yet a word-for-word surface structure translation, that is, "Jean a été donne un livre par Paul" is judged as ungrammatical in French by Ruwet. Both sentences have identical base strings:

(1) Paul + prst + perfect + give + a + book + to + John

(2) Paul + prst + perfect + donner + un + livre + à Jean

In this case the interpreter would have to know that the double passive transformation, in which either the direct or indirect object can become the subject in a passive sentence, is available in English, but not in French. To translate the sentence "John has been given a book by Paul," it seems reasonable to suppose that the interpreter must apprehend the deep structure in which "Paul" is the subject, "a book" the object, and "John" the indirect object in order to carry out the singular passive transformation in French. The sentence would then read "Un livre a été donne à Jean par Paul."

These few examples, though barely touching on the subject, are useful because they highlight the distinction between deep and surface structures, and provide hints as to the type of knowledge an interpreter must have about his different languages. As Nida (1969) points out about translators in general, not only must they know the rules for generating sentences in different languages, but they must also know the levels at which the rule systems correspond. Nida also stresses that this type of knowledge is not all that is required in translation, because the translator does not simply map the syntactic forms of one language onto those of another. In keeping with the foregoing discussion of deep and surface structure, Nida suggests that the translator must first of all decode the source language message into some abstract form before restructuring it in the target language, but that experienced simultaneous interpreters may often short circuit the deeper level of analysis by selecting frequently occurring surface structure correspondences; that is, they will often be able to predict the target language equivalent without analysing the input completely. This suggestion is similar to those of Kade and Cartellieri (1971) and Chernov (1973) discussed above, except that these authors do not suggest that a further level of analysis is required. As the above examples demonstrate, however, a predictive model cannot cope with the more complex analyses required by a linguistically more adequate account of sentence structure.

Output Procedures

In the flow chart it is suggested that the source language message as understood by the interpreter is stored for comparison with the target language transform. While translating, the interpreter has the choice of beginning output immediately or of checking whether his translation is a satisfactory version of that portion of the original message involved before starting his utterance. The evidence for testing before output comes from statements made by professional interpreters, to the effect that they may occasionally hold up the output in order to check it against the source message. However, even if the interpreter does decide to begin output at once, the matching of output with the original message (or with some memory for the context) can still take place. Testing involves decoding the translation and matching of this derived meaning with that of the original message. If the match is satisfactory, interpretation may proceed; if not, output may be stopped or prevented. The interpreter may then decide to loop through the routine again (retry). On the other hand, he may decide, for instance, that too much input will be lost if he attempts to correct his recent output or that the error is not critical. He might then discard the current message and proceed to the next portion of the message in the input buffer.

The evidence for testing after output has started comes from the type of revision and correction made by interpreters in the course of translating shown in Table 1. These are similar to the hesitations (or discontinuities) in the flow of speech described by Maclay and Osgood (1959) as retraced false starts, in which a speaker attempts to correct a word, or words, he has already uttered. In the case of the simultaneous interpreter, the examples in Table 1 show that different levels of analysis can be involved in that parts of words, words and phrases can be modified. Whether or not and to what extent testing and correction take place depend on the interpreter's criteria for adequate performance. When there is time, and when a high value is placed on accuracy, the criteria will be relatively high, but under stress, or when an interpreter does not value accuracy so highly (as is perhaps the case with minor slips), the criteria will be lower.

Additional support for the hypothesis that a source-language message can remain in some form of temporary storage long enough for comparison with its translation comes from an experiment by Treisman (1964). Treisman presented her subjects with similar and different prose passages in both ears, varying the delay between messages. They were instructed to attend to and shadow the primary message, but were given no information regarding the secondary passage other than that it was there to see how well subjects resisted distraction. The experiment hinged upon subjects' spontaneous reports on whether the messages on the two channels were identical. When the primary channel preceded the secondary channel, subjects were able to report that both channels were identical after a mean delay of 4.3 seconds. When the secondary channel preceded the primary, the mean delay in report was 1.3 seconds. Furthermore, when the rejected message was a French translation of the preceding shadowed English passage, 11 out of 18 subjects noticed that both channels were identical.

Treisman's discussion of the way in which information to both channels is analyzed, and that to the nonattended channel attenuated so that the subject can attend to the primary channel, is of interest when considering ways in which simultaneous interpreters could monitor their own output. Treisman suggested that, instead of being blocked as had been previously suggested (Broadbent, 1958), secondary channel information is merely attenuated, and is analyzed along with primary channel information by means of a heirarchy of tests involving simple statistical decisions. Although not precisely specified by Treisman, these tests would presumably involve particular attributes of the signal, such as loudness, type of voice, phonetic, syntactic, and semantic features. Speech on the unattended channel, being attenuated, will not pass tests low in the heirarchy, and will not be recognized, but the criteria for certain types of secondary channel input may be lowered because of their importance for the subject, or because of contextual probabilities. In order to account for the recognition of the translation of an attended channel, Treisman suggested that the occurrence of a word in one language will lower the criteria for its translation.

In comparing the interpreter's translating and monitoring to the type of dichotic listening task studied by Treisman, source-language input that has been translated might correspond to the attended shadowed passage in the primary channel in Treisman's experiment. The translation itself, once uttered, is analogous to secondary-channel information because, when a further portion of input is being translated and uttered, it might only be attended to if criteria for matching with the original message are not satisfied.

Gerver (1971) suggested that the interpreter might compare earlier input with current output by means of a running analysis of sound, meaning, and structure, and that one form such an analysis might take would be similar to the analysis-by-synthesis model of speech recognition proposed by Halle and Stevens (1964). Halle and Stevens suggested that speech recognition involves the internal synthesis of speech patterns according to certain rules and the matching of internally generated speech patterns against the pattern under analysis. The generative rules employed for speech perception would be similar to those used for speech production. As Neisser (1967) pointed out, these rules need not be restricted fo the analysis of speech sounds alone, but can also encompass larger units as well:

Auditory synthesis can apparently produce units of various sizes. The listener can ask himself 'What sounds were uttered?' or 'What was meant?'. In each case he must have a set of rules: phonetic, syntactic, semantic or what you will. . . . Hearing an utterance, the listener constructs one of his own in an attempt to match it. Such matching may go on at 'several levels'—that is in terms of different segment sizes. If a single noise-masked word is presented, the listener's preliminary speech analysis may pick out distinctive features or syllables which suggest a tentative answer; various related words are then synthesised until one fits. If the stimulus is an entire sentence, a few words tentatively identified by the preliminary system may guide the synthesis of whole constituents as units, or even of the whole sentence.

After synthesis of the source language message, the interpreter might generate his translation in an analogous way, the process of translation also involving the synthesis and analysis of possible translations of the source language message, that is, continuous generation, monitoring and testing of the translation against the source language message as understood by the interpreter. According to this view, then, monitoring and possible revision and correction are an integral part of the process of simultaneous interpretation, rather than an additional activity *after* translation. Furthermore, an analysis-by-synthesis model incorporates both a hypothesis-generating procedure similar to that suggested by Kade and Cartellieri (1971), and by Chernov (1973), and the more complex types of analysis discussed above.

This outline can only be regarded as a first approximation to a model of the processes involved in simultaneous interpretation. There is obviously a need for further systematic analysis of the skills involved in simultaneous interpretation, as well as of situational, personal, and linguistic factors, before the various aspects of the model can either be made more explicit or discarded in favor of more likely hypotheses. It could easily be objected, however, that the conditions in which experiments are carried out are so artificial as to render meaningless any conclusions about "what really goes on" in the interpreter's booth. Professional interpreters might, for instance, object that failing to take into account such nonverbal factors as the presence or absence of the actual source language speaker, or an audience, diminishes the value of conclusions based on experimental findings. In spite of the reservations some interpreters have voiced about some of the research discussed in this review (Marquis, 1972; Selskovitch, 1973), and bearing in mind that the results so far may not be typical of different source and target language combinations, it may still be hoped that the research reviewed above will provide both methodological and theoretical guidelines for future workers in this fascinating field.

FOOTNOTES

1. Shadowing is a task often employed in psychological experiments on attention, and involves the immediate vocalization of auditorily presented speech stimuli.

2. Martinet (1960), for instance, distinguishes between professional bilingualism (interpreters, translators) and social bilingualism, that is, the bilingualism of a particular population such as French- and English-speaking Canadians, or Swiss–German- and Romanish-speaking Swiss. As Martinet points out, professional bilingualism is an isolated phenomenon compared with social bilingualism.

REFERENCES

Alpbach, Report of a conference on "interpreters and interpreting", 1968.

Association Internationale des Interpretes de Conference. Health Committee Report, January, 1969.

Barik, H. A study of simultaneous interpretation. Unpublished Ph.D. thesis. University of North Carolina, 1969.

Barik, H. A description of various types of omissions, additions, and errors encountered in simultaneous interpretation. *Meta*, 1971, *16*, 199–210.

Barik, H. Simultaneous interpretation: temporal and quantative data. *Language and Speech*, 1973, *16*, 237–270.

Bergman, H. De simultan-vertaal-installatie. Ergonomische kriteria en overwegingen. Unpublished Doctoral Dissertation. University of Utrecht, 1973.

Broadbent, D.E. *Perception and communication.* London: Pergamon Press, 1958.

Carroll, J.B. An experiment in evaluating the quality of translations. *Mechanical Translation*, 1966, *9*, 55–66.

Chernov, G.V. Linguistic problems in the compression of speech in simultaneous interpretation. *Tetradi Perevodchika*, 1969, *6*, 52–65.

Chernov, G.V. Towards a psycholinguistic model of simultaneous interpretation (in Russian). *Linguistische Arbeitsberichte*, (Leipzig), 1973, *7*, 225–260.

Ervin, S. and Osgood, C.E. Second language and bilingualism. *Journal of Abnormal and Social Psychology* (Supp.), 1954, *49*, 139–146.

Feigenberg, I.M. Probabilistic prognosis and its significance. In M. Cole and I. Maltzman. *A Handbook of Contemporary Soviet Psychology.* New York: Basic Books, 1967.

Gerver, D. The effects of source language presentation rate on the performance of simultaneous conference interpreters. In E. Foulke, Ed. *Proceedings of the 2nd Louisville Conference on Rate and/or Frequency Controlled Speech,* University of Louisville, pp. 162–184, 1969.

Gerver, D. Simultaneous interpretation and human information processing. Unpublished Ph.D. thesis, Oxford University, 1971.

Gerver, D. Simultaneous and consecutive interpretation and human information processing. London: Social Science Research Council Research Report, HR 566/1, 1972a.

Gerver, D. A.S.P.A.-Automatic speech-pause analyzer. *Behavioral Research Methods and Instrumentation*, 1972b, *4*, 265–270.

Gerver, D. The effects of noise on the performance of simultaneous interpreters: Accuracy of performance. *Acta Psychologica*, 1974a, *38*, 159–167.

Gerver, D. Simultaneous listening and speaking and retention of prose. *Quarterly Journal of Experimental Psychology*, 1974b, *26*, 337–342.

Glemet, R. In R. Brower, Ed. *On Translation*. Cambridge: Harvard University Press, 1958.

Goldman-Eisler, F. Sequential temporal patterns and cognitive processes in speech. *Language and Speech*, 1967, *10*, 122–132.

Goldman-Eisler, F. *Psycholinguistics: Experiments in spontaneous speech*. London: Academic Press, 1968.

Goldman-Eisler, F. Segmentation of input in simultaneous interpretation. *J. Psycholinguistic Research*, 1972, *1*, 127–140.

Halle, M. and Stevens, K.N. Speech recognition: A model and a programme for research. In J.A. Fodor and J.J. Katz, Eds. *The structure of language*. Englewood Cliffs: Prentice-Hall, 1964.

Henderson, A.I., Goldman-Eisler, F., and Skarbek, A. Temporal patterns of Cognitive Activity and Breath Control in Speech. *Language and Speech*, 1966(a), *8*, 236–242.

Henderson, A.I., Goldman-Eisler, F., and Skarbek, A. Sequential temporal patterns in spontaneous speech. *Language and Speech*, 1966(b), *9*, 207–216.

Hockett, C.F. Grammar for the hearer. Structure of language and its mathematical aspects. In: *Proceedings of the 12th Symposium on applied mathematics*. Providence, 1961.

Howells, G.W. Personality characteristics of simultaneous interpreters. Unpublished research report, no date.

Hromosová, A. A study of memory in interpreting. *Acta Universitatis*, 17 Novembris, Pragensis III, 1972.

Jaffe, J., Breskin, S., and Gerstman, L.J. On the range of sequential constraint in monologue rhythms. *Psychonomic Science*, 1970, *19*, 233–234.

Johnson, R.E. Recall of prose as a function of the structural significance of linguistic units. *Journal of Verbal Learning and Verbal Behavior*, 1970, *9*, 12–20.

Joostling, P.E. Notes sur l'hygiene du milieu dans les cabines d'interpretes. Delft: Instituut voor Gezondheidts technick TNO, 1970.

Kade, O. and Cartellieri, C. Some methodological aspects of simultaneous interpretation. *Babel*, 1971, *17*, 12–16.

Kahneman, D. *Attention and effort*. Englewood Cliffs, Prentice Hall, 1973.

Kolers, P. Bilingualism and information processing. *Scientific American*, 1973, 220, *3*, 78–86.

Krušina, A. Main factors determining the process and quality of simultaneous interpretation. *Acta Universitatis*, 17 Novembris, Pragensis: Studies on language and theory of translation II/1971.

Lawson, E.A. Attention and simultaneous translation. *Language and Speech*, 1967, *10*, 29–35.

Leont'ev, A.A. Some problems in learning Russian as a foreign language. *Soviet Psychology*, 1973, *11*, 1–117.

Lounsbury, F.G. Sequential psycholinguistics. in C.E. Osgood and T.A. Sebeok, Eds. Psycholinguistics: a survey of theory and problems. *Journal of Abnormal and Social Psychology*, 1954, *49*, (suppl.) 93–125.

Maclay, H. and Osgood, C.E. Hesitation phenomena in spontaneous English speech. *Word*, 1959, *15*, 19–44.

Macnamara, J. The bilinguals linguistic performance—a psychological overview. *Journal of Social Issues*, 1967, *23*, 58–77.

Marquis, M. In Le Courrier des Lecteurs. *Meta*, 1972, *17*, 177.

Martinet, A. *Elements de linguistique generale*. Paris: A. Colin, 1960.

Miller, G.A., Galanter, E., and Pribram, K.H. *Plans and the structure of behavior*. New York: Holt, Rinehart, and Winston, 1960.

Miller, G.A. and Chomsky, N. Finitary models of language users. In R.D. Luce, R.R. Bush and E. Galanter, Eds. *Handbook of Mathematical Psychology*, Vol. II., New York: Wiley, 1963.

Miller, J.G. Adjusting to overloads of information. *Research on Public Assistance for Nervous and Mental Disease*, 1964, *42*, 87–100.

Neisser, U. Cognitive Psychology. New York: Appleton-Century-Crofts, 1967.

Nida, E.A. *Toward a Science of Translating*. Leiden: E.J. Brill, 1964.

Nida, E.A. Science of translation. *Language*, 1969, *45*, 483–498.

Norman, D.A. Toward a theory of memory and attention. *Psychological Review*, 1968, *75*, 522–536.

Oléron, P., and Nanpon, H. Recherches sur la traduction simultanee. *Journal de Psychologie Normale et Pathologique*, 1964, *62*, 73–94.

Paneth, E. An investigation into conference interpreting. Unpublished Master's Thesis. London University, 1957.

Pinhas, R. Les retombés scientifiques des operations "Apollo" sur l'interpretation simultanée. *La Linguistique*, 1972, *8*, 143–147.

Pintner, I. Der einfluss der übung und konzentration auf simultanes sprechen und horen. Unpublished Ph.D. thesis. University of Vienna, 1969.

Posner, M.I. Short term memory systems in human information processing. In A.F. Sanders, Ed. *Attention and Memory*. Amsterdam: North Holland, 1967.

Prucha, J. Soviet Psycholinguistics, Janua Linguarum Series Minor, 143, The Hague, Mouton, 1972.

Rommetveit, R. *Words, meanings, and messages*. New York: Academic Press, 1968.

Ruwet, N. *Introduction a la Grammaire Generative*. Paris: Librarie Plon, 1968.

Schwartz, J., and Jaffe, J. Markovian prediction of sequential temporal patterns in spontaneous language. *Language and Speech*, 1968, *11*, 27–30.

Seleskovitch, D. *Colloque sur l'enseignement de l'interpretation*. Paris. Association Internationale des Interpretes de Conference, 1965.

Seleskovitch, D. Les mechanismes de la prise de notes en interpretation consecutive. Unpublished Ph.D. thesis. Université de Paris, 1973.

Suci, G.J. The validity of pause as an index of units in language. *Journal of Verbal Learning and Verbal Behavior*, 1967, *6*, 26–32.

Treisman, A. Monitoring and storage of irrelevant messages in selective attention. *Journal of Verbal Learning and Verbal Behavior*, 1964, *3*, 449–559.

Treisman, A. The effects of redundancy and familiarity on translating and repeating back a foreign and a native language. *British Journal of Psychology*, 1965, *56* 369–379.

Van Hoof, H. *Theorie et pratique de la traduction*. Munich. Man Huober, 1962.

Welford, A.I. *The Fundamentals of Skill*. London: Methuen, 1968.

Woodhead, M.M. Effects of bursts of loud noise on a continuous visual task. *British Journal of Industrial Medicine*, 1958, *15*, 120–125.

Wundt, W. *Die Sprache* III, Leipzig, 1900.

CHAPTER 6

Perspectives on the Role of Interpreter*

R. BRUCE W. ANDERSON

In the past, sociologists have shown little interest in translation or in the behavior of interpreters or other translators.
Several sociologists have recently focused attention on methodological problems arising from translation in comparative research. Among these are statements by Grimshaw (1969a,
1969b), Deutscher (1968, 1969), and Anderson (1967, 1969)
which attend to translation problems in both *inter*national and
*intra*national investigations. One gains the clear impression
from these reports that translation is potentially a methodological issue whenever the investigator and his subjects differ with
respect to cultural background or the subjects differ from one
another. Though the methodological problems resulting from
(the need for) translation are virtually ubiquitous, their visibil-
ity is clearly greater when cultural differences are paralleled
by language, rather than dialect differences.

Probably as a result of the dominance of survey research in
sociology, much of the concern with translation as a methodological issue has focused on problems of comparability between
paper-and-pencil instruments. Translation of such instruments
is primarily undertaken by bilinguals working more-or-less in
isolation, and it is essentially nonsocial behavior. One need
only read Phillips (1960) account of his experiences in working

*Preparation of this paper was supported in part by Research Training Grant 5T01
HD001 64 of the National Institute of Child Health and Human Development. Addi-
tional support was provided by the Department of Sociology of the University of
Manitoba. This support and the comments of Mahadeo L. Apte, Alan C. Kerckhoff,
Ryali Rajagopal, and Edward A. Tiryakian are gratefully acknowledged.

through an interpreter while interviewing in Thailand to realize that translation also occurs in *social* situations—situations
amenable to sociological analysis. In any such setting the role
played by the interpreter is likely to exert considerable
influence on the evolution of group structure and on the
outcome of the interaction. For a sociologist conducting
interviews through an interpreter, the problem of maintaining rapport with him may give greater bearing upon
data quality than the time-honored problem of maintaining
respondent rapport!

International negotiations concerning trade agreements,
peace treaties, and the like constitute another area of potential
sociological interest in the role of the interpreter. Here sociological interest in the evolving social structure of a small group
of negotiators merges with the interests of social psychologists,
political scientics, and legal scholars in analysis of problem-
solving behavior. Whether one is interested in the legal interpretation of plurilingual treaties (Stevens, 1967; Germer,
1970), the politics of international crises (Young, 1967, 1968),
attitudes of various ethnic groups toward each other in multilingual societies (Gumperz, 1962; Ferguson, 1962; Lambert,
1967) or problems of integration of ethnic and liguistic minori-
ties (Ervin-Tripp, 1967; Gaarder, 1967; Macnamara, 1967) understanding the role and behavior of interpreters is likely to
prove relevant. Even in the context of domestic urban research "aspects of the role and status of the . . . translator in
relation to the researcher, and to the ongoing network of in-
migrant poor persons (especially in relation to the bureau-
cratic institutions of the city)" have been described as important and sociologically interesting by one investigator
(Kirchner, 1968). Understanding the role of the interpreter
may also aid understanding of interaction between people of
different statuses and backgrounds within a single-language
community. For example, paraphrasing, which may be viewed
as a special case of translation, commonly obtains in labor
negotiation, doctor-patient interaction, parent-child interaction, and resolution of disputes between dominant and
minority groups. In each case the parties to the interaction
differ in their vocabulary (e.g., technical versus nontechnical)
and in their understanding of the meanings of terms known in

common. Frequently, the services of an intermediary are needed for effective communication. The remainder of this chapter explores *some* factors that describe and determine the role of the interpreter in relation to others involved in bilingual (or multilingual) interaction.

Basic Elements of Translation Situations

To facilitate analysis of the role of the interpreter a brief outline of a set of minimal conditions that are necessarily present in translation situations follows.

1. Typically, translation occurs in social situations involving interaction among a least three persons.

2. These actors may be identified as producer, interpreter,[1] and consumer. In some cases "producer" and "consumer" are roles adopted interchangably by a single participant. In others they are played by unique individuals. The dual role situation may be illustrated by a multilingual conference, whereas the separate role situation might be exemplified by a translated lecture. At times it may be convenient to refer to both producer and consumer together as clients of the interpreter, since both use his services.

3. It follows that the role of the interpreter is pivotal to the entire social process. In the type case of three participants, two may be assumed to be monolingual. The interpreter is, by definition, bilingual. The two monolingual actors would be unable to communicate with each other without his aid—except through a primitive set of gestures.

Roles of the Interpreter and some Hypotheses about his Behavior

The Interpreter as Bilingual. There is a growing body of literature dealing with the nature and types of bilingualism. For example, studies by Lambert and his associates (1955, 1958) have shown that the linguistic behavior of bilinguals is influenced by the order in which they learned the languages at their command, the relative dominance of their languages, and the extent to which the language systems merge. A bilingual's characteristics with respect to each of these dimensions

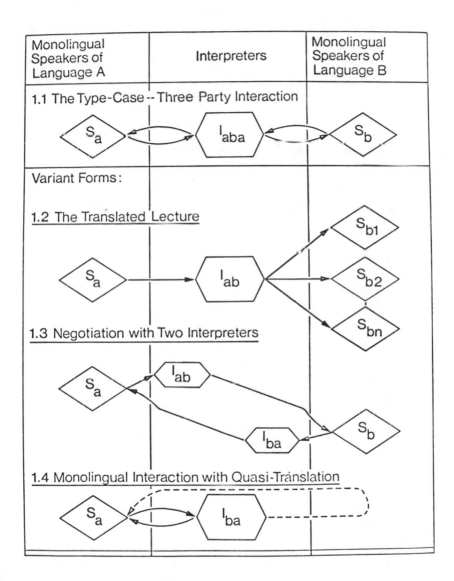

Monolingual Speakers of Language A	Interpreters	Monolingual Speakers of Language B

1.1 The Type-Case -- Three Party Interaction

S_a I_{aba} S_b

Variant Forms:

1.2 The Translated Lecture

S_a I_{ab} S_{b1} S_{b2} S_{bn}

1.3 Negotiation with Two Interpreters

S_a I_{ab} I_{ba} S_b

1.4 Monolingual Interaction with Quasi-Translation

S_a I_{ba}

seem to have implications for the role of the interpreter. Because the empirical studies of bilingualism are imprecise regarding the interrelations among them, they are discussed independently here.

Most bilinguals learn one language first—although second-language learning may take place quite early in childhood. The child of bilingual parents may be an exception to this if his parents speak to him in two or more languages from infancy.[2] If a bilingual mother chooses terms of endearment from one, rather than another language when addressing her child, he is likely that this language will take on the significance of a "mother tongue" (c.f. Pieris, 1951)—even if she uses another language for communicating different sorts of information. Basically the mother-tongue idea implies that the speaker generalizes some of the warm affectual responses to the mother and comes to associate them with the language in question.[3]

It follows that bilinguals are more likely to have positively affective reactions to the first language learned than to languages learned later. This identification with language may be observed in situations in which language choice is unconscious and situationally irrelevant—as with love-making or silent counting (c.f. Vildomec, 1963, p. 14). For the interpreter the consequence is a somewhat greater probability that he will identify with monolingual speakers of his mother-tongue than with speakers of other languages, *ceteris paribus.*

Of course, all other things are unlikely to be equal. Another matter that must be considered is linguistic dominance. A bilingual's dominant language is the one which is preferred or easier to use. Clearly, in many cases this is the first language learned, in which case the situation reduces to that previously discussed. The correlation between primacy of language learning and dominance is, however, imperfect. Many people spend the majority of their lives using a language other than the first one learned—and my even forget their mother-tongue. In these cases the second or later learned language becomes the bilingual's dominant language. For the interpreter, linguistic dominance has two consequences that they may be expected to obtain whether the dominant language is also the first language learned.

First, it is generally easier to understand a language than to speak it with facility. It follows that a bilingual translating to his dominant language may be expected to meet with more success than when he is translating from it, ceteris paribus.

The second consequence of linguistic dominance relates to the interpreter's likely identification with his clients. The situation is similar to that encountered in the case of primacy. Dominance, however, must be treated separately from primacy, because its effects may either reinforce or counteract those of primacy. In general, it is expected that the greater the linguistic dominance the more likely an interpreter will identify with the speakers of the dominant language, rather than with clients speaking his "other" language.

A third aspect of bilingualism to be considered involves the relationships between symbols in the bilingual's languages and their empirical referents. As Haugen (1956, p. 69) phrases it, the issue is "the extent to which two language systems remain *distinct* (coexistent, coordinate) or *merge* (compound, suboridinative)." In learning a second language by the traditional school approach, the student learns that a new word, say, *samfund*, is a translation equivalent of a word in his native language (in this case, society). He equates the meanings entirely. This procedure is followed throughout the language learning process. Ervin and Osgood (1954) term a bilingual who operates in this merged fashion a compound bilingual. In contrast, a coordinate bilingual associates samfund and society with their empirical referents, maintaining two distinct linguistic systems. These two polar types of bilingualism are schematically represented by Figure 2.

Lambert and his associates (1958, p. 243) have shown that conceptual independence is correlated with separation of the context of language learning. Their empirical findings lend support to the Ervin and Osgood (1954) hypotheses. The following remarks from their paper deserve special attention:

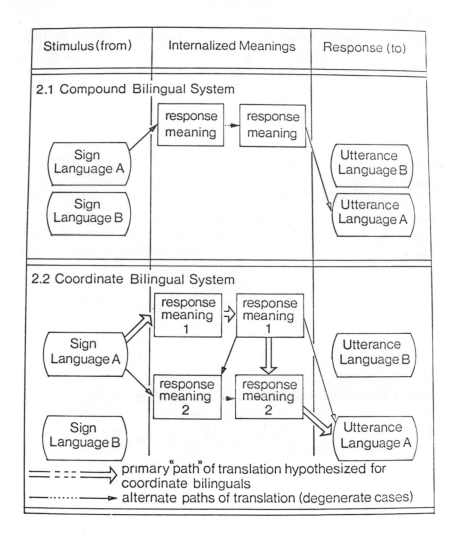

"The coordinate bilinguals, in contrast to the compound bilinguals, appear to have more functionally independent language systems. If their coordinateness has been developed through experience in culturally distinct contenxts, they will have comparatively different meanings for concepts translated into their two languages. Coordinate and compound bilinguals, however, appear to have equal facility in switching from one language to the other." (Lambert et al., 1958, p. 243)

What might be the significance of variation along the compound-coordinate[4] continuum for the interpreter's role? It seems probable that persons who are relatively close to the coordinate end of the continuum will be more likely to render translations that evoke responses among "consumers" similar to those that the original utterances would evoke among monolinguals speaking the producer's language. This seems to follow from the facts that (1) for purposes of translation they appear to image the referent of a given statement in the source language, shift languages with this image in mind, and render a translation based on a closely equivalent meaning, and (2) the "meanings" of two translation-equivalent terms are rarely identical. The compound bilingual, and contrast, is limited to verbal-verbal associations—hence would be more likely to come up with a translation that is equivalent to the source language utterance only to the extent that the two sets of words share a common meaning (c.f. Foa, 1967). Thus we would expect that coordinate bilinguals will produce translations with greater meaning equivalence than compound bilinguals.

Further, with respect to the linguistic identification of the two polar types, differences would also be expected. The compound bilingual is, in one sense, more monocultural even though bilingual. The coordinate bilingual, in contrast, is both bicultural and bilingual. In the present context biculturalism refers to the ability to interpret experiences in the manner appropriate to either culture (c.f. Lambert et al., 1963; Voegelins, 1967). Monoculturalism, in contrast, implies ethnocentric interpretation—regardless of the language or context of the experiences being interpreted. The distinction is one of degree—and individual bilinguals are likely to be more-or-less bicultural.[5]

If coordinate bilinguals tend to be bicultural as well, whereas compound bilinguals are essentially monocultural, then the former's identification with one or another client will be harder to predict than the latter's. A reasonable expectation in the case of the compound bilingual is that he will identify with the client whose culture he shares in preference to a client with whom he is culturally at odds (c.f. Haugen, 1956). This identification would probably be reinforced by primacy and dominance in most instances. On the other hand, the identification of a coordinate bilingual, if any, must be predicted on the basis of other criteria to the extent that his coordinacy approaches the type case. A completely coordinate bilingual operates with equal, separate linguistic and cultural systems. Here, too, linguistic dominance is likely to be minimal, and the effects of primacy may be expected to be at least partially counteracted. The hypothesis suggested by this discussion may be stated as: An interpreter who tends toward compound bilingualism will identify with the client whose culture he shares, whereas one who tends toward coordinate bilingualism is more likely to remain neutral.

Ambiguities and conflicts of the interpreter role. The interpreter commonly serves two clients at the same time. He is the "man in the middle" with some obligations to both clients— and these obligations may not be entirely compatible. Phillips (1960), for example, describes both positive and negative consequences of this situational dilemma for his anthropological research in Thailand. Social psychologists have explored the implications of such situations in terms of role conflict.[6] Juxtaposition of a good summary of this research with Ekvall's (1960) account of his experience as interpreter reveals the relevance of several role-theoretical constructs for the interpreter's dilemma.

For example, Ekvall discusses a number of situations in which the details of his role as interpreter had to be worked out on an ad hoc basis. These illustrate the fact that the interpreter's role is always partially undefined—that is, the role prescriptions are objectively inadequate.[7] The interpreter's position is also characterized by role overload. Not only is it seldom entirely clear what he is to do, he is also frequently expected to do more than is objectively possible. This situation obtains under several conditions noted by Ekvall:

1. When everyone talks at once—the interpreter is simply unable to translate the entire flow of speech.

2. When the translation activity is carried on over too long a time period, introducing fatigue and mental strain.[8]

3. When a client talks extemporaneously with too few breaks and/or with too long between breaks.

The two types of role ambiguity discussed above are essentially problems of inconsistency within a single role. In the first instance the precise nature of that role is unclear. Should the interpreter be a mere echo, or should he be an advisor and ally? Should he inform his client of whispered, off-the-record remarks made by the other party to the interaction, or should he stick to the text? In the second instance, the issue is not what, but how much behavior is expected. In either event, a sociology of interpreter behavior should include propositions about the likely effects of the interpreter's efforts to cope with these ambiguities upon the ongoing interaction. Although there are insufficient empirical data available to allow specification of hypotheses, factors that should be examined may be identified. Among these are the relative power of the interpreter vis-a-vis his clients and his perceived hierarchy of obligations, both of which would influence the ligitimacy of alternative means of ambiguity reduction. For example, a powerful interpreter could solve the role overload problem simply by insisting that his clients take turns talking, pause often, and break off the exchange after an hour or two.

The interpreter, like the foreman, is occupationally vulnerable to counter pressures from his two clients. No matter what he does, one of them is apt to be displeased. Ekvall (1960) notes that in most situations involving international negotiations, such as the recent Paris Peace Talks, each party provides its own translator(s). This serves the purpose of eliminating many aspects of role strain by making the interpreter responsible to a single client. His identification with his principal then become possible without the complications of role conflict, and his linguistic ability becomes a part of the negotiating team's arsenal. In other cases, in which the interpreter is not so closely linked with a single client, role conflict is apt to present considerable difficulty.

In general, the interpreter's role is characterized by some degree of inadequacy of role prescription, role overload, and role conflict resulting from his pivotal position in the interaction network. Research is needed to allow specification of the conditions under which each of these characteristics obtains.

Power and the interpreter. Because the interests of three parties may be discovered in all translation situations, this section focuses on the power relations in the type case, and structural forms that deviate from the triad are not considered here. The previous section attended to the ambiguities of the interpreter's position as the man in the middle. The resulting weakness of his position is mitigated considerably by the fact that the interaction obtains would be impossible without his participation. Bilingualism constitutes a rare skill which the other parties to the interaction are unable or unwilling to acquire. To the extent that qualified interpreters are hard to find, and replace, the interpreter is cast in a highly important role vis-a-vis his clients. Thus his position in the middle has the advantage of power inherent in all positions which control scarce resources.[9] This advantage, when combined with the relative ambiguity of the interpreter's role, allows him considerable latitude in defining his own behavior vis-a-vis his clients. His behavior may, therefore, be expected to have an unusually great impact on the structure of the entire situation.

The interpreter's control over the interaction pattern that develops, and thereby over the structure of the triadic relationship, is founded in his ability to translate selectively. He may translate all that is said by both clients with as great fidelity as he can muster—or he may chose not to. His monolingual clients will be unable to ascertain the difference unless he oversteps rather wide bounds.

If the interpreter acts as a "faithful echo" of the remarks of *both* clients, he is in effect casting himself in the role of the nonpartisan. This, of course, is a difficult task—complicated by the considerations of bilingualism discussed above. There is reason to believe, however, that some interpreters have a neutral self-image, which appears most likely to occur when bilingualism and biculturalism are relatively well balanced. It would also seem reasonable to expect relatively greater impartiality on the part of multilinguals, or other persons for whom *neither* of the language spoken is primary or dominant.[10]

If the interpreter assumes the nonpartisan role, what would be expected regarding group structure and process and translation fidelity? Simmel's (1964, p. 147) classic essay on the triad offers some interesting insights into what might reasonable be expected. He observes that:

"A third mediating social element deprives conflicting claims of their affective qualities because it neutrally formulates and presents these claims to the two parties involved. Thus the circle that is fatal to all reconciliation is avoided: the vehemence of the one no longer provokes that of the other, which in turn intensifies that of the first, and so forth until the who relationship breaks down. Furthermore, because of the non-partisan each party to the conflict not only listens to more objective matters but is also forced to put the issue in more objective terms than it would if it confronted the other without mediation. For now it is important for each to win over the mediator."

This formulation of the mediator's role serves well to describe what we might expect of the nonpartisan interpreter. He would be likely to orient himself toward his listener as if he were echoing the other client with utmost fidelity. This orientation would presumably be the same when translating in either direction—always characerized by apparent personal detachment from the content of his translations. Under this facade would be considerable manipulation of communicative content in the direction of moderation and rationality. Hidden losses in fidelity would blunt angered words and soften rigid stances.

Simmel further develops this argument to note that nonpartisanship may be of different sorts. If the interpreter's nonpartisanship results from equal interest in the ends of both other parties, then we would expect modified transmittal as described above. In this case the interpreter would probably attempt to manipulate the interaction in the direction of a "just" outcome[11] whereby both clients would believe that they had maximized their own gains.

On the other hand, the interpreter's nonpartisanship might result from his total personal detachment from the situation. Rather than being equally pulled in both directions, he might be pulled in neither.[12] In such instances, instead of pseudofidelity, we should expect maximal attention to faithful interpretation—even to reproduction of intonation and gestural signs. The value-laden aspects of any utterance would likely come through with minimal filtering. His detachment would force his clients to work out their own differences, because any outcome would be acceptable to him. Thus the nonpartisan interpreter can either function as a fair, but covert manipulator, utilizing the power inherent in his monopoly of the means of communication, or he can remain a passive element in the interaction network. Factors leading translators to adopt one rather than the other of these orientations merit investigation.

The power of the interpreter need not be used impartially in the interests of both clients. Again, Simmel has anticipated some relevant considerations. It is clear that the interpretor may choose, for whatever reasons, to ally himself with one rather than the other client. The discussion of *Tertius Gaudens* contained in Simmel's (1964) essay on the triad stresses reasons for and implications of an opportunistic motivation. Simmel is concerned with the situation where the man in the middle derives advantage from choosing sides per se. An example of a client "competing for the favor of" (Simmel, 1964, p. 155) the interpreter is found in Phillips (1960) report that informants sometimes confided in his Thai interpreter with the request that their remarks *not* be conveyed to the outsider. It is unclear from Phillips account if there was hostility directed toward him in any of these situations, but it is unquestionable that anthropologists have occasionally been greeted with suspicion if not overt hostility. It is clear that the anthropologist, working through a native interpreter, must encourage his translator to ally with him if he is to accomplish his ethnographic task. Equally obvious is the fact that members of the society under study are likely to view the interpreter as something of a deviant—and may seek to "save" him from the outsider's corrupting influence. The interpreter is then called upon to take sides—and benefits of one sort or another are probably offered to entice him to do so.

The successful anthropologist breaks down suspicion and eventually gains a measure of acceptance into the host society. Simmel (1964, p. 160) has observed that this will inevitably result in the destruction of the favorable position of the *tertius*. Phillips (1960) discusses this in terms of his eventual learning of Thai, after which he was able to obtain information which the interpreter was denied.[13] Ekval (1960) recalls an assignment in the Pacific during World War II in which his duties included reprimanding Chinese officers for inadequate performance of their units in the previous day's attack. He notes that his language ability eliminated the need for an interpreter, with the dual effects that (1) he adhered more closely to the strong language of the original message. and (2) "at the same time there was no one else present to spead an exaggerated version of the reprimand to all the eager ears which had no business to hear" (Ekvall, 1960, p. 31). This is but one of several example Ekvall offers from his experience that illustrate the way in which the structure of the situation changes, and the power of the interpreter disappears, if a client happens to be bilingual. Thus it appears that there are at least three possible ways in which the power of the interpreter might influence the interaction, and their frequency of occurrence and the attendant anticedents and consequences merit empirical investigators.

Summary and Conclusions

This chapter is offered as an initial indication of the relevance of the role of the interpreter for sociolinguistic and sociological theory and research. It has sought to shed some light on determinants of that role and to illuminate some aspects of translation situations. The role of the interpreter in face-to-face interaction has been explored through examination of some implications of selected literature relevant to three aspects of that role:

1. The interpreter as a bilingual.
2. The interpretor as a man in the middle, subject to client expectations that are often conflicting.
3. The interpreter as a power figure, exercising power as a result of monopolization of the means of communication.

There are undoubtedly other aspects of the interpreter's role and of translations situations that merit consideration. Three broad groups of potentially relevant factors are mentioned here, although adequate discussion of them would require expansion of this chapter beyond reasonable bounds. One group of variables that is particularly well known to sociologists as exerting influence on interaction in varied contexts includes the relative statuses of the participants with respect to social class, education, sex, age, and so forth. Other variables that may prove relevant are the situational factors, some of which have been noted in passing here. In addition to variations in the number of participants and in the distribution of language skills among them, one would expect the arena of interaction (whether political, military, academic, religious, and so on) and the level of tension (c.f. Young, 1967, 1968) to influence emergent role relations. Finally, the relative prestige of the national or ethnic groups involved and the associated attitudes toward the languages spoken are of potential interest (c.f. Tucker and Lambert, 1969; Lambert et al., 1965; Lambert, 1967). The addition of these three groups of variables to those discussed in this chapter as factors influencing the role of the interpreter brings us to the clear, if cliched, conclusion: further investigation is required.

FOOTNOTES

1. Clearly the interpreter is both "consumer" and "producer" at once. He "consumes" the utterance in the source language, and "produces" an utterance in the target language. This is true for any item that is conveyed in the interaction, while his clients *either* produce *or* consume any single item—hence the distinction drawn here.

2. Vildomec (1963, pp. 25ff.) cites three studies in which the authors report in detail on the development of their own bilingual children. Of particular interest in the present context is his discussion of reports by Leopold (1939) and Ronjat (1913). The former study is offered as a model of thoroughness, and the bilingualism was developed largely as a result of unsystematic parental influences. The Ronjat child, in contrast, was systematically encouraged in bilingualism by use of the one-person–one-language approach (his mother spoke only German, his father French to him).

3. In this regard it is interesting to note that Louis Ronjat is reported by Vildomec (1963:25) to have preferred German, the language spoken by his mother, for literary self-expression and French, his father's language, when dealing with technical matters. His ability in either language at the time of expression of these preferences (young adulthood) was adjudged equal (note, however, that French was also the language of his early formal schooling).

4. Macnamara (1970) is highly critical of the compound-coordinate distinction. The present writer agrees with his point that ". . . differences between the semantic systems of languages might well give rise to a whole range of bilinguals who vary in the extent to which they keep the semantic systems of their two languages distinct" (p. 30). When considering comparisons among bilinguals having skills in *several pairs* of languages the matter of differences between semantic systems of the several languages clearly muddles the picture presented by the compound-coordinate distinction, and Macnamara's suggestion that a distinction based on degree of sematic interference would be more useful is well taken. On the other hand, if comparisons are made among bilinguals having *a common pair of languages,* then the matter of their relative ability to keep the semantic systems of these two languages distinct must necessarily vary independently of the semantic systems of the languages in question —since the latter are effectively held constant. Under such controlled conditions one would expect interindividual variation, and it is the contention of this writer that the compound-coordinate distinction conceived in ideal-typical terms is conceptually useful for understanding interpreter behavior under these conditions.

5. It would seem likely that any degree of biculturalism must be accompanied by some degree of bilingualism. The reverse, however, is not necessarily true.

6. Excellent summaries of this literature are found in Secord and Back-man (1964), Shibutani (1961), and Newcomb et al. (1965).

7. On the objective inadequacy of role prescriptions, see Newcomb et al. (1965, p. 399). Ekvall (1960, p. 34) describes an experience during World War II when he was assigned the task of interrupting "official" interpretation whenever it seemed to him to be in error. He notes that "It was a thankless job . . . yet slowly the value of a check and recheck of what was transposed from language to language became established." Other instances when the interpreter's role was worked out on the spot are described throughout the book.

8. In order to reduce this difficulty the United Nations, for example, limits translation to 1-hour periods, and considers 2 hours total translation time as a day's work.

9. Among the more interesting examples of power accruing to those who control scarce resources is the case of the French tobacco monopoly where automation has reduced uncertainty to problems of machine breakdown. The ability to repair machines has thus become a highly valued resource—and the maintenance staff has been able to challenge the power of line personnel and officials (Crozier, as cited in Blau and Scott, 1962). Much of the literature on communication networks suggests that persons who are centrally located are likely to exert more influence on the outcome(s) of group interaction than persons who are not so favorably situated with respect to communication channel resources (e.g., Bavelas, 1950).

10. Some evidence of the occurrence of such neutrality may be extrapolated from Useem (1963) and Useem et al (1963). Bohannan (1965) has remarked that "secondary ethnocentrism" is common among biculturals, and suggests the learning of a third culture as a means of counteracting this tendency and attaining a neutral perspective.

11. "Outcome is used here to mean "result of the interaction." The term seems appropriate in most cases in which an interpreter is employed —with the possible exception of instances in which interaction is based on sociability alone. The "justice" of any outcome may, of course, be differentially perceived by the several participants to the interaction. To the extent the manipulative translator, through biculturalism and other mechanisms, is able to perceive the interaction adequately from the perspectives of *both* clients, a shared perspective may obtain.

12. The situation of bidirectional pull seems akin to the psychological concept of approach-approach conflict (Barker, 1942, 1946). The contrasting situation in which there is pull in neither direction is similar to Parsons (1951) notion of affective neutrality.

13. These instances clearly indicate the destruction of the translator's power. For example, "I did not tell Kham Sing because he is a Thai and an expert at gossiping but . . ." (Phillips, 1960:298).

REFERENCES

Anderson, R. On the comparability of meaningful stimuli in cross-cultural research. *Sociometry*, 1967, *30*, 124–136.

Anderson, R. Hidden translation problems in mono-cultural research. *Sociological Focus*, 1969, *3*, 33–42.

Barker, R. An experimental study in the resolution of conflict by children. In Q. McNemar and M. Merrill, Eds. *Studies in personality*. New York: McGraw-Hill, 1942, pp. 13–34.

Barker, R. An experimental study of the relationship between certainty of choice and the relative valence of alternatives. *Journal of Personality*, 1946, *15*, 41–52.

Bavelas, A. Communication patterns in task-oriented groups. *The Journal of the Acoustical Society of America*, 1950, *22*, 725–730.

Blau, P., and Scott, W. *Formal organizations: a comparative approach*. San Francisco: Chandler, 1962.

Bohannan, P. Personal communication, 1965.

Deutscher, I. Asking questions cross-culturally: some problems of linguistic comparability. In H. Becker et al, Eds. *Institutions and the person*. Chicago: Aldine, 1968, pp. 318–341.

Deutscher, I. Asking questions (and listening to answers): a review of some sociological precedents and problems. *Sociological Focus*, 1969, *3*, 13–32.

Ekvall, R. *Faithful echo*. New York: Twayne, 1960.

Ervin, S., and Osgood, C. Second language learning and bilingualism. In, C. Osgood and T. Sebeok, Eds. Psycholinguistics. *Journal of Abnormal and Social Psychology*, 1954, supplement 49, 136–146.

Ervin-Tripp, S. An Issei learns English. *The Journal of Social Issues*, 1967, *23*, 78–90.

Ferguson, C. The language factor in national development. In F. Rice, Ed. *Study of the roles of second languages in Asia, Africa, and Latin America*. Washington, D.C.: Center for Applied Linguistics, 1962.

Foa, U. Differentiation in cross-cultural communication. In L. Thayer, Ed. *Communication concepts and perspectives*. Washington, D.C.: Spartan, 1967, pp. 135–151.

Gaardner, A. Organization of the bilingual school. *The Journal of Social Issues*, 1967, *23*, 110–120.

Germer, P. Interpretation of plurilingual treaties: a study of Article 33 of the Vienna Convention on the law of Treaties. *Harvard International Law Journal*, 1970, *11*, 400–427.

Grimshaw, A. Language as obstacle and as data in sociological research. *Items*, 1969(a), *23*, 17–26.

Grimshaw, A. Some problematic aspects of communication in cross racial research in the United States. *Sociological Focus*, 1969(b), *3*, 67–85.

Gumperz, J. Language problems in the rural development of north India. In F. Rice, Ed. *Study of the roles of second languages in Asia, Africa, and Latin America*. Washington, D.C.: Center for Applied Linguistics, 1962.

Haugen, E. *Bilingualism in the Americas: A bibliography and research guide*. American Dialect Society 26: University of Alabama Press, 1956.

Kirchner, C. Personal communication, 1968.

Lambert, W. Measurement of the linguistic dominance of bilinguals. *Journal of Abnormal and Social Psychology*, 1955, *50*, 197–200.

Lambert, W. A social psychology of bilingualism. *Journal of Social Issues*, 1967, *23*, 91–109.

Lambert, W. et al. The influence of language-acquisition context on bilingualism. *Journal of Abnormal and Social Psychology*, 1968, *56*, 239–244.

Lambert. W. et al. Attitidunal and cognitive aspects of intensive study of a second language. *Journal of Abnormal and Social Psychology*, 1963, *66*, 358–368.

Lambert, W. Evaluational reactions of Jewish and Arab adolescents to dialect and language variations. *Journal of Personality and Social Psychology*, 1965, *2*, 84–90.

Leopold, W. Speech development of a bilingual child: a linguists record. As cited in Vildomec, 1963. (originally published in 1939).

Macnamara, J. The bilingual's linguistic performance—a psychological overview. *Journal of Social Issues*, 1967, *23*, 58–77.

Macnamara, J. Bilingualism and thought. In J. Alatis, Ed. *Report of the Twenty-first Round Table Meeting on Linguistics and Language Studies*. Washington, D.C.: Georgetown University Press, 1970.

Newcomb, T. et al. *Social Psychology*. New York: Holt, Rinehart, and Winston, 1965.

Parsons, T. *The social system*. Glencoe, Ill.: The Free Press, 393–427.

Phillips, H. Problems of translation and meaning in field work. *Human Organization*, 1960, *18*, 184–192.

Pieris, R. Bilingualism and cultural margniality. *British Journal of Sociology*, 1951, *2*, 328–339.

Ronjat, J. *Le developpement du language observe chez un enfant bilingue*. As cited in Vildomec, 1963 (originally published in 1913).

Secord, P., and Backman, C. *Social Psychology*. New York: McGraw-Hill, 1964.

Shibutani, T. *Society and personality: an interactionist approach to social psychology*. Englewood Cliffs, New Jersey: Prentice-Hall, 1971.

Simmel, G. The triad. In K. Wolff, Trans. and Ed. *The Sociology of Georg Simmel.* New York: The Free Press, 1964.

Stevens, L. The principle of linguistic equality in judicial proceedings and in the interpretation of plurilingual instruments: the regime linguistique in the Court of Justice of the European communities. *Northwestern Law Review,* 1967, *62,* 701–734.

Tucker, G. and Lambert, W. White and Negro listeners' reactions to various American-English dialects. *Social Forces,* 1969, *47,* 463–468.

Useem, J. The community of man: a study of the third culture. *Centennial Review,* 1963, *7,* 481–489.

Useem, J. et al. Men in the middle of the third culture: the roles of American and non-western people in cross-cultural administration. *Human Organization,* 1963, *22,* 169–179.

Vildomec, V. *Multilingualism.* Leyden: A.M. Sythoff, 1963.

Voegelin, C., and Voegelin, F. Anthropological linguistics and translation. In *To honor Roman Jacobson, essays on the occassion of his seventieth birthday,* 11 October 1966, Volume 3. Janua Linguarum Studia, Memoriae Nicolai Van Wijk Dedicata, Series Maior 33. The Hague: Mouton, 1967.

Webb, E. et al. *Unobtrusive measures: non-reactive research in the social sciences.* Chicago: Rand-Mcnally, 1966.

Young, O. *The intermediaries: third parties in international crises.* Princeton: Princeton University Press, 1967.

Young, O. *The politics of force: bargaining during international crises.* Princeton: Princeton University Press, 1968.

CHAPTER 7

Approaches Toward Minimizing Translation

HARRY C. TRIANDIS

IT IS OFTEN SAID that one way to define a concept is to circumscribe its limits and to define its opposite. My self-imposed task in this chapter is to discuss how to minimize translation, in order to throw some light on translation itself. In doing so I will present some research tools different than those suggested by Brislin (1970, and his chapter for this volume).

Broad Theoretical Considerations

In their important paper on translation, Werner and Campbell (1970) argued that one way to improve translations is to increase the total context of what is translated. As the message includes more and more redundancy and is set in a larger context, its meaning becomes clearer, any errors of translation become less important, and overlaps in meaning produce common ground in each language that is likely to be equivalent.

In any translation one has to face the problem of the extent to which what he is to translate is culture-specific (emic) or universal (etic). It is easy to see that etic concepts, such as fire, moon, and sun, produce fewer translation difficulties than emic concepts, such as the Greek concept of *philotimo* or the Anglo-American concept of *fairness*.

By definition, it is impossible to translate perfectly an emic concept. One can discuss the context in which the concept might be used, its antecedents and consequences (see Triandis et al, 1972, Chapter 7), its synonyms and antonyms, if any, but exact translation is extremely difficult, if not impossible. Even native speakers have difficulties giving really good definitions of emic concepts.

In fact, many abstract concepts, such as *beauty* are so culture specific that one can use linguistic conventions to translate them, but really can not do so adequately. For example, the concept *sympathy* in English, connotes *pity*. The *Britannica Dictionary* defines it as the "quality of being affected by the state of the other with corresponding feelings in kind" and gives *pity* as a third choice. Yet American subjects tested by Triandis et al. (1972, p. 251) considered pity and compassion as the salient aspects of its antecedents, rather than similarity of affect when thinking about *sympathy*. Greeks, on the other hand, clearly favored the primary definition (after all, it is a Greek word) and saw *goodness, good character, trust, good behavior,* and *admiration,* rather than *pity* or *compassion* as antecedents of *sympathy*. The point is that because of the derivation of the English word from the Greek, a translation of one into the other is reliably done, yet although the dictionary gives a definition that is close to the Greek, the American users of the word deal with it in ways that are somewhat different from the primary definition. Furthermore, sympathy is not an enduring quality of a person in English, but a temporary emotional state. In the languages of the Latin family (sympatique, sympatico, etc.) it is a relatively permanent quality of individuals. The "equivalent" English translation, although not quite adequate, is the word *nice*.

In short, in order to translate one needs to relate the concept to context, antecedents-consequences, or other settings in which it might be used.

One way to do this is to define an emic concept in terms of etic attributes. This is essentially the approach used by Osgood (1971), Triandis, Vassiliou and Nassiakou (1968), and many others. We return to a discussion of the details of this approach shortly, but before we do this it is worth noting some universal attributes of human behavior.

There is considerable evidence now that some basic dimensions of social and cognitive behavior are universal. We can think of these as the etic dimensions that can be used to define emic concepts. These dimensions appear in studies of the meaning of words, behavior or emotions; in studies of interpersonal behavior; in animal and human data; in analyses of mothers' behaviors toward their children; in personality studies; and so on. A review of many studies from different areas of psychology suggesting such convergence can be found in Triandis (1976). Briefly, the basic dimensions of connotative meaning as discovered by Osgood (1971) are evaluation, potency, and activity. The basic dimensions of behavioral intentions (Triandis, 1964; Triandis, Vassiliou and Nassiakou, 1968; Foa and Foa, 1974; Benjamin, 1974) include association-dissociation and superordination-subordination, as well as hostility, which turns out to be quite "active", and intimacy. The dimensions of emotion (see Schlosberg, 1954; Triandis & Lambert, 1958) include pleasant-unpleasant, attention-rejection (which turns out to be related to "control" or potency), and tension which related to activity. Animals are described as engaged in grooming or as having pecking orders (e.g., Mason, 1967). Mothers are described as warm-cold versus autonomous-controlling (e.g., Schaefer, 1971). Personality theorists describe variations in personality along the dimensions warm-cold and dominant-submissive (e.g., Leary, 1957). These dimensions are emerging up and down the phylogenetic scale, cross-culturally and developmentally. In short, they provide a universal framework. If we relate our emic concepts to this framework we will be able to achieve equivalence, by measuring what is unique (emic) in terms of a common yardstick (etic dimensions). Of course, much of the surplus meaning of emic concepts is lost in such translations. For example, if we learn that apple flavor is related to price in the same way as orange flavor is related to price, we realize that an apple or orange flavor is "a good thing" but we do not know much more about the essential qualities of these attributes.

Factor Analysis as a Method to Produce Equivalence of the Framework

An example of studies that employed this approach and hence minimal translation comes from the work of Osgood (1971). In this project 100 "culture fair" nouns were translated, via double translation, into some 25 different languages. By "Culture fair" is meant that these nouns were easy to translate, and double translation resulted in easy retrieval of the original word in many cultures. For example, concepts like house, fire and stone apparently are culture fair.

This was the only translation used by Osgood and his colleagues. From that point on, all the work was done following identical procedures, but independently in each culture. Specifically, subjects gave qualifiers as responses to each noun. For example: "The *house is . . .*"; "The . . . *house.*" The most frequently obtained qualifiers, which were generated as responses to diverse nouns, were employed in *semantic differentials.* Thus, for example, one item was

house

good_'_'_'_'_'_bad

In each culture, the 100 concepts were judged on 50 scales. The 5000 judgments required for this step were divided among different subjects so that each judgment was made by 20 or more subjects. The mean judgment from these 20 subjects was recorded in a 100-by-50 matrix. Correlations among the 50 scales, based on 100 observations per variable, were the basis of a factor analysis. Only after the analysis were the highest loading scales translated into English. It was generally found that in all cultures the highest loading scales form similar clusters, reflecting the dimensions of evaluation *(good, clean, honest)* potency *(strong, large, heavy)* and activity *(fast, active, alive).*

As a further check, a pan-cultural factor analysis was performed. Here the data from k cultures were lined up so that the 100 common nouns represented one side of the matrix and the $50k$ scales represent the other. The $50k$-by-$50k$ matrix of intercorrelations, based on 100 observations was computed. A principal factor analysis, with unities in the communalities, was used to reduce the complexity of the data. Thus factors emerged with loadings on each of the scales. At that point translation permitted the discovery of "what scales are used equivalently in each culture." It turned out that the evaluation, potency, and activity factors (clusters) emerged again from this analysis.

The scales that loaded highly on the same factor appeared

to have similar meanings in *common.* For example, the American scales might be *good, beautiful* and *fair,* and·the Kannada Indian *nectarlike, good* and *desirable.* Obviously, such sets of concepts have similar *common* meanings; in both cases they imply evaluation.

Note that the etic dimension is at a higher level of abstraction than the emic. This is probably true in most other investigations. In analyses of cognitive structures, at very high levels of abstraction we reach the point where biologically transmitted mechanisms play significant roles, while the effects of culture become unimportant. The unity of mankind is clear at that level.

This can be seen even better when we examine other kinds of data. First, consider what happens when instead of factor analysis we use multidimensional scaling. Multidimensional scaling requires no prior assumptions whatever about translation. One takes a sample of stimuli from some domain—say, pictures of emotions—and asks people from different cultures to make some kind of judgment of distance. A popular judgment involves three stimuli, *A, B,* and *C,* and the subject is asked to choose one that is most different from the other two. This is a simple judgment of dissimilarity. If he chooses *B,* this means that *B* is further from *A* and *C* than the latter are from each other. After making several such judgments, a subject provides the psychologist with the basis for the construction of a "map" of the way the stimuli are organized in the phenomenal field of the subject. It is only after this "map" is available that one needs to ask what the dimensions which contrast the different parts of the map do represent. When this is done, we find that the dimensions have much in common with evaluation, potency, and activity. In short, these dimensions emerge even when we use very different methods.

Second, consider what happens when we change the kinds of concepts and scales that we use. In studies by Triandis, Vassiliou, and Nassiakou (1968) and Triandis et al. (1972) samples of students from many parts of the world were asked to indicate how they would behave. This was done with respect to two kinds of concepts: stimulus persons and roles. The latter judgment, for instance, asked subjects whether in their culture it was considered appropriate for a father to beat his son:

Father-son

would_'_'_'_'_'_'_'_would not

beat

In most studies, 60 roles were judged on 30 behaviors, with a complete replication with another 60 roles and 30 behaviors in each culture. The highly replicated factors from each culture were compared across cultures. Typically, four factors were obtained in each culture: association versus dissociation, superordination versus subordination, active hostility versus no hostility, and intimacy versus formality.

The first two factors, which did account for most of the common variance, have a strong similarity with the evaluation and potency factors. Furthermore, they are similar to factors obtained in analyses of the behaviors of mothers toward their children in different cultures (Minturn and Lambert, 1964), to analyses of the conditions under which people use *vous* versus *tu,* which, according to Brown (1965) depend on solidarity and dominance; analyses of the social behavior of apes (Mason, 1964), which also show the dimensions of solidarity (grooming, playing with) and dominance (pecking orders); analysis of personality (Leary, 1957); studies of interpersonal behavior (Bales, 1950); leader behavior (Stogdill and Coons, 1957); emotion (Schlosberg, 1954); and reported own behavior (Lorr and McNair, 1965). When similarities emerge across both the phylogenetic level and cross-culturally, it is reasonable to assume that the dimensions are independent of culture (Klineberg, 1954).

In short, one must recognize that at least at the level of abstraction used by Osgood, the dimensions of qualification of nouns have equivalence that suggests universality and a biological emphasis.

The great advantage of discovering such universal, etic dimensions is that it is possible to use them as the framework for comparisons. Emic dimensions that are related in reliable ways to etic dimensions can be compared using the etic dimensions as a bridge.

The argument can be summarized as follows: If two constructs, concepts, or dimensions behave equivalently, in a particular theoretical network, they can be employed as equivalent. Of course, we must remain fully aware that this is a useful convention, rather than reality. For many situations it does not matter that the constructs are not identical. In fact, it is better to deal with such nonidentical constructs, fully realizing that they are not identical, rather than to assume that they are identical simply because one has obtained, say, a good translation from one to the other.

Facet Analysis for Equivalence of Framework

Guttman (1959), Foa (1965), Jordan (1968), and others have used facet analysis as an approach toward avoidance of translation. The basic idea is simple. To increase specificity, consider stimuli that have four elements a, b, c, and d in common, and imagine that each element takes two values: $+$ and $-$. One can construct 16 stimuli with all possible combinations of these elements. Each element is a *facet*. The logic of construction of such elements makes specific predictions about the relationships among such stimuli. For example, using the convention that an element that has no sign is positive, we might compare the following three stimuli: a, b, c, d; a, b, $c-$, $d-$, and $a-$, b, $c-$, $d-$. The logic requires that reactions to the second and third stimuli be more highly correlated than reactions to the first and second, if each of the four elements is of equal weight. The reason is that the second and third stimuli have three elements in common, whereas the first and the second have only two. The first and the third are even more different, having only one common element. In short, the logic of stimulus construction tells us what to expect concerning the correlations of the responses toward the stimuli.

The assumption that the four elements are of equal importance is very limiting. However, if we know or can hypothesize a rank order of importance, then we can incorporate it in the analysis. Let us say that we know that the most important element is b, followed by d, c, and a, in that order. Let us arrange the stimuli as follows:

Note that as we move from top to bottom, the value of the least important elements changes many times, whereas the

$b+$	$d+$	$c+$	$a+$
$b+$	$d+$	$c+$	$a-$
$b+$	$d+$	$c-$	$a+$
$b+$	$d+$	$c-$	$a-$
$b+$	$d-$	$c+$	$a+$
$b+$	$d-$	$c+$	$a-$
$b+$	$d-$	$c-$	$a+$
$b+$	$d-$	$c-$	$a-$
$b-$	$d+$	$c+$	$a+$
$b-$	$d+$	$c+$	$a-$
$b-$	$d+$	$c-$	$a+$
$b-$	$d+$	$c-$	$a-$
$b-$	$d-$	$c+$	$a+$
$b-$	$d-$	$c+$	$a-$
$b-$	$d-$	$c-$	$a+$
$b-$	$d-$	$c-$	$a-$

value of the most important changes only once. What this means is that the elements are arranged so that they produce few dramatic changes of meaning. Now if we compute the 16-by-16 matrix of intercorrelations we should obtain a simplex matrix, that is, one in which the entries near the diagonal are large whereas those far from the diagonal are either very small of negative. Such a pattern *confirms* the hypothesis concerning the relative importance of the elements.

Now suppose that in each culture we have made hypotheses about the relative importance of the elements in each stimulus, and we tested them by computing the correlations among the stimuli and confirmed our results. Then we can argue that the rank order of importance in each culture is the one that was hypothesized, which could be either the same order (a case that is usual) or even a different order (logically possible). For example, we know (Triandis and Triandis, 1962) that prejudiced Americans object to blacks as neighbors, but object to black physicians less than to black truck drivers; Greeks object to the religion of a person (if it is different from their own) more than to his race, so they will reject a Mohammedan or Jew more than a black. We can predict, then, the following orders of social distance in the two cultures:

If we obtain simplex matrices from the American and Greek data and confirm our hypotheses, we can state that differences in religion in Greece have similar implications for social organization as do differences in race in the United States. How-

	In America	In Greece
Small		
	White, physician of same religion	Same religion, white, physician
	White, physician of different religion	Same religion, black, physician
	White, truck driver of same religion	Same religion, white, truck driver
	White, truck driver of different religion	Same religion, black, truck driver
	Black, physician of same religion	Different religion, white, physician
	Black, physician of different religion	Different religion, black, physician
	Black, truck driver of same religion	Different religion, white, truck driver
	Black, truck driver of different religion	Different religion, black, truck driver
Large distance		

ever, some caution is required when making such a statement, because the thresholds of rejection are at different points on an etic social distance scale. For example, Greeks may not accept people of a different religion as "good friends", but they generally accept them in formal settings—neighborhood, jobs, schools, and the like. Some Americans do not accept blacks even in such formal settings. Hence we have a situation in which the facets have equivalent functions, but there are some important differences in the way the subjects respond to the equivalent facets that are not captured by this approach.

To deal with this difficulty it is useful to take the dimension of social distance as the focus of our study and to establish equivalence in what is meant by social distance in the two cultures. This we did in some other studies.

Establishing Equivalence on a Single Dimension

Consider the concept of social distance. As a theoretical construct this concept exists in many cultures. However, the way the concept is operationalized in each culture may be quite different. Thus although some behaviors, such as marrying somebody, are generally very positive, and some, such as killing somebody, generally negative, there are many behaviors that are quite ambiguous. For example, to exclude someone from the neighborhood has definite meaning in the United States but makes little sense in Japan. In Japan one would normally invite his neighbor to tea even if he strongly disapproved of him. To be polite to one's neighbor is a very important norm in Japan.

To describe the solution to the problem of equivalence, in the case of the dimension of social distance we need to engage in a brief digression.

For many years social psychologists have been asking people how they intend to respond to hypothetical persons, whom they described by mentioning their nationality, race, religion, or what have you. Studies of social distance examine the relationship between these characteristics of people and the way typical members of different cultures react to them. In some cultures people give a large weight to one characteristic and a small weight to another, whereas in other cultures the reverse happens. It is important to learn which cultures are particularly sensitive to which particular characteristic.

The methodology developed by Triandis and Triandis (1960) provides information about such weights. Hypothetical persons formed by systematically varying different characteristics —race, nationality, religion, social class—are presented to samples in each culture.

After pretests, in which students in each culture rank-ordered a large number of racial, national, religious, and occupational groups, we selected one racial group that was liked and one that was disliked, a national group that was liked and one that was disliked, and so on—and thus constructed $2 \times 2 \times 2 \times 2 = 16$ hypothetical stimulus persons. Each stimulus person had a high or a low value on each of the four dimensions under study. We then asked new samples of students to react to each stimulus. These reactions were obtained on a scale, which was precalibrated to represent a continuum from maximum social distance (I would gladly kill this person) to minimum social distance (I would marry this person).

Of course, most of the responses were at points intermediate between these two extremes. Using a procedure developed by

Thurstone in the 1930s (see Edwards, 1957) it is possible to obtain a "value" for each statement along the social distance scale. Thus, for instance, if the person agrees with the statement "I would invite this person for tea" this implies less social distance than if he agrees only with the statement "I would accept this person as a citizen in my country."

In order to find scale values, as required by the Thurstone procedure, the approach is as follows. First, one constructs many (say, 100) emic statements that probably represent different positions on a social distance scale. Second, the statements are presented to pretest persons from the same culture as the persons who will be used in the study, who are asked to judge these statements. The judges look at each statement and place it in one of 11 piles, depending on how much social distance they believe is implied by agreement with this statement. If a statement is placed by most judges in a particular pile, or its neighbor piles it must be that the statement communicates its meaning unambiguously. If this does not happen the statement is eliminated. Those statements that do meet the criterion of a small interquartile range are retained and used for a scale.

Once the stimuli have been pretested and the statements have been scaled, the preparations for the study have been made. New samples are then presented with hypothetical stimulus persons and asked to indicate which of the behavioral statements included in the scale they are willing to endorse. For example, "if a Japanese coalminer who is of the same religion as you were visiting your town would you invite him to dinner?"

The answers that respondents give can be analyzed by analysis of variance, because the stimulus persons are generated by a factorial design. Thus it is possible to find out how much of the variance in social distance scores is accounted for by race, religion, nationality, or occupation. The final output of the study is a table that lists the amount of variance accounted for by each of these sources of variance and their interactions.

In the American study (Triandis and Triandis, 1960) we found that race accounted for more variance than occupation; nationality and religion accounted for almost no variance. However, this was only true for the average American student.

There were some students who paid much attention to religion; there were also some students who emphasized occupation more than race. This led to a typology of students and an analysis of personality scores. But this is too much detail; suffice it to say that we found relationships between characteristics of persons, such as their race, occupation, or religion, and the way others responded to them. When extending the study to Greece (Triandis and Triandis, 1962) Japan and Germany (Triandis, Davis, and Takezawa, 1965) we only translated the data-collection procedure; it was not necessary to translate any of the items. In each culture we asked; "What are the recognized races, religions, occupations, and nationalities here? How are they ranked in this culture?" We selected stimulus persons that represented these dimensions. We generated 100 statements that imply social distance in each culture and did the Thurstone scaling of these statements separately in each culture. Thus the social distance scale was scored with values scaled and calibrated in each culture. The items of each scale were different. Only the procedure was translated.

To sum up—translation is done with the focus on the procedure for doing the study. Procedures involve explicit steps or behavior. One can work with his counterparts in the other culture, answer their questions, restate points that are critical, check their work as they implement the procedure developed in one culture in another culture. All this can be done in explicit terms. At the same time he may find that the procedure he developed in one culture is not general enough, that is, it does not translate well. Then, a modification of the procedure to take into account such realities can be carried out. The result is that the procedure that is finally used is decentered in Werner and Campbell's (1970) sense.

In the study that was just described the translation of the procedure resulted in similar operations carried out in each culture. Thus the generation of the stimuli was based on pretesting of various potential stimulus characteristics on four dimensions—race, religion, occupation, and nationality. Stimulus values were selected so as to give maximum contrast on each of the four dimensions, for persons in each culture. The respondents used scales calibrated in each culture. Thus although the stimuli and responses were "culture appropriate" or emic, the results could be compared at a higher level of abstraction on dimensions like race, nationality, or occupation which have universal meaning, that is, are etic.

Conclusion

The basic concept behind the present argument is that to get good translations one needs to have much context. To understand the meaning of unique culture-specific concepts one needs a common framework of universal concepts. This can be accomplished by (1) factor analyses that derive a universal framework within which the specific meaning of concepts can be understood, (2) facet analyses that check if theoretically derived frameworks are equivalent, and (3) translation of the procedures for data gathering, but allowing the specific stimuli and responses used in each culture to be maximally appropriate for that culture. In each case translation is minimized by translating only the stimuli in (1), by translating only the facets in (2), and by translating only the procedures in (3).

REFERENCES

Bales, R. F. *Interaction process analysis: A method for the study of small groups.* Cambridge, Mass.: Addison-Wesley, 1950.

Benjamin, L. S. Structural analysis of social behavior. *Psychological Review,* 1974, *81,* 392–425.

Brislin, R. Back-translation for cross-cultural research. *Journal of Cross-Cultural Psychology,* 1970, *1,* 185–216.

Brown, R. *Social psychology.* New York: The Free Press, 1965.

Edwards, A. L. *Techniques of attitude scale construction.* New York: Appleton-Century, 1957, *120,* 148.

Foa, U. New developments in facet design and analysis. *Psychological Review,* 1965, *72,* 262–274.

Foa, U., and Foa, E. B. *Societal structures of the mind.* Springfield, Ill.: C. C. Thomas, 1974.

Guttman, L. A structural theory of intergroup beliefs and action. *American Sociological Review,* 1959, *24,* 318–328.

Jordan, J. E. *Attitudes toward education and physically disabled persons in eleven nations.* East Lansing, Mich.: Latin American Studies Center, 1968.

Klineberg, O. *Social psychology.* New York: Holt, 1954.

Leary, T. *Interpersonal diagnosis of personality.* New York: The Ronald Press, 1957.

Lorr, M., and McNair, D. Expansion of the interpersonal behavior circle. *Journal of Personality and Social Psychology,* 1965, *2,* 823–830.

Mason, W. A. Sociability and social organization in monkeys and apes. In L. Berkowitz, Ed. *Advances in experimental social psychology.* New York: Academic Press, 1964.

Minturn, L., & Lambert, W. W. *Mothers of six cultures.* New York: Wiley, 1964.

Osgood, C. E. Exploration in semantic space: A personal diary. *Journal of Social Issues,* 1971, *27,* 5–64.

Schaefer, E. S. From circular to spherical conceptual models for parent behavior and child behavior. In J. P. Hill, Ed. *Minnesota Symposia on Child Psychology.* Vol. 4. Minneapolis: University of Minnesota Press, 1971.

Schlosberg, H. Three dimensions of emotion. *Psychological Review,* 1954, *61,* 81–88.

Stogdill, R. M., & Coons, A. E. *Leader behavior: Its description and measurement.* Research Monograph No. 88. Columbus: The Ohio State University, 1957.

Triandis, H. C. Exploratory factor analyses of the behavioral component of social attitudes. *Journal of Abnormal and Social Psychology*, 1964, *68*, 420–430.

Triandis, H. C. *Interpersonal behavior*. Monterey, Cal.: Brooks/Cole, 1976.

Triandis, H. C., and Lambert, W. W. A restatement and test of Schlosberg's theory of emotion with two kinds of subjects from Greece. *Journal of Abnormal and Social Psychology*, 1958, *56*, 321–328.

Triandis, H. C., and Triandis, L. M. Race, social class, religion and nationality as determinants of social distance. *Journal of Abnormal and Social Psychology*, 1960, *61*, 110–118.

Triandis, H. C., and Triandis, L. M. A cross-cultural study of social distance. *Psychological Monograph*, 1962, *76*, No. 21 (Whole No. 540).

Triandis, H. C., Davis, E. E., and Takezawa, S. I. Some determinants of social distance among American, German and Japanese students. *Journal of Personality and Social Psychology*, 1965, *2*, 540–551.

Triandis, H. C., Vassiliou, V., and Nassiakou, M. Three cross-cultural studies of subjective culture. *Journal of Personality and Social Psychology Monograph Supplement*, 1968, *8* (4), 1–42.

Triandis, H. C., Vassiliou, V., Vassiliou, G., Tanaka, Y., and Shanmugam, A. *The analysis of subjective culture*. New York: Wiley, 1972.

Werner, O., and Campbell, D. T. Translating, working through interpreters and the problem of decentering. In R. Naroll and R. Cohen, Eds. *A handbook of method in cultural anthropology*. New York: American Museum of Natural History, 1970, 398–420.

PART 3

Applications

CHAPTER 8

An Operational Machine Translation System

PETER TOMA

ALL HUMAN LANGUAGES follow rules. Any precisely formu lated rule can be programmed. An entire set of programmed rules comprises a computer translation system. The feasibility of computer translation is determined by the extent to which the rules of human language can be defined.

I.

Translation is one of the most fascinating—and complicated —intellectual tasks man performs. In fact, Richards (1953) has gone so far as to describe this type of communication process as "what may very probably be the most complex type of event yet produced in the evolution of the Cosmos." Perhaps it is this complexity that lends such fascination to the job of automatizing this human process on today's fastest and largest computers.

When humans translate, they first read the text in its original (source) language. To do this, they need to know

1. What the individual words mean.

2. the role each word plays in any particular sentence.

3. whether the denotation of any word(s) is affected by its context.

After the translator has determined these, he transfers the information content into the target language; that is, he produces the translated text. When the translator is human, it is virtually impossible to produce a translation free from the translator's *interpretation* of the original textual information. Necessarily, an interpretation is tinged by the human translator's ability to grasp the concept expressed in the source language, and, depending on the type of material to be translated, his own reactions to that concept.

Machine translators or computer translation systems need to know the same things, basically, that human translators do. Therefore, they must have adequate dictionaries ("vocabularies"), syntactic analysis programs, semantic analysis procedures, and target language synthesis programs.

There have been many publications devoted to computer translation and many discussions of the problems that arise in developing, or attempting to develop, computer translation systems. The first, Locke and Booth's *Machine Translation of Languages* appeared in 1955. Yet the first demonstration of a real translation system did not occur until June 6, 1959, when, at the Pentagon, the Georgetown (SERNA) system (described in Toma, 1959) translated over a hundred thousand words of text it had never "seen" before.

The SERNA system ran on second-generation computers, whose input-output operations as well as core processing operations were so slow that it seemed impossible that computer translation would ever be economically feasible.

Work with the SERNA system, and with other systems designed during the ensuing years, made it apparent that it would be necessary to know a great deal more about human languages and the rules we follow to use them than anyone knew at that time.

In optimizing and refining SYSTRAN, the operational system described below, we find that this is still true. In too many instances there are no grammar books or linguistic analyses to turn to for answers. Rather, programs are written to have the machine produce appropriate corpora for linguists to analyze. The results of the linguists' work are then programmed into the translation system.

SYSTRAN has been in operation since 1969, when the U.S. Air Force first started using it to translate Russian scientific and technical texts. Since then, the Air Force has come to depend on it more each year; NASA now uses it for the translation support activities (English to Russian and Russian to English) so vital to the success of the Apollo-Soyuz docking maneuvers. Despite the fact that computer translations may still sound stilted in places, NASA and the Air Force rely on this system's speed (300,000 words per hour) and its ability to produce consistent translations which accurately reflect the information content of original texts.

II.

This chapter describes SYSTRAN as it is today, and as it performs today. The expounding of theories of a hypothetical, ideal system which might exist someday is left to others—who may build one, someday.

Because SYSTRAN translates from more than one language (Russian, Chinese, German, English), the term *source language* is used to denote the language translated *from,* and *target language* to denote the language translated *to.* All the languages SYSTRAN translates have some basic things in common. SYSTRAN expresses the presence of these commonalities with the same codes, regardless of language. Thus one might say that the system uses a common denominator for all source languages. The simplest examples of common properties of languages are

1. Words to express action or a state of being (or equivalence: "*X* is *Y*").

2. A relationship between the action and that which performs the action ("John hits").

3. A relationship between the action and that which is affected by the action (*"(X)* hits Mary").

Of course, all languages use vocabularies or dictionaries, even if they are not written. The first thing SYSTRAN does when presented with a text[1] is to look the words up in its dictionaries. Random access and sequential lookup procedures are combined to make computer use maximally efficient. For example, all idioms are selected on a longest match basis, using sequential lookup, whereas grammar codes are found via random-access procedures. Techniques using the attachment of addresses only and the attachment of all dictionary information are also combined. High-frequency words are given the address of their dictionary information, whereas low-frequency words are supplied with the information itself.

Dictionary information is represented as codes[2], reflected by the appearance of specific bits in specific bytes. There are three types of codes:

1. Part of speech (signifying noun, particle, preposition, etc.) and subdivision within part of speech group (reflexive finite verb, adverb which may function as predicate, etc.);

2. Syntactic properties (allowable inflection pattern, object-type requirement, ability to govern infinitive, ability to govern preposition, ability to function impersonally, etc.);

3. Semantic features (human, combustible, sound device, malleable, measurable, mechanical process, etc.).

Although translation processing begins with dictionary lookup, the whole translation procedure is initiated at the moment the text is read into the computer. INITCALL, SYSTRAN's master control program, calls for the execution of the dictionary lookup programs and calls all subsequent programs. There is no human intervention; INITCALL relinquishes control only when the translated text is ready to be printed.

Once the text words have been looked up in the dictionaries[3], those that comprise idioms will have been given their idiomatic meaning, those that are homographic will have been given a homograph type identification, and contiguous declinable words that have special meanings when in sequence will have been recognized and given appropriate meanings.

The first set of structural analysis routines (called PASS1) is called after PASS0 has established the function of all the homographs in the sentence. (Homographs are words like stand in English, which can either be a verb—stand there—or a noun —a stand of trees.)

Each analysis (and synthesis) program depends on the fact that each word in the sentence has, in the analysis area in core, 160 bytes for information about that word. Some of the information is supplied by the dictionaries; other information (a far greater percentage) is supplied by analysis and synthesis routines. To say that a word has 160 bytes reserved for it means that there are 160 spaces that can hold information. Each byte (space) can be thought of as being divided into 8 bits; any combination of these may be used to signify specific types of information. Each program also depends on the fact that INIT-CALL has assigned each word in the sentence a sentence sequence number (a number identifying each word as the first word, second word, third word, etc. of the sentence).

PASS1 moves word by word through the sentence, turning on switches so that the location of nouns, verbs, and so on can be remembered, and establishing basic syntactic relationships[4]:

1. Noun + adnominal genitive
2. (Adverb +) adjective + noun
3. Adverb + verb
4. Verb + object
5. Preposition + object
6. Governor + infinitive
7. Governor + subordinate clause initiator (e.g., ČTO or ČTOBY in Russian).

The establishment of these syntactic units is reflected by byte relationships. That is, byte 18, for example, of the verb will contain the sentence sequence number of its object. Its object, in turn, will contain the verb's sequence number in byte 28. Thus, for SYSTRAN, an 18–28 byte relationship signifies a [governor + governed word] syntactic relationship. All syntactic relationships have equivalent SYSTRAN byte relationships. The syntactic signification of any byte relationship remains the same, no matter what language is being translated.

To establish syntactic units like those listed above, PASS1 depends heavily on the syntactic codes supplied by the dictionary for each word. For example, in determining whether a given Russian noun is the object of a particular preposition, the routine checks the byte information for the declension the preposition may govern. If the declined noun meets the preposition's requirements, and all other syntactic requirements are met in the context, government is established.

PASS2 extends the relationships established in PASS1 by recognizing enumerated noun modifiers, enumerated objects, enumerated adnominal genitives, appositives, and the like, and by establishing the function of enumerative commas and conjunctions, as well as the function of commas that set off parenthetic phrases.

At this point the full extent of prepositional phrases, noun phrases, and verb phrases has been defined. In other words, nouns have been linked with all their modifiers (single word modifiers, enumerated single word modifiers, participial phrase modifiers), their appositives, their adnominal genitives, relative clauses for which they are head nouns, and the like, and verbs have been linked with their objects, modifiers, modals, auxiliaries, and the like.

Therefore, it is appropriate that the program which determines types and extent of clauses be called. This program establishes whether clauses are main clauses or subordinate clauses, marks each word in the clause with type indicator (first main clause, third main clause, relative clause, that-S complementizer clause, for-to complementizer clause, etc.), and sets up byte pointers to allow ensuing subject-predicate searches to "jump over" embedded clauses.

The subject-predicate search routines depend on the clause boundaries, types, and pointers established by the preceding program to limit the extent of their search and also to find all sections of interrupted clauses: the subject and predicate of any clause must be *within* that clause. Clause type indicators are important for determining types of allowable predicates. In Russian, for example, ČTOBY clauses need not contain finite verbs; infinitives suffice.

Subject-predicate searches must also depend on dictionary information. Number, gender, and case information is important for determining potential subject candidates and for matching proper subject candidates with predicates; codes attached to verbs may indicate, for example, that the verb is always used impersonally and never takes a subject or that the verb's subject usually follows, rather than precedes, it.

The above discussion briefly highlights the major functions of the analysis phase of translation processing. Further analysis routines determine the function of prepositional phrases and handle special structures idiosyncratic to the source language (such as "ratio" expressions in Chinese and the passive transformation in Russian).

When the analysis phase is completed, synthesis into the target language begins. These routines not only supply proper source-language inflections (or preposition insertion to denote case, such as to for the dative in English) and article insertion, but also perform conversions such as $[\text{VERB} + \text{ADJ}_{(\text{OBJ})}] \Rightarrow$

[VERB + THAT WHICH + VERB₂] where VERB₂ is reconstructed from the adjectival form. These functions, again, depend on the presence of proper dictionary codes for allowable
endings, restrictions on article insertion, cross-reference verb
stems, etc.

After lexical synthesis has been effected, sentential constituents are rearranged to conform to target-language word-order
requirements. In translation from Russian to English, the most
frequently necessary rearrangement procedures are

1. Converting OBJECT + VERB + SUBJECT to SUBJECT
+ VERB + OBJECT order.

2. Converting MODIFIER + PREPOSITIONAL PHRASE
+ MODIFIED WORD to MODIFIER + MODIFIED WORD
+ PREPOSITIONAL PHRASE.

III.

It is simple enough to say "PASS1 does this, PASS2 does that,
PASS3 does something else, ..." Most people, however,
would probably want to ask *how* computer programs can do
these things.

There is certainly nothing magic or mysterious about it. As
we pointed out earlier, any rule that can be precisely formulated can be programmed. Hence the most difficult part of the
job is uncovering the rules that govern languages. We know
these rules exist; if they did not, everyone would speak his own
version of the language, and no one would be able to understand anyone else.

Another indication that these rules exist is the fact that we
can understand what a sentence is "talking about," even if we
don't know the meanings of all the words. For example, in the
sentence

Gorly gruk gobbers rogurtted the tobers, blikking mewsp in a
pousap botorov.

we know that gobbers, which are gruk, even gorly gruk, did
something: they rogurtted something(s) called tobers. At about
the same time they did the rogurtting, something called a
mewsp was blikked in something called a pousap.

To a computer all sentences are like this. Nether the machine nor the syntactic analysis programs knows the meaning of any word, even though a dictionary lookup program attaches target-language meanings to source language words. Rather, the programs called into the computer's memory look for codes attached to the words. When looking at any particular word to examine its syntactic environment the programs look for specific codes on the other words in the sentence. Such words could supply the following information:

1. "Gorly" is an adverb.
2. "Gruk" is an adjective/noun homograph.
3. "Gobbers" is a nominative noun.
4. "Rogurtted" is a verb (third person plural, past perfective) that requires an accusative object.
5. "Tobers" is a noun and may be either genitive if singular or nominative or accusative if plural.
6. "Blikking" is a present active participle formed from the verb blik, which requires an accusative object.
7. "Mewsp" is an adjective, either accusative or genitive.
8. "In" is a preposition requiring either an accusative or locative object.
9. "Pousap" is a locative noun.

SYSTRAN would decide in PASS1 that "gorly gruk" modified "gobbers"; that "tobers" is the object of "rogurtted" and is, therefore, accusative plural; that "pousap" is the object of "in"; that "mewsp" does not modify "botorov", but is the elliptical object of "blikking"; that "botorov" is the adnominal genitive of "pousap."

Had it been the case that "blikking" required a genitive object, SYSTRAN would have established that "mewsp" modified "botorov," that "botorov" was the object of "blikking," and that the prepositional phrase "in a pousap" had to be postposed after "botorov."

In other words, SYSTRAN depends on grammar codes supplied by the dictionary and on the position of lexical items relative to each other. Word order is always an important consideration, but it must be remembered that word order rules vary from language to language. For example, if the nonsense sentence given above were Russian, structural analysis programs would be written to expect the preposition's object to follow the preposition and to expect an adnominal genitive to follow its head noun. On the other hand, if the language were Chinese, the preposition might be the type that follows its own object. In addition, in Chinese, adnominal genitives precede their head nouns, the structure being marked by the particle *de*.

Grammar codes and word order are not always sufficient. When source language words are polysemous (i.e., have two or more different meanings), their different meanings will require different target language equivalents. For example, the Russian word TSEL' may be translated as target or as purpose (or objective, etc.). In order to determine which meaning the word is intended to convey, it is necessary to examine the word's semantic environment and the syntactic relationships between the word in question and other words that may affect or determine the choice of a target-language equivalent. To do this, SYSTRAN programs look at semantic codes attached to the polysemous word and to words that have the potential to influence its target-meaning selection. For example, a projectile may be fired at a target, but not at a purpose. A phase of a mission may have a purpose, but not a target (except, perhaps, figuratively).

At present, the system has multiple-meaning disambiguation routines only for those words that were chosen to be included in a semantic study effort. These routines are called after the structural analysis routines, in order that they may depend on previously established syntactic relationships. As time permits, more and more source language polysemous items will be included in semantic analysis routines.

On the other side of the coin, the use of semantic characteristics can be a great aid in disambiguating syntactic structures. Here, again, though, the surface has barely been scratched. To a limited extent, SYSTRAN's structural passes include semantic tests for allowable relationships. For example, a structurally plausible [head noun + adnominal genitive] may be disallowed because establishing such a relationship would create a semantic anomaly.

IV.

As we said earlier, a good computer translation system depends on proper linguistic analysis. Perhaps it also should be pointed out that it is essential that the results of the linguists' work be accurately reflected in the programs. Generally, qualified programmers are not trained as linguists; by the same token, qualified linguists are not trained as programmers. This situation gives rise to the possibility of a serious communication gap: linguists investigate problems and devise rules that are meaningful to them; unless the programmer, however, knows exactly what the rules are supposed to do (*i.e.,* what type of language problem necessitated the rules and what the desired effect of the rules is), there is every chance that something will be lost in the "translation" of linguistic rules into programmed instructions.

For that very reason, SYSTRAN's systems analyst devised a set of macro instructions that comprise a natural-language-oriented programming language. These macros are mnemonic, look like English, and sound like the procedures a linguist might use.

For example, if you want to look for a particular word, type of word, or type of grammatical feature in the sentence, you scan the sentence: SCANL means scan to the left (of some fixed point you choose in the sentence); SCANR means scan to the right. To limit the part of the sentence you want to look over, you use "MAX" (maximum) operands, specifying the beginning or end of the sentence, the clause, particular number of words, previously fixed point, specific word, and the like. To ask questions about a property of any word in the sentence, TEST instructions are used. CMPWD is used to ask if a word is specifically X (red, house, walked, etc.). Other instructions ask how the word ends or begins.

SYSTRAN's linguist finds this programming language easy to learn because its instructions do not seem arcane and because they represent the types of operations he wants to effect. Moreover, when a linguist finds the need for operations for which no macro instruction exists, he simply presents the problem to the systems analyst, who creates a new macro.

In this way the potential problem of a communication gap is obviated, because the linguist does his own conversion of linguistic rules into programmed instructions. We have found an ancillary benefit in this approach in that the linguist who programs learns how precise his rules must be before they can be programmed and implemented with efficacy. Because of this, he soon learns not to make spurious generalizations, but to limit his rules to environmental restrictions so far as is necessary. That is, when his rules are context sensitive, as opposed to context free, the sensitivity and the character of the context must be programmed into the rules via as many "tests" as necessary.

SYSTRAN helps the linguist at his work in another significant way: diagnostic programs can be used to extract from extensive corpora of "live" text any number of sentences containing the specific type of problem (defined by structure, by co-occurrence of specific words or classes of words, etc.) he is working on. A linguist usually feels more confident about his analysis when he can examine 500 "actual" sentences instead of 25 or 50 he made up himself. Thus he simply has SYSTRAN do his field work for him.

V.

At this point, you may be asking yourself either "Why isn't computer translation more widely used?" or "If it's been around since 1959, but still hasn't become popularly used, why talk about it now?"

The answer to the first question is simple: machine translation is economical only for large amounts of translation. Therefore, only those like the Air Force and NASA, who need to have thousands and thousands of words translated, find it cheaper to use machine translation. However, it might be worthwhile to note that if many people or groups with lesser translation requirements organized a translation center, then computer translation could also be economical for them.

The second question cannot be answered so readily. First, as pointed out earlier, machine translation of the late 1950s and early 1960s was limited to second-generation computers. Not only were these slower than the ones we use today, but they had a lot less memory. The latter factor meant that analysis programs had to be much smaller than now. That meant chopping programs into smaller parts, which could severely affect programs that operate most effectively when they are able to keep track of everything in the sentence (for example, PASS1 and the subject-predicate program, discussed earlier).

More than that, linguistics has come a long way since the 1950s as has the position of the linguist in machine translation.

The SERNA system and others of the same genre and/or era, were inherently weak because of these factors. The Georgetown system did have several small "passes" (where SYSTRAN has PASS1) to establish basic syntactic units; it depended on input structures fitting into programmed sentence patterns which were used almost as templates, whereas SYSTRAN depends on linguistic generalizations about how languages tend to behave. The systems and programming staffs were not linguists; the linguists were not programmers. Hence when the computer translation required modification, no one knew exactly where the changes should be made. The system became a black box whose inner workings could not be modified as new facts about language were uncovered because no one dared put his hand in.

This is not to say that this system sprang full-grown from an omniscient creator's forehead. Rather, the system grew out of the 1960s, benefitting from the work spent on its predecessors, and from the constant effort expended in overcoming its own problems. Easily amenable to change, it is always being changed, as new techniques of software management and better linguistic analyses are implemented to improve translation quality.

FOOTNOTES

1. Texts are inputted either on keypunched cards or magnetic tapes. No text is ever preedited or modified in any way other than by standard transliteration (Romanization).

2. Naturally, all these codes are supplied to dictionary entries by (human) linguists.

3. The plural is used because SYSTRAN employs specialized dictionaries as well as a general dictionary.

4. The routines that establish these relationships are called by the part of speech of each word in the sentence.

REEFERENCES

Richards, I. Toward a theory of translating. *Studies in Chinese Thought.* American Anthropological Association, Vol. 55, memoir 75, Chicago: University of Chicago Press, 1953, pp. 247–262.

Toma, P. *SERNA System.* Washington, D.C.: Institute of Languages and Linguistics, Machine Translation Research Center, 1959.

CHAPTER 9

Multi-Dimension Translation: Poetry

LILA RAY

"OUR NEIGHBOUR lost his sheep on the highroad because there were many forks, the ferryman's apprentices lost their lives because there were many methods. The root of what they were learning was one and the same, but you can see how far the tips of the branches had diverged. Only return to where they are one, go back to where they are the same, restore the missing and find the lost." Yang Chu in the Book of Lieh-Tzu.

The languages of men are the diverging branches, and in order to restore the missing and find the lost we must return to where they are one, in the human breast. A translator starts at the tips of the branches, works his way back to the source, and journeys out again, down another limb of man's experience. For experience is what we receive from language. No two languages, no two texts, codify exactly the same area of experience. A man has an experience about which he wishes to tell others. He has discovered something, perceived something, as a result of that experience. If what he has discovered is of value to them, other men listen to him. It adds to their own experience and becomes the possession of the group to which he belongs, a part of their cherished lore.

So it is that the languages of men are a major human resource, if not *the* major human resource, and translation plays a key role in their utilization, addition and expansion. How much would we know or understand about ourselves without the Rosetta stone? More modern methods of training translators are fully as important as more modern methods of training teachers.

Many regard the problems of translation as not different from problems of language in general. Translation introduces us to a language in the first instance. It is an indispensable adjunct to language learning. Traditionally, a student begins to make use of it from the first exercise in the first lesson in every language textbook. It is not surprising, therefore, that many find it difficult to disassociate translation from the learning of a language. They are accustomed from childhood to regard it as a useful subsidiary activity of minor importance.

That translation has another role to play, a role of major importance, is not widely enough realized. No individual can learn more than a few of the many languages men speak, and that imperfectly. Translations can be made from all of them however. Translation eliminates the need for learning a language. It can make our world heritage accessible to an increasing extent, and it is the only activity that can. The translator alone is able to overcome language barriers. Nobody else can. We do not read the English Bible to learn Aramaic or Greek or Latin. We read it so we will not have to learn these languages to know what Jesus said and did and Moses before him.

Nowhere in my reading have I found this dual function of translation clearly set forth. It is both an aid to language learning and a substitute for it. Its role is reversed at the higher levels of its operation. It is clear that, though translation begins with

je, ich, ami, o,

I, mu, hum, yo,

it does not end there.

Translation that is a substitute for language learning keeps languages apart while bringing cultures closer together. It is an aid to the acquisition of understanding rather than syntactical skill. If the translator is competent no language problem exists for the reader. Multilinguilism remains what it is, an asset, because of the wide freedom of expression it makes possible and the broad range of artistic and intellectual creation it provides scope for. The varied richness of language diversity is preserved. The distinctive character of each language is protected and its individual growth encouraged. Linguistic loyalties have nothing to fear and much to gain from translation of this kind.

Translation is concerned, therefore, not only with the problems of language in general but with the entire range of human experience, yet a translator, like a grammarian and a lexicographer, is a student of meaning, and, like them, has to make use of a large variety of empirical sciences. Yet the age-old debate between literal and free translation goes blindly on. Words are still transferred brick by brick from one language to another and a text reconstructed in a second language piecemeal in the optimistic hope that the text will come through undistorted because of the conscientious but clumsy efforts of the bricklayer. Some translators do not even stop to read the text through before they start to work on it. Others set about translating as though it were a semi-magical or intuitive process that comes mysteriously right if the translator runs through the text a number of times and regurgitates it in an unobstructed flow of fluent verbiage.

Translators in general and in India in particular are as reluctant to share their knowledge of their craft as snake charmers. They guard it as closely as a trade secret. But translation is much less lucrative than snake charming, and it profits little to be mysterious about it. It is possible that translators do not share their knowledge because they do not know themselves what they do or why they do it. Their approach is too intuitive and traditional. An adequately objective attitude is sadly lacking.

This is of course far truer for translators of literature than for scientific and technological translators. Scientific translators have been thinking about exactly what they do for a long time. But translators of all kinds must, to a greater and greater extent, set about the reconstruction of texts in a conscious and deliberate manner without adhering to any specialist theory or reverting to outdated methods. The realization that they have much to gain from the pooling of their experience is slowly growing.

My own experience is limited to the translation of literature, and my remarks will be most humbly confined to what I have learned and observed in the course of my own work. My training is a continuing process. From every text I take up I learn something.

What would people think of an architect who started transferring bricks from one site to another without taking a look at the building he undertakes to construct or making measurements of any kind? Without a blueprint?

All construction requires blueprints; translation is no exception. From the tips of the branches down to the root, every inch of the way must plotted out accurately before construction can begin. This is done by analysis. The aim of the translator is to give the sound, the sense, and the feel of a text in a language other than that it which it is originally written. His work begins at the preverbal level, in the examination of the event that has resulted in an experience and perception the author feels the urge to communicate. This is where the sense is. For the sound we must study the physical components of the text and to get the feel of it we must study the author's use of syntax. In the following pages I explain the type of analysis I do to help me in my translation efforts. The categories are my own, developed because they are useful to me. I hope that they may be helpful to others, perhaps after they are adapted to the special needs of a given translator.

There are two types of analysis: surface analysis and analysis in depth. I shall run through them briefly, touching on points I have not found sufficiently elaborated elsewhere. Three sets of blueprints are made, one for the sense, one for the sound, and one for the feel of a text. Surface analysis is concerned with sound and syntax. Let us start with them.

Surface Analysis
I. Sound: the physical components of a text.
A. Letters

The rarity or commonness of the letters used in a text, particularly poetry or dialogue, is of significance. If letters of uncommon occurrence are used by the author the translator should also try to choose equivalent words with rare or uncommon letters.

Six letters out of the twenty-four that comprise the French alphabet supply more than half the total number of around 40,000 words in the average French dictionary. They are C, A, P, E, M, and S; two vowels and four consonants.

More than half the entries in the average Bengali dictionary consists of nine letters, six consonants and three vowels. They are A, U, long A, K, M, P, B, T, and Sh.

The two languages share: M, P, C=K, short A=E, long A, S =Sh. All the French letters are available in Bengali. Bengali has three letters not available in common French usage. They are U, B, and T.

Example: The usefulness of this kind of analysis can be demonstrated in the translation of nursery rhymes. I give one line from English.

    Hickory dickory dock

    i o y i o y o : 7 vowels: note pattern of recurrence

    h ck r d ck r d k : 8 consonants: note pattern

Bengali:

    dyakho re dyakho re dyakh

    ya o e ya o e ya : 7 vowels: note pattern similarity

    d kh r d kh r d kh : 8 consonants: note pattern similarity

Compare the Bengali translation with the English.

Vowels: The 'o' is short in both and occurs in the same place except at the end where, in Bengali, the first vowel is repeated.

              For 'y' in English the Bengali has 'e'. The sound of two vowels is not very different.

              The 'i' is short.

              The 'e' is short. The 'e' is in exactly the same place.

              For the English 'i' the Bengali 'ya' is substituted. It is equally short and emphatic. The Bengali 'ya' occurs in the same places the English 'i' occurs and also at the end, in place of the English 'o'. This does not interfere with the movement of the line.

Consonants: The same consonants are used in the same places with one exception: 'd' is substituted for 'h'.

    B. Vowels

Vowels are the transmitters of feeling and emotion in all languages. In poetry they are patterned. Comparable patterns can be constructed and set in the same places, if not with the same vowels, with vowels similar or related in sound. The use of vowels often identifies the characters in a drama or story.

They are used to define types and individuals.

C. Consonants:

Consonants indicate movement, gesture, action. They describe events, either physical or mental.

Patterns of consonants add emphasis to vowel patterns, and can either intensify or subdue their effects.

D. Pitch:

Vowels and consonants both have pitch contours. So have words. Changes in levels of pitch must be noted and imitated.

There are four: (a) high rising (b) high falling (c) low rising (d) low falling.

There may be more than one pitch level within a word or a sentence. How and where the switch from one level to another is made should be noted.

Words have four shapes: (a) high-high (b) high-low (c) low-high (d) low-low.

There are four pitch contours: (a) high-rising-falling (b) high-falling-rising (c) low-falling-rising (d) low-rising-falling.

The balance between high and low pitch should be noted. Pitch patterns are keys to emotive meaning.

Pitch is affected by the length and duration of vowels and consonants and their position in the text.

II. Syntax: the feel of a text is to be found in what a writer does with his own language. The translator must try to do the same with the second language.

A. Words

Words represent cognition. Sound and meaning come together in words. Words are of three kinds: (a) event words (b) object words (c) abstract words.

Every word has four aspects: (a) sound (b) role (c) as metaphors (d) meaning.

Meaning is altered by the interplay of these factors.

Word patterns: Certain words tend to recur, either as key words or as mannerisms. So do phrases and sentence patterns and patterns of inflection. Characteristic turns and twists of syntax identify the author and/or the actors in his story or novel or poem.

B. Vocabularies for given texts are useful compilations. The same word should be translated by the same equivalent as often as it recurs. So should phrase and sentence patterns or patterns of inflection. A translator will find that such vocabularies will greatly simplify his job.

C. Sets of equivalents: Alternative sets of equivalents are available for any given text. The translator makes his choice in the light of his understanding of the text.

D. Area of meaning: In the use of words meaning areas have to be matched. The word run in English has 54 numbered meanings as a verb, 33 numbered meanings as a noun, and 4 numbered meanings as an adjective, a total of 91 meanings.

To accurately define areas of meaning in a second language some words may require to be added to the text. No word can be added that does not contribute to that definition.

E. This brings us to the formal patterning of word groups. There are four sentence patterns in English. What are the equivalent patterns in other languages?

F. Language levels:

Every text is on one of the seven language levels. The level may change in the course of the text many times. A graph can easily be made plotting its course. This is a useful guide to the translator. He should aim at designing an equivalent course. The relationships between the components of a message is more important than the components themselves. The relationships can be reconstructed with different components.

G. Style:

Style is the sum total of all the factors noted up to this point. Language is inseparable from style. Style may be defined as the context of language as purposeful language variation. It comprises tone of voice, inflection of pitch, idioms used, and the concern focused on a particular event or experience. Sources of style: There are three:

(a) The individual himself

(b) The form chosen from alternatives offered by social groups

(c) The form assigned by social group as an approved way of fulfilling a particular need.

Styles of language, in general, also differ. English is less formal than French. Persian is ceremonious, Bengali luxuriates in adjectives, and so on. A writer does not deal with passive material. He uses the properties and resources of language for his own ends, reshaping it to his own purpose. A translator must know what the author is doing and how he does it. He has to re-enact what the author does. Style is the manner in which a writer utilizes available resources. Style gives us the feel of a text (see also the chapter by Nida).

Analysis in Depth: Sense and Meaning
A. Experience:

Every poem, every story, every drama, every essay, every novel records an experience. Experience is associated with events. Not every event is an experience. Events are taking place all around us constantly. An event becomes an experience only when it impinges on us personally, intrudes into our lives and consciousness. As a result of an experience we perceive something of which we were not so acutely aware before, if at all. This perception may be so important to us we feel like telling others about it. It is then codified in a text of one kind or another. No event takes place in a vacuum. There are parties too. Objects are involved.

The translator's job is to re-enact the original experience of the author, working as he did, from the inside out. He enjoys the advantage of having a completed structure to guide him. The author has to create the structure. The translator seeks and tests equivalents. Unless the original experience is re-created, no form, however perfect, can be anything but lifeless. The translator has to enter into the mind and heart of his author, relive his circumstances, refeel what he felt, reperceive what he perceived.

Meaning is of three kinds: connative, referential, and emotive. These may be said to start where linguistic meaning leaves off. Linguistic meaning precedes them, providing the antecedent conditions, the take-off point.

B. Dimensions:

Meaning has many dimensions, some of them unexplored and unrealized. Take, for instance, the Bengali word, bhadralok. It is usually translated as gentleman. That is correct and accurate. A bhadralok is a member of the gentry, a man of some education and refinement, not working class, not a peasant. But a bhadralok in Bengal will not do things a person of the same class does in other social contexts. He will not, for instance, throw out the garbage as an American pater familias does. When we are confronted with class categories of this kind, it is often necessary to define them by the *response* method. The only difference between a mlechha and an untouchable is, for the orthodox Hindu, that the latter is expected to be obsequious, whereas the former is usually regarded as arrogant and condescending, which is resented. Meaning is often, therefore, defined socially by what a person will not do more than by what he actually does. No Bengali bhadralok will do menial work, manual work, or work that is ritually unclean. Thus we see unemployed young men idling around heaps of uncleared garbage in the streets. Unless we are aware of these inhibitions, how can we appreciate the revolutionary character of Tolstoi's action in taking to cobbling or Gandhiji's in cleaning latrines?

C. The Matching of Meaning:

Meanings have to be matched. World images have to be matched. The frame of meaning has to be fitted over natural concepts. These do not often coincide exactly. Where they do not, adjustment must be made in order to present them intelligibly. The separate components are of less importance than the pattern. Equivalent patterns must be built out of letters, words, syntax. Angularities of strange syntax must not obtrude into natural and familiar syntax, attracting attention by their awkwardness, disturbing the reader.

The translator focuses attention on the text or message and is justified in doing what he finds necessary to bring it into the new language in an authentic and effective manner, building it back to the surface level of the original from the blueprints he has made by analysis. Before going on to consider the examples of my methods of analysis which follow, I wish to show briefly what happens to a translation when the person who makes it does not take the trouble to analyze the experience behind it. This three-line poem by Quasimodo was translated into English by Allen Mandelbaum. The original is as follows:

> *Edé subito sera*
>
> Ogmeno sta sole sur cuor della terra
> traffito da un raggio di sola:
> edé subito sera

Mandelbaum's English runs as follows:

Each alone on the heart of the earth
impaled upon a ray of sun:
and suddenly it's evening.

It roughly means (this rough step might be taken at a very preliminary stage):

Alone we stand upon an earth pierced by rays of
the sun, each alone on its breast.

I humbly submit that Allen Mandelbaum did not realize what it was the poet was saying. The experience he was recording was the comfort of companionship, of being together in the heart of the earth and at the same time accorded individual recognition. The event is a sunset that the poet and his friend or friends watch. Darkness follows the moment of illumination swiftly. The poem makes sense when this is visualized. The translation should run something like this:

As we stood together in the earth's lap
the rays of the setting sun touched us,
piercing our breasts separately with light.
The evening was sudden.

Study of the Sound Properties of a Four-Line Mantra

This is the seminal mantra of Manasa, the snake goddess. The four lines are given here. They will be studied one by one and then together. The mantra is

I   *phani phona mani gana bhusitāmaste*
II   *khara tara bisa dhara kankana haste*
III *bahujana janita jayā dhvani tuste*
IV   *bhāgavati bisahari devi namaste*

I

phani phona mani gana bhusitāmaste

(she whose hood is thickly encrusted with gems)
The number of letters in the line is 27.

Consonants

ph n ph n m n g n bh s t m s t

There are 14 consonants or chest pulses, indicating movement. The number of separate consonants is as follows:

n - 4
ph - 2

m - 2
g - 1
bh - 1
s - 2
t - 2

The difference in frequency of consonants is small, indicating narrow range of movement; 'n' occurs four times, 'm' twice, 't' twice, 'ph' twice. These are dry, even, and low-placed letters on the same level of pitch. The 'ph' or 'f' adds an implosive, blowing of breath, also dry. The pitch range is as limited as the movement. The absence of any sibilance should be noted. The dry light movement of a snake is perfectly imitated, both in the short turns from side to side as the line progresses and the low connectedness of the pitch. Leaps are avoided. The highest pitch is at the end of the penultimate, or fifth, word, bhusitā, the emphasis falling on the long 'a'.

Vowels

This brings us to the vowels.

a i o a a i a a u i a a e

There are 13.

All the vowels, with one exception, are short, reflecting the shortness of the consonants. The long vowel comes in the fifth word, marking the highest point in the line.

The vowels occur as follows:

a - 8
i - 3
e - 1
o - 1

The short dry 'a' is obviously the most important.

The three 'i's are evenly planted, one in the first word, one in the third word and one in the fifth. In each instance it comes at the end of the word. The single 'o' comes toward the beginning. This is almost a short 'a' and can be written as such.

The single 'e' comes at the end.

The line consists of twelve short vowels and one long one.

The consonants and vowels are arranged in alternate succession.

No two vowels occur together.

Consonants occur singly, with one exception, in the last syllable, where 's' and 't' come together, creating an emphasis.

There are six words.

The line is descriptive of a snake's motion, climaxing in a strike on the long 'ā' in the fifth word. Vowel changes just before strike are portents, creating suppressed excitement and alarm. Sound, sensation, and movement are synchronized accurately. Consonants coil around the reiterated 'a', moving above and below but staying close to it.

II
khara tara bisha dhara kankana haste
(who bears swift poison in golden hands)

The number of letters in the line is 27. They are contained in six words.

Consonants
kh r t r b sh dh r k n k n h s t

There are 14 consonants. The last 's' and 't' are pronounced together making a combined consonant. The number of separate consonants is as follows:

kh - 1
r - 3
t - 2
b - 1
s - 2
dh - 1
k - 2
n - 2
h - 1

There is greater diversification in the consonants, indicating a greater degree of movement but the range is still restricted.

Four consonants occur once.

Four consonants occur twice.

One consonant occurs three times. This is 'r'.

In the first line (I) there is a total of seven consonants. In the second (II) a total of nine consonants. The number of 't' s in the two lines is the same. So is the number of 's' s. There are two aspirated letters, 'kh' and 'dh'. In the first line (I) the two were 'ph' and 'bh'. There is no 'r' in the first line, no 'm' in the second. No 'g' in the second and no 'h' in the first. There is no 'k' in the first. The 'k' introduces a sensation of cold apprehension, the chill of shaking fear.

Vowels

a a a a i a a a a a a a e

There are 13 vowels, the same number as in I. All are short. There is no long vowel.

The number of separate vowels is as follows:

a - 11

i - 1

e - 1

The short a is the pitch setter. The voice is kept to a single note. This gives a sense of rapidity, even and menacing because it is concentrated. The 'n' and 'k', coming together in the fifth word, give the highest point, climaxing in a tremor.

There is no vowel change before climax. Climax is made by consonants, not by vowels. It is muted.

Vowel change after the climax; as in line I, relieves tension.

III

bahujana janita jayā dhvani tuste

(is appeased by praise and paeans of the multitude)

There are again six words and 27 letters.

Consonants

b h j n j n t j y dhv n t s t

There are 14 consonants.

The number of separate consonants is as follows:

b - 1

h - 1

j - 3

n - 3

t - 3

y - 1

dhv - 1

s - 1

Three consonants occur three times. Of these two have already been introduced in I and II. The new one is 'j'. It takes its place beside 'n' and 't' as of equal importance.

Six consonants occur only once, highlighting the importance

of the three. Of these six, four have occured in the first two lines.

There is no extension in the range of physical movement.

Vowels
a u a a a i a a a a i u e

There are again 13 vowels. All but one are short. The long vowel occurs at the end of the fourth word and marks a rise in the pitch of emotion.

The number of separate vowels is as follows:

a - 8 one long
u - 2
e - 1
i - 2

The 'a' is again the most important vowel, but a new vowel is introduced for emotional depth, the 'u'. Both the 'i' and the 'e' have occurred before. The 'e' always comes at the end of the line.

The tension which has been built up throughout line II, with a minor enhancement by the combined consonants 'n' and 'k' in the fifth word breaks in a climax on the long 'ā' at the end of the fourth word. This long 'ā', after the long build-up, comes like a triumphant shout.

IV
bhagavati bishahari devi namaste
(fortune's deity, goddess of poison, accept our homage)

Again there are six words and 27 letters.

Consonants
bh g v t b sh h r d v n m s t

There are 14 consonants.

The number of separate consonants is as follows:

bh - 1
b - 1
g - 1
v - 2
t - 2
h - 2
d - 1

sh - 1
s - 1
n - 1
m - 1
The maximum number of different consonants is present.

No single consonant dominates, as eight consonants occur once and three occur twice.

With the exception of three, all the consonants in the first three lines, I, II, III, are present. The three are p, ph, k, kh, and j.

No new consonant is introduced.

There is a winding up of a movement inauguarted by 'p' and 'ph', brought to a maximum agitation by 'k' and 'kh' and resolved in the triumphant 'j'. Less emphatic consonants take over and brake the motion of the four lines to a stop.

Vowels

a a a i i a a i e i a a e

There are 13 vowels.

The number of separate vowels is as follows:

a - 7 one of which is long
i - 4
e - 2

The long 'ā' comes at the very beginning of the line. The mood of the mantra is changed to one of strong assertion and appeal. There is no more haste or trepidation.

The 'a' is the dominating vowel in all the four lines, I, II, III, IV. There are eight 'a' s in the lines I and III; eleven 'a' s in the line II; and seven 'a' s in line IV.

The vowels in lines I and III are the same: a, i, u, e and o.

The vowels in lines II and IV are the same: a, i, e.

There is an 'e' in each line and it always comes at the end.

In line II the series of short 'a' s is unbroken, climaxing in line III.

In line IV the series of 'a' s is broken by the 'i' and the 'e', slowing down the motion.

The last vowels are 'a', 'a', 'e', making a kind of coda.

There are three long vowels, all 'a' s in the entire mantra. They mark the highest pitch to which the voice rises. They are placed in I, II and IV lines at points of emphasis.

The equal balance between the number of vowels, 17 and 13, throughout is maintained unbroken.

The regular alteration in their spacing, one consonant, one vowel is also unbroken except for the last consonants in each line. These are the same in every line, 's' and 't', and are pronounced together.

The perfection of the structure of this mantra becomes very clear when it is analyzed in this way.

Another Example

The way syntax governs the feel of a text is well illustrated in the following Bengali translation of the French poem, *Déjeuner du Matin*, by Jacques Prévert.

The feel of the poem is in the handling of the third person singular pronoun, 'il', which occurs 13 times in 31 short lines, at the beginning of the first and every alternate line down to the sixteenth, a total of nine times in the first half of the poem. The remaining four times it occurs in lines 23 and 25.

There are five possible equivalents for 'il' in Bengali. They are (1) se, (2) ini, (3) uni, (4) o, and (5) the omission of the pronoun altogether, as the verb form does not really require it.

The pronoun 'il' is masculine. None of the Bengali alternatives denotes gender. That 'il' is masculine has to be indicated in some other way.

The situation described in the poem has to be studied. The event is a departure. The scene is the breakfast table. It is the morning after something has happened to cause hard feelings. There is no communication between the two people present, the man, and presumably, the woman. Both are silent. The woman is the guilty party. She is consumed with anxiety. What will he do? She watches him helplessly. He is cold and indifferent, ignoring her. Then he walks out into the rain without a word or look of farewell, leaving her in the rain of her tears.

To solve the problem of gender we must take the help of Bengali taboos. A woman does not address her husband by name and always refers to him indirectly as the One, the Respected One or just Him. If she is forced in circumstances to pronounce his name, she will change the first letter. The pro-

APPLICATIONS 277

noun she usually uses is 'uni' which denotes esteem or 'ini'
which denotes respect. She seldom uses 'se' which is ordinary,
just him. She may use 'o' which is intimate.

It was the fifth alternate that proved to be the most satisfactory. Intimacy is indicated by the indirectness of omitting the
pronoun altogether, and Bengali decorum preserved while at
the same time showing clearly that the 'il' is a man who stands
in the relationship of a husband to the woman. The woman is
hurt, indignant, angry, alarmed. There is no need to make a
show of esteem or respect.

Her apprehension is shown in the irregularity of the eleven-
line stanza. The first stanza is a regular one, containing eight
lines. Uncertainty develops in the second. The third stanza of
nine lines is broken with grief-stricken realization. The last
three lines are a sobbing summary.

The language is deceptively commonplace, the speech of
every day. It is charged with feeling.

Dejeuner du Matin	*Pratarash*
1. Il a mis le café	dallo kaphi*
2. dans la tasse	peyālāte
3. il a mis le lait	dallo dudh
4. dans la tasse de café	kaphite
5. il a mis le sucre	dilo chīnī
6. dans le café au lait	peyālāte
7. il a tourné	nere dilo
8. avec la petite cuiller	chhōtta chāmuch diye
9. il a bu le café au lait	dilo chumuk
10. et il a reposé la tasse	kaphite
11. sans me parler	rākhla peyālā
12. il a allumé	nāmiye
13. une cigarette	kathā nā bole
14. it a faut des ronds	dharālo cigārette
15. avec la fumée	uriye dilo dhōyā
16. il a mis les cendres	jhere dilo chhāi
17. dans le cendrier	chhāi dānōte

*The translation has been written in Romanized Bengali. This translation was done
under the direction of Lila Ray at the Translators' Workshop of the (now inactive)
Translators' Society of India. (Ed.)

18. sans me parler   kathā nā bole
19. sans me regarder   chōkh nā phiriye
20. il s'est levé   ute parlo
21. il a mis   māthāy tupi dilo
22. son chapeau sur sa tête

                              nilo tule
23. il a mis son manteau
    de pluie   barshātitā
24. parcéqu'il pleuvait   bristi parchhilo
25. et il est parti   · gelo beriye
26. sons la pluie   bristir jole
27. sans une parole   kathā nā bole
28. sans me regarder   chōkh nā phiriye
29. et moi j'ai pris   hāte māthā rekhe
30. ma tête dans ma main

                              kāndte lāglām
31. et j'ai plueré   ajhōre

Conclusion

For the poet, the original creator of these poems, awareness
of these dimensions may be intuitional more than conscious,
and likewise, the deployment of them. But for the translator,
faced with the task of restructuring the poem in another language, detailed and accurate knowledge is indispensable.

CHAPTER 10

Linguistic and Cultural Implications of Bible Translation

RUDOLF KASSÜHLKE

The Special Problem of Bible Translation

Bible translation holds a special position within the broad field of translation work. First, more translations of the Bible have been made than of any other book in the history of mankind; second, it is not really a book, in the sense of a homogeneous literary product, but more a collection of writings belonging to a wide variety of literary genres. Besides folk poetry in the form of legends and sagas, we find all kinds of lyric poetry, collections of laws and regulations, folk wisdom, philosophical reflections, biographical elements, letters to individuals and groups, and so on. Not even individual biblical writings—with a few exceptions—conform to a uniform literary genre; most of them are a mixture of different genres.

Moreover, a period of more than a thousand years separates the oldest and most recent parts of the Bible. The authors come from widely differing social backgrounds and testify to differing educational levels. They lived in different cultural and political periods. Accurate historical classification is made particularly difficult by the fact that most biblical writings have undergone a variety of editorial revisions and extensions, to adapt old expressions to a changed situation.

Today the Bible translator is confronted with the seemingly overwhelming task of making this diverse collection of documents available to the people of his own language and culture.

How is he to bridge the span of approximately 2000 years? And how is he to overcome the gap that separates his language and culture from the language and culture of the biblical texts?

Methodologically, there are two possible ways of solving the translator's problem: *formal correspondence* and *dynamic equivalence*.[1] The first of the two methods sees the specific form of the source text as its most important feature and seeks to produce a counterpart in a receptor language whose form corresponds to the original as nearly as possible. To achieve this aim, a word in the source language is reproduced as far as possible in concordance with a word in the receptor language. Whenever possible, both the word order and the syntactic structure are preserved. But, in particular, the idiomatic and figurative expressions of the original text are translated literally. This method of translating is held to make the reader aware of the strangeness and the great antiquity of the Bible as well as the uniqueness of the biblical language. The reader should be transported, as it were, into the unknown world of the biblical authors.

A formal correspondence translation suffers from a serious deficiency: the effect on the reader is unnatural and tiring, because the fresh impact of the original has been lost in favor of more formal elements.[2] A knowledge of this foreign world demands of the reader a lengthy learning process with the help of secondary literature such as commentaries and Bible dictionaries. Very few readers are prepared to undertake such a strenuous task, to say nothing of the fact that in most languages resources of this kind do not even exist. A formal correspondence translation is from the beginning largely not understandable and in many places actually misleading.

Through the increasing use in the theological field of the results of general linguistics, formal correspondence translations are becoming rarer. Today the prevailing practice is that the sentence structure of the receptor language is taken more seriously; for example, the long, highly wrought sentence constructions of the Greek New Testament are reproduced in shorter sentences. On the level of individual lexical items, also, concessions are more readily made to take into account the content of the statement, thereby moving away somewhat from a concordant literal reproduction. Unfortunately, this cannot be said of the so-called theological key terms such as faith, grace, justice, and the Kingdom of God, even though these terms present the greatest problems of understanding. The normal German reader understands "the justice of God," the reproduction of the Greek *dikaiosune theou* in Romans 1,17, as an attribute of God: God is just because he acts as everyone expects him to. The exegetes have generally agreed that Paul is speaking here, not of an attribute of God, but of the process by which God brings mankind into a proper relationship with God. A literal translation does not reveal this meaning. Another example: most traditional translations offer a literal translation of Luke 1,69: "He raised up a horn of salvation for us in the house of his servant David." How is a reader without special theological knowledge to understand that this means: "He has sent us a powerful Saviour, a descendant of his servant David"?

The second method of translation aims at a dynamic equivalent translation of the source text. This translation should affect the reader in the same way the original text affected the first readers or listeners. The aim is to enable the biblical authors to express their thoughts and concepts in the language of today. However, a complete equivalent is not possible because of the time span and cultural gap between the biblical writings and ourselves. It will be shown later that the cultural gap can vary considerably.

Some people have urged that the Bible, as the document of God's revelation, should be reformulated in the respective receptor languages, taking full consideration of the receptor culture, in order to give an exact equivalent of its message. This demand overlooks the fact that the revelation of God happened in very concrete historical and cultural situations. This concrete embedding and unfolding of revelation, whose stages can be clearly perceived in the Bible is, however, of inalienable significance for theology. A Bible translation should not give the impression that the reported events took place at close proximity a few years ago. Acculturation, the transferring of the biblical message into the time and thoughts of today, its application to the present situation, is a problem of the sermon, not of the translation.

A dynamic equivalent translation does not attempt to fill the cultural gap. On the contrary, it makes the difference between the cultures of the Bible and the culture of the receptor language as clear as possible. Through consistent use of colloquial speech and careful avoidance of technical terms and expressions, through an unequivocal reproduction of the content, taking fully into consideration the structure of the language, the reader should be placed in a position that enables him to take cognizance of the "foreignness" of the biblical world. Incomprehension of the language and possible misunderstandings on the part of the reader, which are unavoidable in formal correspondence, should be recognized and eliminated by the translator. We believe that only in this way can the intention of the biblical authors be made known to the reader. How this is possible and where the limits of translation lie, is discussed in part 3. Now we must speak of the factors that play a role in interlingual communication.

Factors in Communication[3]

The point of departure for any examination of the process of communication between different languages must be intralingual communication. The three basic factors of every communication are the source (S), the message (M) and the receptor (R), which may be diagrammed as follows:

Actually, this diagram is greatly simplified. For a more complete description of the process of communication, see Nida (1964, pp. 120–125). In the context of this paper further development of this point is not necessary. It is, however, important for understanding any communication, that for each of the given basic factors, a series of subfactors should be taken into consideration.

As regards the source, the most important factor is to discover as much as possible about the writer's education, social status, profession, and religion, and also his mother tongue, the language in which he may have been educated, the influence of other literature on his work, and the source of his references and citations. Paul, for example, often quoted the Old Testament in his letters. Even though he knew the Hebrew text, most of his citations are taken from the Greek translation, the Septuagint. One can hardly prove from this fact alone that his readers were most accustomed to the Septuagint, for then he would have used it throughout. What is more probable is that the Greek text supported his argumentation better than the Hebrew text.

In regard to the message it is enough in this context to point out the essential subfactors without going into the more subtle differences. The essential factors are form and content.

Some elements of form are obligatory. How the particular sounds are presented by the alphabet is regulated by convention within the ethnic group. The building up of words and sentences is prescribed by the structure of the language itself, in some languages by the use of active or passive, or of direct or indirect speech. Other elements of form are, on the contrary, optional, for example, the thought sequence in expository discourse, the choice of the literary form (such as parable, allegory and proverb), and the use of rhetorical devices (such as rhetorical questions, chiasmus, parallelism or double negation for the purpose of emphasis).

The meaning of the content of a message can be taken from two different sets of relationships. first, from the relationship of words to each other (syntactical or relational meaning); second, from the relationship of these words as linguistic symbols to objects, events, and qualifications in the nonlinguistic "real" world (referential meaning). When one speaks of the meaning of a message, the referential meaning is generally meant. In connection with the Bible two very different levels of meaning are spoken of: first, of the direct linguistic meaning of a certain account; second, of the higher or theological significance of the account. The accounts of the crucifixion of Jesus, for example, can, on the one hand, be understood as a chain of events; on the other hand, they are more often interpreted according to their symbolic meaning in the framework of the "History of Salvation". In regard to the parables, the dissimilarity of the two levels of understanding is intended from the beginning. For the purposes of this chapter, referential meaning always has to do with the first level of meaning because it is the prerequisite of the second level[4].

Both factors of a message, not only form but also content, imply two aspects: the cognitive and the emotive. The cognitive aspect concerns the intellectual comprehension of the relational and referential aspects of a message, as well as the logical links that are expressed through the form of the message. The emotive aspect has to do with the emotional reaction to the form and content of the message of those persons participating in the communication. Good literature will always show an effective combination of both aspects of form and content.

What is valid for the source is also valid for the receptor. For purposes of analysis it is important to find out as much as possible about the receptors' ethnic backgrounds, their religious ideas, their level of education, their mother tongue, other languages (if any), and the like. If a message is addressed to a larger group, it must normally be assumed that the group represents varying levels of education and interests, and that therefore the reaction to the message will certainly not be uniform. Most of the writings of the New Testament clearly show that they presuppose two or more different groupings with whom the author identifies himself or enters into discussion.

In addition to the communication facts mentioned above, the analysis must also consider the situational (locatory) factors. These include time, place, the relationship of the participants to one another, as well as the medium and channel of communication.

Important in regard to time are (1) events that preceded the communication, (2) the time of the communication itself, (3) subsequent events, to which the reaction of the receptor also belongs. It is difficult to reach an understanding of many Bible texts because we have no or only insufficient knowledge about the preceding events and the reaction of the receptors. In some cases such gaps in our knowledge can be partly filled up by information from contemporary sources.

As regards place, it is important to know whether the source and the receptor were in the same or in different places, and to what local conditions the communication refers.

The analysis of a communication must also examine the relationships of the participants to one another. Were the source and the receptor related to one another as teacher and pupil, as superior and subordinate, as colleagues of equal rank, or in any other way? In any case, the actual setting affects the form and content of the message.

Communication may use various media: word, picture, rites, spontaneous actions, and so on. It also has followed different channels, in the past as an oral message or written document, today also by means of radio and television. Biblical texts very often show earlier stages of oral transmission, the complex problems of which are the concern of literary criticism.

For the Bible translator the results of this kind of research are very useful for a better understanding of certain aspects of the text. However, he is not primarily concerned with the earlier stages, but with the final wording as a written document. In translating the gospels, for example, he must understand and translate what the evangelists wanted to say to those for whom they wrote, not what Jesus "might really" have said.

Cultural factors of communication. All the above-mentioned factors are still not enough for the understanding of a message. Its sense only becomes clear when it is seen in the broad frame of its cultural thought and behavioral structures. This concept can be illustrated by the following diagram:

$$\boxed{S{-}M{\rightarrow}R}$$

The process of communication is embedded in a three-fold cultural frame. The inside frame (the unbroken line) represents the interpretation of the events in a particular culture. The second frame stands for the patterns of behavior that are common in this culture. Finally, the outer frame represents the common presuppositions within the culture group in question. Basically, there are not three clearly distinguishable borderlines treated here, but rather degrees of intensity of the same presuppositions which range from the most common ideas to the evaluation of specific events.

As common presuppositions we term all the fundamental thought patterns of the people of a certain culture. They are apparently so self-evident that they need not be expressly defined. They become distinct only in contrast to other types of thought patterns in another culture. In the entire Bible, for example, we find no attempt to prove the existence of God; God is simply presupposed, he is part of the biblical presupposition. Other examples of this presupposition are the connections between blood and life, sin and illness or death, the three-storied world view, the distinction of animals as clean or unclean, without clear, logical characteristics for classification. Unique in ancient history is the concept of the linear passing of time, in contrast to the then usual cyclic pattern. This new understanding of history is related to another typical biblical concept: the coming kingdom of God, and the expectation that peace and justice will then determine the social life of mankind. In other questions the Bible shows variations of this presupposition, and one can certainly speak of an evolution of concepts. According to the older writings of the Bible, the life of man ends in the grave or in the world of the dead, whose inhabitants slip more and more into oblivion. The later writings, on the other hand, include the concept of the resurrection of the dead, and relate the final destiny of man to his earthly life: for some an eternal life in the heavenly world, for others a punishment in Gehenna. These few examples may be sufficient; even a partially complete list would be beyond the limits of this examination.

Patterns of behavior are constantly recurring happenings that illustrate the presuppositions of a culture group to questions of daily life. They are not accidental customs, but build within the culture a meaningful whole. The ignoring of these behavior patterns would not only evoke disapproval, but would be judged as an offense against the norms of society. If a largely homogeneous culture appears strange to us today, it is only a sign that our increasingly pluralistic society has other thought patterns.

Examples of the behavior patterns, which today seem strange to us, in the so-called world of the Bible are sexual abstinence before and during battle, the great importance attributed to names, and the value of blessings or curses. These presuppose an idea of the power of the word, which we find incomprehensible. Also the high estimation of virginity, the use of levirate marriage, and the begetting of children by the maid of a barren wife, whereby these children would then be ascribed to the wife, indicate presuppositions about marriage and sex which we cannot follow. What alienates us most is the fact that guilt and innocence were decided by lot.

The interpretation of particular events also gives us important clues to general presuppositions. In Joshua 7 it is reported that Achan and his whole family were stoned because he had seized the spoils of war from the town of Ai. This punishment is only understandable against the background of the then general practice of *herem*, according to which in a decisive war all persons, all animals, and the whole booty of the conquered city were consecrated to God and therefore had to be destroyed. Achan's theft was nothing less than sacrilege. The punishment of his whole family with him was the natural consequence of the presupposition that the guilt of an individual always affects the collective in which he lives. Only much later did the prophets of the Old Testament consider this concept as false. The present-day arrest of relatives, as practiced by totalitarian governments, seems in this light to be an anachronistic reversal.

To take another example, in John 4,27 it is reported that when returning from buying food, the apostles were highly surprised to meet Jesus conversing with a woman. This surprise is only understandable on the basis of Jewish tradition, according to which no rabbi spoke to a woman. In cultures with different presuppositions, this same account can give occasion to a serious misunderstanding. When, in the absence of other persons, a man asks a woman for something to eat or drink, it can only be interpreted in some cultural groups as a clearly sexual proposal. In translating this account for such a culture group, the misunderstandings must be ruled out through an annotation to the text.

Communication between different languages. The above-mentioned examples of factors in intralingual communication have been discussed in contrast to other languages and their thought patterns, and in this way give an indication of the difficulties of an interlingual communication. Communication between different languages could be presented in a simplified way as follows:

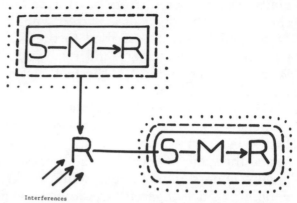

Interferences

Besides communication in the source language, there is a repetition of the communication process in the receptor language. Both are embedded in their particular cultural frame. The link between them is the translator, who is both the receptor of the original message and the source of the secondary message. The interferences signify difficulties that concern both the translator and the translation process.

It is to be remembered that our communication diagram is presented in a very simplified way. Normally, one would also have to take into account interferences in intralingual communication. These can be of various types. Oral communication is often disturbed by outside noise which hinders the receptor from hearing the message in its entirety. In written communication there can be technical "noise," such as illegible writing or unclear print. There is also psychic "noise," such as when a receptor is expecting another message or interprets it differently from the intention of the author. Such types of interference are presupposed in connection with this examination. They are of secondary importance and do not require further discussion here.

By contrast, the interferences that influence the process of interlingual communication are important. In Bible translations a very significant disturbance factor is that in many cases we no longer have at our disposal the background information which the author and primary receptors all had at their disposal. Insufficient information of this type often prevents us from understanding certain accounts clearly. There is also linguistic "noise." Fortunately, in addition to the New Testament, we have in Greek a collection of contemporary writings that can help us in the semantic analysis of lexical items and the finer points of grammar. However, there is no Hebrew literature parallel to the Old Testament that can show the development of the language to the same degree.

For this reason, any attempt to understand *hapax legomena,* especially frequent in the Old Testament, is largely conjectural. Reference to corresponding words in closely related semitic languages can sometimes help, but it does not give the certainty one would wish, because these words or roots in the neighboring languages can have very different meanings.

The Double role of the translator. A quite distinct kind of "noise" is bound up with the person of the translator. As receptor, he participates in the original communication and belongs within the cultural frame of this communication. In the case of Bible translation, however, he is always a secondary receptor who had to learn the source language and its thought patterns. At the same time, he is the source of the message in the receptor language which, as a rule, is his mother tongue. Thus he belongs within the cultural frame of the communication of the receptor language. In his double function, he is exposed to dangers from both sides. If he overestimates his own language and culture, he will inevitably underestimate the source language and culture, and so distort the message and purpose of the author. He can, however, become so enamored of the source language and its culture that he does not take his own seriously enough and expects of the receptors of the message a knowledge they cannot possibly have. Any deviation from his function as an objective mediator is, then, a disturbance of interlingual communication. The role of the translator becomes even more complicated if he has become acquainted with the language and thought patterns of the Bible indirectly, through a language other than his own. This is true of many translators in Africa, Asia, and Latin America, who received their education in a world language. They are happy to identify with this acquired language and its thought patterns because they have learned in this language to reflect on difficult structures and are therefore in danger of rating it higher than their mother tongue.

The case of a missionary translator is no less complex. As a rule he learns the biblical languages and also the receptor languages through his mother tongue, but sometimes also through other languages in which he was educated. His own or the acquired language works like a filter through which he sees and interprets the other languages and their thought patterns. As a result, there is always a danger of distorting the communication.

The receptors of the translation. In the formulation of the original message, the writer kept his receptors in mind and tried to foresee their reactions. Accordingly, he chose his words and utilized patterns of speech that appeared to be the most effective in passing on his message. In the same way the translator has to keep his receptors in mind and foresee their possible reactions, conditioned by the presuppositions and the behavior patterns of their culture.

Unlike the author of the original communication, the translator may not communicate his own thoughts and interpretations, but must pass on the message of the various biblical authors to the receptors of the translation. If the receptors are to understand this message in their own language and culture, then they need not only a linguistically clear reproduction, but also a minimum of information about the thought patterns and values of the source culture. For this purpose the translator must make certain adaptations, but these must be minimal. A translation cannot replace a commentary. Neither can it be a complete acculturation of the biblical message, because a translation is not a sermon.

Measuring the Distance Between Languages and Cultures

These examples of cultural factors in communication given the impression that the Bible translator is always concerned with a homogeneous "biblical culture," which is separated from his own culture by an enormous gap. This impression would be a false one. It has already been stated that no uniform biblical presupposition exists, but that its various parts have various presuppositions and that the authors' respective senses of value differ.

In speaking of presuppositions and patterns of behavior within a culture, we must distinguish various levels. The individuals of a given culture group follow a series of common thought patterns. Within these there are, however, also subcultures based on professional specialization, or conditioned by age, sex, and social standing. All these subcultures have specialized thought patterns and evaluate human events in a different way. Parallel to this fact, there develops a specialized use of the language, which can strongly influence reciprocal communication. Every translator of the Bible who wants to reach the widest possible range of receptors must recognize this fact and therefore avoid as far as possible every type of specialized language, in order to guarantee the highest degree of commonly understood and acceptable communication.

If there are such differences even within a culture group, then greater dissimilarities are to be expected between distinct cultures. Nevertheless, when one examines more closely the gaps between particular cultures a very diverse picture is revealed. Cerrtainly, the breach between the secularized, scientific presuppositions of our Western technological society and presuppositions of the biblical texts is enormous. Conversely, many of the so-called primitive cultures in Central Africa and elsewhere come relatively close to the world of the Bible. A whole series of practices and ideas in the Bible that appear strange to us are generally common in these cultures: polygamy, animal sacrifice, certain forms of revenge, blessing and cursing, slavery, belief in miracles, communication with the supernatural world through dreams and visions, and many other features. Ethnologists estimate that there are approximately 2000 clearly distinguishable culture groups, but they always emphasise that the cultural differences of these groups are fewer than their similarities. Difficulties in understanding between representatives of different cultures never concern the broad expanse of human experience, only particular aspects. The practice of Bible translation gives evidence to this fact. Of all the religious books of world history, the Bible is the easiest to translate. The area from which it originates has experienced in its history more cultural and political upheavals than any other region on earth. No other area has produced as many creative ideas, and nowhere else have so many diverse languages and cultures influenced and enriched one another. For this reason, it is not surprising that for centuries, disregarding all cultural barriers, the Bible has appealed to man. Another reason for the attractiveness of the Bible is its theme, which differentiates it from other writings of world religions.

The Hindu documents mainly consider the heroic acts of the gods. The Buddhist writings primarily contain philosophically elevated ethical principles. The Koran concentrates on instructions on how to follow faithfully the teachings of the Prophet. All these writings are considered to be essentially timeless and of universal application. The Bible, however, is deeply rooted in history. It tells of God's dealings with man. Its primary purpose is to point out what God does and what he wants, not to teach what he is like. His dealings with man are not generalized, but described by means of very concrete examples. What God does always relates to people with their concrete needs and problems. And these needs and problems are very similar to those which people had and have everywhere and at all times. They are the questions of life and death, of guilt and punishment, the wish to be able to cope with temptations, to love and be loved.

Linguistic and Cultural Adaptations in Bible Translation[5]

The foregoing theoretical discussion must now be illustrated by practical examples from Bible translation. As far as possible this is done by comparing translations of particular biblical phrases and passages in European and African languages. This comparison will clearly demonstrate the diverse problems which arise from language structure and culturally-conditioned presuppositions.

JHVH Elohim 'Jahwe God' is a designation of God that frequently occurs in the Hebrew Old Testament. The particular problem is posed by the proper name JHVH, whose correct pronunciation and meaning can no longer be ascertained with complete certainty. From early times it became common practice among Jews to substitute *Adonai* 'Lord,' for fear of misusing this holy name. Later the vowel signs of *Adonai* and sometimes also of *Elohim* were added to the consonants JHVH, to

remind the reader of this. The Greek translation, the Septuagint, follows the ancient Jewish practice by replacing JHVH
throughout by *kurios* 'Lord.' The same is true of the Latin
Vulgate, which uses *dominus*. Most translations in European
languages followed this tradition. Some translations tran-
scribed 'Jehovah,' the form most used in vocalized Hebrew
texts. Dynamic-equivalent translations today normally use
'Lord,' because this designation has a stronger emotive value
for readers than the unfamiliar proper name. The compound
form *JHVH Elohim* however causes further problems. In German the word 'God' is considered as a name and is used without an article. The expression *der Herr Gott* (the Lord God) is
unnatural and has led to the compound noun *der Herrgott* (the
Lordgod) in colloquial language. Because of the structure of
the German language even Luther translates as *Gott der Herr*
(God the LORD). In current German *der Herr* must be in
apposition to *Gott*, that is, *Gott, der Herr*.

In Fulani (Foulfoulde) adaptation is required for both linguistic and cultural reasons. A first-draft translation had *Jawmiraawo Allah* 'the Lord God.' In Fulani two or more nouns
side by side can be either a genitive construction or nouns in
apposition. Because it is the language of an Islamic people,
Allah is considered as a proper name. *Jawmiraawo Allah* can,
therefore, only be understood as a genitive construction 'the
Lord of Allah.' In the eyes of every Moslem, however, this is
blasphemy. The only acceptable form is *Allah Jawmiraawo*
'Allah, the Lord.'

For the same reason the words 'I am the Lord, your God'
must also be adapted, using either *Min woni Allah Jawmiraawo mon* 'I am God, your Lord' or *Min woni Jawmiraawo,
min woni Allah mon* 'I am the Lord, I am your God'.

The opposite is true in Fulani when another proper name is
added to *Allah*. *Allah Ibrahiima* would indeed be understood
as a genitive construction 'the God of Abraham,' but there is
a danger that this might indicate that Abraham had God in his
power. There is no indication at all of this in constructions with
a possessive pronoun like *Allah am* 'my God.' On the basis of
this presupposition the translation must read: *Allah mo
Ibrahiima sujidani/dowtani dum* 'God, whom Abraham wor-
shipped/whom Abraham obeyed.'

In quite a number of African languages the only name that

can be used for 'God' is of feminine gender. All pronominal references to this name must also use the feminine form. Venberg (1971) reports on deliberations at the time of the translation of the NT into Peve (in the South West of the Republic of Chad). The usual name for God there is *Ifray,* a compound of *ya* 'mother' and *fray* 'heaven.' The suggestion of using the designation *Bafray* 'father in heaven' instead of *Ifray* was declined by the Peve, because it seemed to them to represent the introduction of a foreign God. For God to be introduced as Father contradicted their idea of creation. For when has a man ever given birth to a child? A feminine name for God is not a problem in itself. But it becomes a problem when the designation 'father' is linked with the name of God. In the phrase 'the Father of Jesus Christ' it is difficult to make the father into a mother, for the mother of Jesus was Mary. A possible translation is 'God, who gave us Jesus Christ.' This is a functional translation, for in this context the word 'father' does not have the meaning of 'procreator,' but rather expresses the close relationship between God and Jesus. The prayer formula "Our Father in Heaven" must also be adapted: 'Our God (fem.) in heaven, we are your children' or something similar.

In almost all languages psychological functions are also attributed to certain organs of the human body, and this is particularly striking in idiomatic phrases. In Hebrew, as in European languages, the heart is the seat of feelings of joy and sorrow. The heart also has this function in Fulani, whereas in the languages of Chad it is attributed to the liver. In many places (in the Bible) the 'heart' refers to the seat of conscience. 1 Sam 24, 5 is translated in the Authorized Version as 'his heart smote him,' whereas the New English Bible has 'his conscience smote him' and thus follows current English usage. *Die Gute Nachricht* translates 1 John 3, 20, the Greek *kardia* 'heart', with 'conscience', as does the New English Bible.

Special care is needed with idioms using 'heart.' 'To harden one's heart' is the Hebrew expression for 'not being willing to see something.' Today's English version translates this expression by 'stubborn,' *die Gute Nachricht* by 'verstockt.' In Fulani *sattingo ɓernde* 'to make the heart hard' does not mean the

same as in the Bible, but 'to pluck up courage' or 'be brave.'
The biblical expression must be translated by *sattingo hoore*
'to make the head hard.'

Pneuma hagion 'holy spirit', *pneuma akatharton* 'unclean
spirit,' and *daimonion* 'Demon, evil spirit' present difficulties
for almost every translator. This is not surprising, for ideas vary
enormously with regard to the designation of the invisible
phenomena to which man feels himself exposed. The biblical
concept of 'spirit' is partly determined by the fact that both the
Hebrew *rûah* and the Greek *pneuma,* besides 'spirit,' can have
the meaning 'wind/breath.' In the Old Testament *rûah* is first
of all the life-giving breath of God, and then the power with
which God equips man to fulfil particular tasks. Whether the
spirit of God works good or evil depends on the obedience or
disobedience of men. Not until later did the concept of Satan,
God's wicked adversary, develop, with many evil spirits at his
disposal to induce men to evil deeds and turn them from God.
The concept of 'spirit' becomes more and more personal: the
spirit speaks to men, he inspires the writers of the Holy Scriptures, evil spirits can possess a man, torment him, and so forth.

The rational thinking of Western cultures cannot make
much of this biblical concept of 'spirit.' Admittedly there are
representations of the occult, but most people reject these as
irrational. Spirit is generally understood to be the opposite of
matter, and is therefore connected with thought. 'Geist haben'
(to have spirit) is almost a synonym in German for 'to be intelligent.' The Western understanding of the word 'holy' is also
different from the biblical concept. Used in connection with
God, the Hebrew *qados* and the Greek *hagios* have the meaning of 'morally perfect, separated from evil.' Used in connection with other beings, places, and things, they have the meaning of 'consecrated to God' (and therefore withdrawn from
profane usage). In Western languages there has been a shift in
the meaning: 'holy' used in connection with beings, is understood almost exclusively as 'morally perfect.' In the Bible 'to
have the Holy Spirit' means 'to have God rule over all one's
thinking, feeling and wishing.' In Western languages it tends
to mean 'think on a high moral plane.' In most cases this misunderstanding is partly corrected by the context, but it is not
completely excluded. The reader, therefore, needs to be given

additional information in the form of an explanation of the concept.

The rational thinking of the West places 'evil/unclean spirits' in the realm of psychology. Some modern translations have turned the Bible's 'possessed man' into a psychopath. But this type of cultural adaptation alters the concept of the biblical authors and is illegitimate. It is true that it is alien to Western thought to think of evil spirits in a personal form, but this idea can be grasped fairly easily, since demonic power is thought of as influencing man from outside, by confusing his thinking and feeling.

In many Asian and African Islamic cultures, the idea of 'spirit' in a personal form raises no problems. A literal translation of 'Holy Spirit' would, however, be understood as 'some pure spirit created by God,' which would refer to the angels and Jesus. In order to preserve the biblical meaning as far as possible, the translation in these languages must read 'Spirit of God' or 'Spirit of the Holy One (=God)'.

In the languages of Chad, there is no generic term for 'spirit,' but instead many specific designations for spirits with precisely defined functions. For example, a group of spirits is responsible for the harvest, another for success or failure in hunting. Yet more spirits cause colds, epilepsy, madness, or the like. According to what effects they have, it is very easy to find the specific term for the evil spirits described in Bible stories. It is, however, extremely difficult to find an equivalent for 'the Spirit of God' or 'Holy Spirit.' There is no word for 'holy' in the biblical sense. The suggested equivalents mean either 'taboo' or 'clean' or 'white.' None can be used in connection with 'Spirit.' For the translation of spirit, some missionaries had suggested going back to the etymological meaning of 'breath.' This suggestion was, however, rejected by the Africans, because in their languages that could only be understood literally and not figuratively. Instead, they suggested a term that is normally translated as 'shadow.' This infers a kind of metaphysical 'double' of man: as long as man lives, this 'shadow' is in him. When man dies, this 'shadow' leaves him and continues to lead an independent existence. This 'shadow' is not identical with a visible shadow, yet, in an inexplicable way, the two are connected. No one treads on the visible shadow of another for fear of hurting the person himself. Also, if the person is asleep, his 'shadow' can leave him and act independently. During this time the person is as dead. Since the Holy Spirit appears in many Bible passages as one who acts independently, the question was raised as to whether God is asleep or as dead when his 'shadow' appears separately from him. Some translators said no; no one would think of such a thing in connection with God. Other translators from the same language family thought that such a misunderstanding could not be ruled out and thought it preferable to borrow the quite well-known word *ruuhu* 'spirit' from Fulani, the trade language of the area.

Deut. 11,10 says literally: '. . . Egypt . . . where you sewed your seed and watered it with your foot like a vegetable garden.' The French translation by Dhorme explains this expression 'to water with the foot' in a footnote which says that the foot serves to tread firm the earth of the irrigation channels. A note in the Bible de Jérusalem sees in this expression an allusion to the water wheel, which is moved with the foot. The first explanation is not very probable, the second refers to a method of irrigation that today is unknown in most cultures. A literal translation is, therefore, incomprehensible in most languages. At any rate, the context indicates the burdensomeness of this work. If there is no cultural equivalent, therefore, it suffices to translate '. . . and you had the laborious task of watering it like a vegetable garden.'

Psalm 14,2 (53,3) reads: 'The Lord [God] looks from heaven on the children of men . . .' The Hebrew *benê 'ādām* is an idiom: *'ādām* is the proper name 'Adam,' but it is also used as a collective noun for 'mankind' (in the form *hā'ādām* with an article). From here come the literal translations 'sons of Adam' or 'sons of men.' Most European translations use one of these expressions. Even the New English Bible which often translates using the dynamic equivalence method, has here 'all mankind.' In Today's English Version the translation 'men' fully suffices. In Fulani *bibbe Aadama* 'children of Adam' is a completely natural, idiomatic designation for 'men.' The translation *yimbe* 'men,' which is full of content, is not only unnecessary here, but would lose the impact of the idiom. On the other hand, in Fulani one cannot translate literally '. . . looks from heaven . . .' The preposition *diga* 'from' can only be used with verbs of motion. In this case, therefore, the translation must read 'The Lord is in heaven and looks at men. . . .'

Genealogies have a monotonous and tiring effect on Western readers. Therefore Die Gute Nachricht has varied its translation of the Greek *egennesen* 'begat' used throughout Matthew 1. The expressions used are '. . . was the father of . . .', 'whose son was . . .' or 'there followed . . .' (plus a list of several names). African and Asian listeners and readers seem to react in quite a different way to genealogies, for all the translators from these parts of the world who were questioned valued a full, detailed translation.

The first verses of Romans are a particularly interesting example of compressed information with many implicit elements, which makes too great demands on most readers of today. A literal translation would read: 'Paul . . . called apostle, set apart for the gospel of God, which he formerly promised through his prophets in holy Scriptures, concerning his Son . . . our Lord Jesus Christ . . .'

An analysis using generative transformational grammar makes some of these implicit elements clear. Today's English Version, on the basis of such an analysis, translates: 'Paul . . . an apostle chosen and called by God to preach his Good News. The Good News was promised long ago by God through his prophets, and written in the Holy Scriptures. It is about his Son, our Lord Jesus Christ . . .' In German it is unnatural to say '. . . the Good News, which he had promised.' One cannot promise news, one can only promise to send or give news. Exegetically the gospel is the news of the fulfilment of the promise. Die Gute Nachricht, therefore, translates: 'God has called me, Paul, to be an apostle. He has chosen me to make known the Good News that he has now fulfilled what he had promised through his prophets in the Holy Scriptures. For he has fulfilled all his promises through his son, our Lord Jesus Christ.'

The above text was analyzed at a working conference in Chad with translators of Sahel languages. It turned out that even the German text was too complicated. The structure of these languages requires even greater adaptation. A relative clause like 'what he had promised' is not possible. The content of the promise must be clearly expressed. With reference to the prophets it would be in a word 'salvation.' The translators' objection was that in their languages they did not have a noun for 'salvation,' and would have to translate the content of the promise with a verb, but that the verb 'to save' required a grammatical object. Moreover, the whole statement would be unclear in their languages if the individual pieces of information were not given in normal chronological order. The results of the analysis on the translation were as follows: 'God called me, Paul, and sent me to men. I am to make his Good News known. (Paragraph) A long time ago God promised that he would save men. His messengers/speakers said it. We can read it in the books of God. Now he has fulfilled it. His son Jesus Christ, our Lord, has done it.'

FOOTNOTES

1.   cf. Nida (1964, pp. 22–29 and 1969, pp. 1–32).

2.   This type of translation is most consistently represented in German
      by the Buber/Rosenzweig OT, the Concordant Translation of the
      NT, the Elberfelder Bible and the New World Translation.

3.   In chapters 2 and 3 I refer frequently to expositions and diagrams
      used by Nida and Reyburn in *Translating Across Cultures*, which has
      not yet been published.

4.   In many passages one can even distinguish between several "higher"
      levels of meaning.

5.   The background to the examples given in this chapter is my work as
      a translator in German and Fulani, also as a translations adviser in
      Eastern Europe and Cameroon/Chad.

REFERENCES

Texts and Translations Consulted: The Bible

Biblia Hebraica, Rudolf Kittel, Ed. Stuttgart: Württembergische Bibelanstalt, 1937.

Septuaginta, Alfred Rahlfs Ed. Stuttgart: Württembergische Bibelanstalt. The Greek New Testament, second edition, by Kurt Aland, Matthew Black, Carlo M. Martini, Bruce M. Metzger, and Allen Wikgren Eds. in cooperation with the Institute for New Testament Textual Research. New York, London, Edinburgh, Amsterdam, Stuttgart: United Bible Societies, 1968.

The New English Bible. Oxford University Press, Cambridge University Press, 1970.

Good News for Modern Man, the New Testament in Today's English Version, third edition. New York: American Bible Society, 1971.

Die Gute Nachricht, the New Testament in today's German. Stuttgart: Württembergische Bibelanstalt, 1971.

La Bible, Vol. 1 The Old Testament, under the direction of Edouard Dhorme Bibliothèque de la Pléiade. Paris: Gallimard, 1966.

La Bible de Jérusalem, fully revised and augmented new edition. Paris: Les Editions du Cerf, 1973.

Bonnes Nouvelles Aujourd'hui, the New Testament in français courant London: United Bible Societies, 1971.

Deftere Allah (the Bible in Fulani) (Yaoundé: Bible Society: Cameroun-Gabon) in press.

Selected Bibliography

Capell, A. Names for 'God' in Oceanic languages. *The Bible Translator*, 1969, *20*, 154–157.

Doke, C. M. The points of the compass in Bantu Languages. *The Bible Translator*, 1956, *7*, 104–113.

Grether, Herbert G. Some problems of equivalence in Amos 1:3. *The Bible Translator*, 1971, *22*, 116–117.

Hesselgrave, David J. Dimensions of crosscultural communication. *Practical Anthropology*, 1972, *19*, 1–12.

Kassühlke, Rudolf. Problems of Bible translating in Europe today. *The Bible Translator*, 1971, *22*, 124–133.

Kassühlke, Rudolf. An attempt at a dynamic equivalent translation of 'basileia tou theou'. *The Bible Translator*, 1974, *25*, 236–238.

Kelly, L. G. Cultural consistency in translation. *The Bible Translator*, 1970, *21*, 170–175.

Kramers, R. P. On being polite in Chinese. *The Bible Translator*, 1963, *14*, 165–173.

Lithgow, David R. Change of subject in Muyuw. *The Bible Translator*, 1971, *22*, 118–124.

Loewen, Jacob A. Culture, meaning, and translation. *The Bible Translator*, 1964, *15*, 189–194.

Margot, Jean-Claude. And His Love is Eternal (Psalm 136). *The Bible Translator*, 1974, *25*, 212–217.

Newman, Barclay M. Towards a translation of "the Son of Man" in the Gospels. *The Bible Translator*, 1970, *21*, 141–146.

Newman, Barclay M. Translating "the Kingdom of God" and "the Kingdom of Heaven" in the New Testament. *The Bible Translator*, 1974, *25*, 401–404.

Newman, Barclay M. Some comments on the Common Malay Gospel of John, *The Bible Translator*, 1974, *25*, 432–438.

Newman, Barclay M. Some translational notes on the Beatitudes, *The Bible Translator*. 1975, *26*, 106–120.

Nida, Eugene A. *Customs and Culture*. New York: Harper & Brothers, 1954.

Nida, Eugene A. Are we really monotheists?, *Practical Anthropology*, 1959, *6*, 49–54.

Nida, Eugene A. *Toward a Science of Translating*. Leiden: Brill, 1964.

Nida, Eugene A. Formal correspondence in translation. *The Bible Translator*, 1970, *21*, 105–113.

Nida, Eugene A. Communication and translation. *The Bible Translator*, 1972, *23*, 309–316.

Nida, Eugene A., and Taber, Charles R. *The Theory and Practice of Translation*. Leiden: Brill, 1969.

Nida, Eugene A. and Taber, Charles R. *Theorie und Praxis des Übersetzens* (adaptiert von Rudolf Kassuhlkc und Jacob A. Loewen). Stuttgart: Weltbund der Bibelgesellschaften, 1969.

Noorduyn, J. Categories of courtesy in Sundanese. *The Bible Translator*, 1963, *14*, 186–191.

Reyburn, William D. The transformation of God and the conversion of Man. *Practical Anthropology*, 1957, *4*, 185–194.

Reyburn, William D. The Message of the Old Testament and the African Church. *Practical Anthropology*, 1960, *7*, 152–156.

Reyburn, William D. Sickness, Sin, and the Curse. *Practical Anthropology*, 1960, *7*, 217–222.

Reyburn, William D. Cultural equivalences and nonequivalences in Translation I. *The Bible Translator*, 1969, *20*, 158–167.

Reyburn, William D. Cultural equivalences and nonequivalences in Translation II. *The Bible Translator*, 1970, *21*, 26–35.

Smalley, William A. Vocabulary and the preaching of the Gospel. *Practical Anthropology*, 1959, *6*, 182–185.

Swellengrebel, J. L. Bible translation and politeness in Bali. *The Bible Translator*, 1950, *1*, 124–130.

Swellengrebel, J. L. Politeness and translation in Balinese. *The Bible Translator*, 1963, *14*, 158–164.

Taber, Charles R. Exegesis and linguistics. *The Bible Translator*, 1969, *20*, 150–153.

Taber, Charles R. Explicit and implicit information in translation. *The Bible Translator*, 1970, *21*, 1–9.

Takahashi, Masashi. Use of honorific in Japanese. *The Bible Translator*, 1963, *14*, 174–177.

Venberg, Rodney. The problem of a female deity in translation. *The Bible Translator*, 1971, *22*, 68–70.

de Waard, Jan. The translation of some figures of speech from Psalms in Bamileke and Bamoun. *The Bible Translator,* 1969, *20,* 143–149.

de Waard, Jan. Do you use "Clean Language"? *The Bible Translator,* 1971, *22,* 107–115.

de Waard, Jan. Biblican metaphors and their translation, *The Bible Translator,* 1974, *25,* 107–116.

de Waard, Jan, and Nida, Eugene A. *A Translator's Handbook on the Book of Ruth.* London: United Bible Societies, 1973.

Wilson, W. A. A. 'But Me No Buts', *The Bible Translator,* 1964, *15,* 173–180.

Wilson, W. A. A. Who Married Herodias? *The Bible Translator,* 1970, *21,* 138–140.

Wonderly, William L. *Bible Translation for Popular Use.* London: United Bible Societies, 1968.

Wonderly, William L. Some principles of "Common-Language" translation. *The Bible Translator,* 1970, *21,* 126–137.

Author Index

Subject Index